AUBREY BEARDSLEY

Brian Reade

Antique Collectors' Club

© Brian Reade 1987
First published in 1967 by Studio Vista,
Cassell and Collier, Macmillan Publishers Limited.
Reprinted 1971 and 1974
Designed by Gillian Greenwood

Revised edition published 1987
by the Antique Collectors' Club

ISBN 1 85149 048 5

British Library CIP Data
Reade, Brian
  [Beardsley]. Aubrey Beardsley.
  1. Beardsley, Aubrey
  I. [Beardsley] II. Title III. Beardsley,
  Aubrey
  741′.092′4   NC242.B3

Printed in England by the Antique Collectors' Club Ltd.
5 Church Street, Woodbridge, Suffolk

Portrait of Beardsley by Sickert

The Antique Collectors' Club

The Antique Collectors' Club was formed in 1966 and now has a five figure membership spread throughout the world. It publishes the only independently run monthly antiques magazine *Antique Collecting* which caters for those collectors who are interested in widening their knowledge of antiques, both by greater awareness of quality and by discussion of the factors which influence the price that is likely to be asked. The Antique Collectors' Club pioneered the provision of information on prices for collectors and the magazine still leads in the provision of detailed articles on a variety of subjects.

It was in response to the enormous demand for information on "what to pay" that the price guide series was introduced in 1968 with the first edition of *The Price Guide to Antique Furniture* (completely revised, 1978), a book which broke new ground by illustrating the more common types of antique furniture, the sort that collectors could buy in shops and at auctions rather than the rare museum pieces which had previously been used (and still to a large extent are used) to make up the limited amount of illustrations in books published by commercial publishers. Many other price guides have followed, all copiously illustrated, and greatly appreciated by collectors for the valuable information they contain, quite apart from prices. The Antique Collectors' Club also publishes other books on antiques, including horology and art reference works, and a full book list is available.

Club membership, which is open to all collectors, costs £15.95 per annum. Members receive free of charge *Antique Collecting,* the Club's magazine (published every month except August), which contains well-illustrated articles dealing with the practical aspects of collecting not normally dealt with by magazines. Prices, features of value, investment potential, fakes and forgeries are all given prominence in the magazine.

Among other facilities available to members are private buying and selling facilities, the longest list of "For Sales" of any antiques magazine, an annual ceramics conference and the opportunity to meet other collectors at their local antique collectors' clubs. There are over eighty in Britain and more than a dozen overseas. Members may also buy the Club's publications at special pre-publication prices.

As its motto implies, the Club is an amateur organisation designed to help collectors get the most out of their hobby: it is informal and friendly and gives enormous enjoyment to all concerned.

For Collectors — By Collectors — About Collecting

The Antique Collectors' Club, 5 Church Street, Woodbridge, Suffolk

Contents

Acknowledgments

The revival of international interest in Aubrey Beardsley started with the exhibition I organised at the Victoria and Albert Museum, London, in the summer of 1966. Work for it began several years before then, and I became indebted to all those people whose names were recorded in the exhibition catalogue of over 600 items by Frank Dickinson and myself.

In 1964 I had been working on a biography of Beardsley which, for reasons I need not explain here, had to be discontinued. Meanwhile Lord Clark's lectures on this artist at Aldeburgh and at the Victoria and Albert Museum in 1965 (for which we exchanged books and information) paved a way to the exhibition of 1966.

It was Mr Raymond Rohauer's enterprise that enabled a large part of the exhibition to be set up in New York in 1967 under the patronage of Mr Huntington Hartford at Columbus Circle; and at the end of that year it was due to Mr Rohauer again that a similar Beardsley exhibition was undertaken by the County Museum of Art in Los Angeles. The 1967 book was issued in time for both these American exhibitions.

Since then I have taken part with loans and texts in the exhibitions held, with the help of the British Council, in Japan during 1983 and in Munich and Salzburg in 1984, and in Rome in 1985, composed mainly of the Victoria and Albert Museum collection under the supervision of Miss Susan Lambert.

With the 1985 exhibition in Milan I had nothing to do, otherwise the publication in the catalogue of leaves from a forged sketch-book might have been avoided.

In this revised version of the 1967 book Sir John Rothenstein's introduction has not been included. I was not happy with the first draft, which he very kindly altered; but he was not happy with the inclusion of the *Lysistrata* series in my selection. This series had been published in Beardsley's lifetime in a limited edition; also in 1925 by Philip Sainsbury; and also in various foreign editions, so it was pointless to object to its appearance in a representative selection of Beardsley's work. And with that the Director of Public Prosecutions agreed.

I did, however, draw the line in those days at 'The Impatient Adulterer': it has been published since.* Also I was unable to include that interesting drawing 'The Child Standing by its Mother's Bed' (which had been supposed lost) simply because I bought it at Sotheby's where it surfaced in 1967 some time after the 1967 book had been put together.** I have discussed the significance of this drawing in *Beardsley Re-Mounted,* where I have also recorded a fresh approach to Beardsley based on a closer look at his drawings and what that suggests. This approach has led me once again to point out that the leaves from the sketch-book first reproduced in Lane's *Uncollected Work* of 1925, and more recently in the catalogue of the Beardsley Exhibition at Milan in 1985, are forgeries; which is why I excluded them also from the 1967 selection. Certain other exclusions, mainly of early works, might not have been made by me now, twenty years later, though it is difficult to see how I could have included them without making a larger book.

I am glad to reaffirm my continued indebtedness to the following people for help, both direct and indirect, and for information and discussions in the making of the 1967 book: the late Mr David Carr of Starston, the late Lord Clark, Dr Malcolm Easton, Mr W.G. Good, Miss Gillian Greenwood, the late Mr Ralph A. Harari, Mr David Herbert, the late Mr Vyvyan Holland, Mr Henry Maas, Mr Anthony d'Offay, Sir John Rothenstein, Sir Sacheverell Sitwell, Bt, Mr Timothy d'Arch Smith, Mr Donald Weeks.

The present edition uses the text of the 1967 edition with some minor amendments. The reader should note, however, that where Mr R.A. Harari (Ralph A. Harari, O.B.E.) is noted as the owner of certain objects, these passed, by purchase, into the Department of Prints and Drawings at the Victoria and Albert Museum, London, after his death in 1969. The drawings shown in Plates 106, 113, 157 and 189 were acquired by Harari after the writing of the 1967 book so, with the rest of his collection, they now belong to the Victoria and Albert Museum. An exception was the drawing in Plate 125 which remained with his son, Dr Michael Harari.

Private and institutional owners of drawings in 1967 were recorded in all cases, except when photographs of certain drawings were available with no identification of present ownership. The owners of rare books, posters, etc., were recorded also; otherwise when no acknowledgment was given, the reproductions were made from works out of copyright.

BRIAN EDMUND READE

AUGUST 1987

* Simon Wilson, *Beardsley,* Phaidon, Oxford, 1976.
** *English Literature in Transition 1880-1920,* a Beardsley symposium published by the University of North Carolina, U.S.A., 1987.

Aubrey Beardsley

After hearing and watching the reactions of people who visited the two exhibitions devoted to Beardsley in London in 1966 and in New York and Los Angeles in 1967-8, it could be said, I believe, that those who first see any quantity of drawings by this artist feel a strong impact, beginning with a sense of his power to draw attention to his art. This power is not given to all artists: it was not given in comparable measure to Blake, or to Charles Keene, for example, though Keene had another power, a more extroverted power of observation, which Beardsley lacked. A pause at the moment of discovering Beardsley, at that initial and hypnotic stage when he claims our attention, is usually followed by curiosity, by wonder, by admiration, in fairly quick succession, or it may be by distaste, by detachment or incomprehension. Incomprehension may involve some rejection of opportunities to note certain regions of the mind, while detachment may lead one to cold shoulder a whole stretch of human nature and to walk, as it were, away from the shadow of oneself.

For those who are willing to accept the fact that in Beardsley's art there is something that waits to be understood, one way of pursuing the subject is by the use of a metaphor. In a sense all words are metaphorical, and the easiest thing therefore is to choose one — not necessarily the right word because no particular word would be 'right' for Beardsley — but the first word that suggests itself in the context of graphic art, or of any art, and which we can use, as in long division, to discover how many times it goes into our subject, and what is left over.

Without apology therefore I suggest the quite ordinary word Ideal. This word is useful because it is linked to the notion of effort, to the means by which any ideal is sought; and since theory should not be confused with practice, be it understood that ideals are never reached and that nobody identifies, or can identify himself, with his End.

A study of the drawings and designs reproduced in the present book may be undertaken to find out if the sense of an ideal goes into them at all. Quite soon I think it will be seen that it does. In the first place nobody would dispute surely that Beardsley's craftsmanship reflects a presence in him of the urge to define, and of what arises from this urge, coherence: or that the means of achieving his coherence was mostly by drawing lines which give the impression at normal focal length that they are 'perfect' — for of course they can be magnified in such a way that any detail may seem like a smudge of ink. At the point of convention which links the artist and the onlooker, these drawings were made, and we become aware of them, as tokens for ideal definitions by line and by area of the forms conceived. This is true of Beardsley's craftsmanship at its best, and also at its worst, because the same approach to craftsmanship was always there, the standard of performance on occasions varying short of his potential. Thus, it was an ideal elegance of form that was made to embrace both the sweet and the macabre in 'The Coiffing'. Sometimes hideously grotesque conceptions stand alone, as in the *Bon-Mots* series, and the ideal has to be seen as a minus quantity. In *Le Morte Darthur* what is left over often is an element of journalism, linked with the medium of the line-block for which so much of his work was contrived, a medium which lent itself too easily, because of its cheapness, to ephemeral illustration. At other times Beardsley crosses the grotesque with the handsome, as in *Salome,* and what we find left over is sensationalism. In *The Rape of the Lock* the comeliness of the figures is weakly supported by the technique, while the ornate, sarcastic and realistic qualities of the drawings are increased by it. What we have left over here is escapism, to accord with Beardsley's unfitness to travel a life-span in the Victorian age.

That any artist should go to such lengths to convince both himself and the spectator that his conceptions exist and that they could be put down in black and white with such clarity, is evidence of the discipline that goes before skill, of the disposition which lies behind the strength of character that in turn maintains the discipline. But this skill and its discipline were themselves means to ends; and what, we may ask, was Beardsley coherent about? What does this impressive work of the hand reveal, or describe or convey? And when we turn the pages of the present book once more we may note that there seem to be often some signs of a conflict between the inventions of the artist and his ideals as a craftsman: that the lines and black masses and meaningful reserves of white paper are clear enough usually, but that something corresponding to the ideal of this sort of craftsmanship, which disdains suggestion, does not always go into the reading of the drawing, and we are left at the mercy of all kinds of suggestions, some of them pathetic, some burlesque. Our attention then is held no longer by the initial impact of the drawing upon us (assuming we have not turned away), but by a curiosity which obliges us to wait and to watch, as though someone were climbing a precipice and might fall. And after a time we may agree that this balancing act is the act of balancing factors into which perfection does *not* go, against other factors into which it goes with ease. So we find languid looking arabesques which seem to have been drawn with energy in order to hold them precisely in that quality. We find arabesques again which seem to have graceful assumptions but which hold linear descriptions of monsters and abortions. We find a craft of great delicacy, which also implies great steadiness of mind and hand, employed to insinuate a meaning that if left to itself would escape from our thoughts like a gas.

We look further and suspect the artist of a pleasure in these balancing acts like the pleasure of a humorist in his own wit, but also like the mischievous pleasure of a comedian in some tragic part. Finally, as this curiosity develops and we look over all the pages before us, we become alarmed perhaps that a suspense produced in us by the sight of certain drawings by Beardsley is a suspense we cannot avoid because we ourselves have helped to produce it: the drawing itself being a convention which is so coherent that it is, as an object, conclusive. The balancing feat is now seen to be often the feat of the ironist, including the self-ironist, and his art the art of horror-comedy in terms of this word ideal, that is in terms of the comparatively simple graces within the range of a black-and-white draughtsman, all mounted and executed with marvellous precision.

To such generalizations there are numerous exceptions. For instance, the striving towards an ideal content — a content which required little or no balancing feat to present — is obvious in a drawing like 'Ave Atque Vale' (Plate 441), which illustrates with a sort of holographic sadness, in spite of imperfections of observation, a poem of Catullus translated by Beardsley and itself an epitaph ready-made for the end of his life. Or we can note the feelings of pleasure in feminine forms and clothes which he recorded in drawings like the one of Miss Emery (Plate 370), where there is only the merest glimpse of sub-irony in the slightness of line.

As I have mentioned one very well-known illustration by Beardsley, 'Ave Atque Vale', it is convenient to emphasize that his careful but inexperienced representation of the young man's hand is the kind of defect that can lead us to consider what species of artist he was not. He was not an academic, not an impressionist in any sense, not a realist. He had not been trained, as in those days French artists were trained, in a long gruelling process of observation, comparison and rationalization of what he saw before him — models dead or alive, nudes, draperies and chairs. He lacked therefore the benefit of a great luxury trade in picture-making with its satellite arts of designing and illustrating, or of the long tradition which Paris preserved of technical exercise in manual and mental dexterity. Rather, in England, the tradition was one of adventure, of adventure of the spirit, of exploiting academic opportunities of lesser range and breaking free — like Hogarth or Blake or Constable, to quote the names of widely differing artists and men, whose one common factor was their obstinate courage. To Beardsley likewise this courage was given, dying as he was from his youth up, undermined by tuberculosis and yet fevered by that very destructive force to the pitch of a kind of obsession. There came a time in his short life of twenty-five years when he was too ill to do much, when he was either dying or drawing or reclining and thinking; when the old days of concerts and parties and popular infamy were gone and when his friends had become mere letters in the post to be answered; when the small sums he earned from Leonard Smithers to illustrate or decorate limited editions were inadequate to keep him in comfort and he became a pensioner of his admirer, Raffalovich. With his mother, Ellen Beardsley, his oedipal relationship was classically strong. A short time before he died she left him alone in bed with his drawing materials. In the space when she was gone the ideal, this time the ideal of a super-ego, drove him to exert himself and to begin drawing; while the special gold-nibbed pen he used for this purpose fell or was thrown to the floor, to remain there like an arrow until after his death.*

He had been provocative rather than aggressive. He had indulged erotic curiosity and the fantasies of youth, and he had the nerve to externalize those fantasies for publication in Victorian England. He had been astute, sarcastic, bold, shy, amusing and, on occasions, charming. From perversity he had professed to admire the French without reservation, as if 'French' were another word for Freedom, and as a boy might admire his uncle in order to spite his own father. Up to a point all this was sincere. And yet he was essentially un-French. That curious humour, that mischievous irony, the innuendoes, the spleen, the stoicism — these were quite basic English, and of all English artists of the nineteenth century he most distilled that spirit of negligent grace admired in the Dandies by Baudelaire.

He was plunged into life on 21 August 1872, nearly twelve months after his sister Mabel was born on 24 August previously. And their birthplace was Brighton, on the south coast of England, where the atmosphere is brilliant, the trees few and the Neo-Classic buildings of the Regency stand terrace by terrace like so many regiments — or at least they stood then. Beardsley's father was a ne'er-do-well descended from London jewellers, and his mother forced by poverty after her marriage to become a governess in London, was the daughter of a retired surgeon-major living in Brighton. His parents never had any home there, but he and his sister were brought up in the house of his father-in-law, the surgeon-major. From earliest times brother and sister were much in each other's pockets, as used to be said, and this accounts in some degree no doubt for Beardsley's curious erotic life. It was Mabel who took the lead: her brother was closer perhaps to her than to their mother, upon whom he was also dependent; indeed, he seems to have resented his mother, sometimes, as a force in the way of his own development.

During those early years Mabel and Aubrey would sing and recite at the houses of their mother's patrons, and Aubrey would even play little pieces on the piano in his role as an infant prodigy. For his mother's friends too he would design dinner cards and make small pictures in the style of Kate Greenaway. Both children were keen on acting, and by the time they reached late adolescence their amateur performances at home were quite remarkable.

Aubrey went first to a preparatory school in Brighton, then to a boarding school at Hurstpierpoint in the same county, and finally — his last academic submission — to

* From an unpublished account by Mrs Ellen Beardsley given by Mr Donald Weeks to the author.

Brighton Grammar School, where at first the little boy's breeches that showed his knock knees made him feel vaguely inferior, and he soon took to trousers and an air of self-mastery. Beginning as a day-boy lodging with his maternal great-aunt, who also lived in Brighton, he became a boarder at the school at the beginning of 1885. He brought with him accomplishments learnt from his mother, a little French, a taste for music and a will of iron, and moreover a strange arrogance as of far-off patrician ancestors. It was an arrogance which manifested itself in facetiousness rather than downright conceit, and in self-consciousness rather than self-knowledge. From the first he gave an impression of being orientated heterosexually. His relations with his father deteriorated, his mother became the staff of his life, and he turned, it appears, to his playmate of a sister in the holidays for early sexual experience. Nevertheless, an attachment with a Brighton girl sprang up while he was at the Grammar School, although the letters that remain as evidence of this affair* suggest that he may have been too deficient in physique and too agile in mind to risk taking his correspondent very seriously. As he wrote he also drew, for he had decided he could draw. And in these letters to Miss Felton, his adolescent drawings were comic and self-conscious, while from his schoolmates he earned popularity in a short while by the countless numbers of caricatures he made for their amusement. His form-master at one stage, H.A. Payne, and his house-master, A.W. King, both encouraged the young eccentric, who was not strong enough to play games like the other boys. They encouraged him to read grown-up books, to compose literary effusions, to exercise his French in little French plays organized partly for his benefit — and for the benefit of his best friend among the boys, Charles Cochran, who later became the well-known impresario; and they encouraged him to draw when inclined, though they criticized him for not rising above the style of caricature in which he redeemed himself, so he thought, for not being as other boys were. He made caricatures of everybody, including the head-master; and instead of studying Virgil's texts he would shed his school hours in illustrating Virgil's stories in the burlesque manner of Gilbert à Beckett's *History of England*. His Brighton days ended in a sort of triumph, with Beardsley designing the costumes, and illustrating the libretto of the school Entertainment, 'The Pay of the Pied Piper', and acting too in this comic opera — although it was performed in the Christmas season after he had left, and he appeared in it strictly as an Old Boy (one who had left the school).

Having left the school, Beardsley had no alternative but to accept a job as clerk, first in a surveyor's office in London, and shortly afterwards in the offices of the Guardian Life Insurance Company. The struggle between his image of himself and his restricted view of life became so acute he relieved it by aping the assumptions of Aesthetic cliques of the period, by a snobbery derived from Whistler's *Gentle Art of Making Enemies*. Beardsley himself was so different from Whistler that his behaviour during this period must be counted affectation; whereas Whistler's affectations were psychologically functional. While still a clerk, Beardsley was able to spend lunch hours in the bookshop of Jones and Evans in Queen Street near the Guardian Life Insurance offices, and evening hours as often as possible at concerts. It was during his early London period that a passion for the operas of Wagner was sown in his mind, to be cultivated in its first growth by Alfred Gurney, a High Church parson from Brighton, who had obtained by that time a living at St Barnabas, Pimlico, not far from where the Beardsley family, now united, had come to live.

Meanwhile Beardsley went on drawing. His premonitions of a short life at this date, 1891, were expressed in a circumscribed use of his energy. Tuberculosis, inherited from the paternal side of his forebears, had been diagnosed in 1879: and it was not long after he had been working in London as a clerk that he began to experience the shocks and the exhaustion of consumptive attacks. Interested though he was at first in all the visual arts, he had insufficient strength to experiment consistently in oils or to investigate in this

* In private possession. Two letters, each on two sheets folded. From Brighton Grammar School, not dated.

medium the values of colour and three dimensional representation, though he did make attempts to imply those dimensions in his drawings. They were the dimensions explored in Venetian painting of the sixteenth century: by the nineteenth century it was the Impressionists, the masters of Touch, who had inherited something of the Venetian approach. Beardsley soon lost interest in this type of art, turned to the other North Italian Schools, to engravings by Mantegna and Blake, and was led away from any sort of current actualism to the elaborate linearism of Burne-Jones. Whistler's decorations in the Peacock Room at 49 Princes Gate, which Beardsley went to see with his sister, made a deep impression on him, but this did not prevent him from idolizing Burne-Jones, from imitating his drawings, going to visit him, and even winning from the elderly painter encouragement to aid him in deciding that he would make his own living as an artist. Accordingly he went for a year to evening classes at the Westminster School of Art, the only art training he ever had, and the old comic strain of his schooldays fell dormant. In the middle of 1892 he went to Paris, called on Puvis de Chavannes with a letter from Burne-Jones, and gave him a sample of his work. And it was then no doubt that he became aware of posters by Toulouse-Lautrec, in which the figures of Parisian night life were represented in silhouetted, or nearly silhouetted, shapes. In this year, too, Beardsley's taste reflected the current vogue for all that was Japanese in his 'Japonesque' style, in which arabesques and areas of black ink, given texture by slight abrasions, were artfully balanced, or dis-balanced, in order to dramatize the subject of the drawing without lifting it much from an almost geometrical purity of line. This was his tribute to the Japanese print-makers of the eighteenth and nineteenth centuries.

In the paintings of Botticelli, which he could see in the National Gallery, Beardsley found, too, an ideal, a second-hand ideal already evolved by the Pre-Raphaelites. In Dürer, Pollaiuolo and Mantegna he found other ideals, distressed by awareness of harsher feeling, and this awareness corresponded in him to his former sense of the burlesque. When late in 1892, on the recommendation of Frederick Evans of the bookshop he used to visit, he was suddenly commissioned by John Dent to illustrate a new edition of Sir Thomas Malory's *Le Morte Darthur* — his first professional undertaking — he gave up his post at the Guardian Life Insurance Company, getting Mabel's approval for this step, but not consulting his parents. Over 350 drawings were required for the book, to be reproduced by the line-block process, a photo-process of facsimile reproduction then coming into wider use and limiting him to a style of drawing in black and white, without intermediate tones. The work lasted him for eighteen months and to begin with he was obliged to lean heavily upon his assimilation of motifs and mannerisms, especially those of Burne-Jones and Walter Crane and William Morris and other outstanding book decorators of the day. A concurrent commission from the same publisher brought him the series of miniature *Bon-Mots* to illustrate with vignettes, and in these little books he let himself go in an opposite direction, with calligraphic fantasies in a grotesque vein that sprang from his earlier resource of the burlesque.

Shortly after this beginning with Dent, Lewis Hind, the editor presumptive of *The Studio*, which was still at the planning stage, was so impressed by some drawings by Beardsley that he arranged for Joseph Pennell to write an article around reproductions of them in the first number of the new magazine. It was then that his experimental illustration to a passage in Oscar Wilde's *Salome* appeared, 'J'ai Baisé Ta Bouche Iokanaan' (Plate 272), which led in a short time to a commission from Elkin Mathews and John Lane of The Bodley Head for Beardsley to illustrate a translation of Wilde's play from the French. This was published in the following year, 1894.

The *Salome* illustrations are so well known we will not linger on them, except to point out that they were really the last of his early works. They were novel at the time and still have the power to amaze by their qualities, largely because as abstract patterns the compositions are individual, because the short cuts and evasions defy all the law and order of descriptive drawing as understood at that time, and because the sense of drama conveyed by the designs is so intense. It was as though he were an actor manqué — his sister became a professional actress and he might well have become one also — who had learnt the manner in which actions and gestures could be translated on paper, not in three-dimensional realism, but in the two values of black and white in flat areas, linked by lines that varied in strength to suggest something of the arrested quality in the outlines of a bas-relief. Beardsley's art was enhanced at this date by his study of the paintings on Greek vases at the British Museum.

Then, after numerous commissions for posters, title-pages and frontispieces, came *The Yellow Book*, founded by Beardsley and the American writer, Henry Harland, in London on the first day of 1894. As art editor of this periodical the young artist's financial situation was so much improved that his sister and he were able to continue the lease of the house they had taken, 114 Cambridge Street, in Pimlico. A phase began of being sociable, in the Victorian sense, when tea-parties held by the Beardsleys attracted the young writers and artists of the *Yellow Book* circle, not to speak of Oscar Wilde (who never contributed to the Bodley Head periodical) and some of his friends. And Mabel's charm and her physical attractions served to bring other visitors, who for Aubrey himself would never have gone out of their way. Aubrey himself was still apt to give an impression that he followed Whistler, and for that matter Gautier and Baudelaire, in despising the middle classes from which he had sprung and in justifying almost any activity from strange sins to Black Magic, provided such activities had Style. Beardsley's style at this time was that of a dandy, an epigrammatist, a close critic, a polite listener and to some extent a nostalgist of the mire like George Moore before him, whose *Flowers of Passion* was published as far back as 1878, containing the translation of a poem 'Le Succube' by Catulle Mendès with verbal images anticipating the lilies in Beardsley's 'Iokanaan' drawing. It was Moore too who showed the ways in which emancipated young men were to arrive, after reading Gautier and Swinburne, glancing at the 'Nocturnes', or better still at the Impressionists, going to Paris and concluding that to shock their elders and each other was better fun than to Succeed. Only Beardsley began to succeed — a success of disesteem — for his illustrations in *The Yellow Book* made it notorious, while his name was plugged in the journals of 1894 as a Decadent, a disciple of Evil, as if he were the fulfilment of some strange dream by Joris Karl Huysmans, something the empirical English thought better to be left in French yellow wrappers than permitted to blazon itself in a magazine sold on the bookstalls of W.H. Smith.

Happy in defiance, Beardsley noticed the world around him, and his art during 1894 and 1895 reflects his excitement at London life, its Lady Golds, its Wagnerites, its Night Pieces and its Éducation Sentimentale (such as that was). The end of this phase came with the trial of Oscar Wilde in 1895, beginning with the failure of Wilde's case against Lord Queensberry in April, and the mistaken belief among the public that Wilde and Beardsley were brothers under the skin, a belief which inspired William Watson, Alice Meynell and Francis Thompson, egged on by Mrs Humphry Ward, the novelist, to blackmail John Lane to get rid of this youthful art editor of *The Yellow Book* and to remove the plates after his drawings for the current number — otherwise their names would be withdrawn from the Bodley Head publishing list. Lane gave in: Beardsley went. For months afterwards he suffered a reaction against the kind of life he had lived, took care to be seen about with women, and in due course his art took a fresh turn, this time away from the world he saw around him and towards an imagined world of the eighteenth century, based on the ideal art of that century from Watteau to the *petits maîtres* of the *ancien régime*. Fortune in the shape of Leonard Smithers came to his aid, and this enterprising publisher of erotic books started yet another magazine, *The Savoy,* with Arthur Symons as literary editor and Beardsley as the regular source of drawings for reproduction, mostly in line-blocks again, and as adviser on the graphic art contributed to it. The magazine began in the first, and ended in the last, month of 1896. In the same year Smithers published *The Rape of the Lock* with Beardsley's 'embroiderings', and, in a very limited edition, *The Lysistrata* of Aristophanes translated by Samuel Smith, again with illustrations by Beardsley.

The Rape of the Lock was praised universally by critics at the turn of the century, after Beardsley was dead. In the illustrations his ironic disposition was safely contained within the meaning of Pope's urbane, antiquarian verses. Moreover a new technical device occurred to the illustrator: he began to use dotted lines in quantity to give stippled effects. Because of the emphasis laid by him on ornate embroideries and those flounces of lace that he mistakenly associated with the epoch of the poem, a notion took hold of these critics and their readers that Beardsley was a supreme decorator, and nothing much more. In fact it is hard to see how these illustrations stop at being decorations. In most of them the scenes are treated as pictorial dramas with great restraint: space is understood and implied by the artist's completely personal craft, and in this respect the drawings are richer than those for *Salome;* but the extraordinary black fields and arabesque lines of the *Salome* period are absent and with them has gone all trace of those curvilinear forms which he bequeathed to the practitioners of *art nouveau.*

The Lysistrata is another matter. In these eight drawings there was a return to something like the manner of decorations on Greek pottery, so far as Beardsley with his deliberated lines and dots and modest areas of black could approximate the spontaneous execution of the ancient Greeks, which arose from constant practice in doing the same thing in the same way. None the less, the *Lysistrata* series, and the illustrations to Juvenal's Sixth Satire, never completed and never published in book form, contain among them the only successful examples of true satire in all Beardsley's output. The old burlesque spirit of his schooldays was revived in the roughest of them and mixed with a controlled aggression, delivered against both sexes, and unlike anything to be found in the satirical works of other artists, since or before.

What unites Beardsley's drawings of 1896 and of the second half of 1895 is the renewed and open assertion of Neo-Classical values — the profile character of the bas-relief — emerging despite the rococo exaggerations of *The Rape* and the bawdy exaggerations of *The Lysistrata.* If space is implied, it is implied by way of the whole design; there is no aerial perspective, the outlines are all closed, and the forms are rationalized so that they expound very clearly ideas in the artist's mind. There is no chance for anyone contemplating these drawings to stage a romance of his own, except by non-visual means, for visual suggestion is reduced to a minimum; and this may have been a factor that influenced critics in the twentieth century, tiring of imitators in particular, to dismiss the whole ethos of Beardsley as literary. That it is literary because the subjects had literary sources is of course fallacious.

In his next major works in a new style, the *Illustrations to Mademoiselle de Maupin,* also published by Smithers, Beardsley dropped his severely black-and-white technique for a technique of line and wash, and the intermediate tones thus introduced had to be reproduced by photogravure. It was an attempt to go beyond the limitations of most of his previous drawings and to imitate aquatint. But it showed him pretty clearly as a master of tone-grading as well as of tone contrasts. The same neatness, precision and uncompromisingly definitive exposition of ideas is to be seen in these drawings in terms of the new technique. His growing sense of three dimensions, which formerly he had implied, he now wished to exploit, as in 'The Lady at the Dressing Table' (Plate 490) where his constant preoccupation with toilet scenes — an indication of narcissistic and transvestite moods — is expressed all the more vividly by his play on vanishing points, a primitive feat on similar lines to the jagged exploits of Cubists in 1910.

In the *Volpone* illustrations, Beardsley's last undertaking, there appears a strong effort to achieve two kinds of perfection: the perfection of a certain kind of seventeenth-century line-engraving, which was the reference for the frontispiece reproduced in line-block; and the Baroque dramatization of light, in order to vivify and make quasi-tangible, more real if you wish, his sense of the form of an idea, which he introduced in the designs for initials reproduced in half-tone and photogravure. Whether his intellectual approach could ever have been enriched by the sensuousness needed to mature such a technique as this last, must remain one of those queries that has anybody's answer. Beardsley died on 16 March, 1898, before the *Volpone* illustrations were completed.

From the time of the Wilde trials in 1895 and the termination of his association with the *Yellow Book* staff, Beardsley was a dying man. His condition was undoubtedly aggravated by these events: in a sense it might be said that he never recovered from them. His life became literally dislocated. The Cambridge Street house had to be given up. There were visits to Dieppe in the late summer of 1895, when he occupied his time either planning *The Savoy* with Arthur Symons who was there too, or watching the gamblers in the Casino, intermittently writing passages down in a portfolio as he progressed, laboriously enough, with his never-to-be-finished *Story of Venus and Tannhäuser,* parts of which, expurgated, came out as 'Under the Hill' in *The Savoy.* After a winter in London in chambers at St James's Place, he paid a short visit to Paris early in 1896, going on later to Brussels where he collapsed. When he returned to London in the early summer he consulted a specialist, Dr Symes Thompson, and learnt that he was seriously ill. 'I am beginning to be really depressed and frightened about myself', he wrote in a letter at this time. In July he spent a short period at The Spread Eagle Hotel, Epsom, where he finished the *Lysistrata* drawings, and at the end of that month he was in Boscombe, Bournemouth, reduced to a state of great weakness. He recovered sufficiently to make a brief visit to London in August, but this exertion set him back more than ever, and he was not to leave Bournemouth again until April 1897, having been converted meanwhile to Roman Catholicism. He left there finally on his doctor's advice for the South of France, but a stay in Paris which he enjoyed did him little good, and he had to be taken out to St Germain-en-Laye. In July he was once more in Dieppe, and in the autumn he was back in Paris. But although he cheered up in Paris, medical advice was not in favour of him risking a winter in that city, and in November 1897 he and his mother, who had been with him most of the time since Bournemouth, set off for Menton in the south of France, where in the Hôtel Cosmopolitain, bed-ridden at last, but still working whenever possible on the *Volpone* drawings, he died some four months later. Indeed he had seldom given up working unless incapacitated by the chills and the haemorrhages that ravaged him; and his feverish productivity, when he was active, was linked indirectly with the fever produced in him by illness. His life became transposed into work: it became concentrated by the restrictive force of tuberculosis into mental adventures. Running parallel with the development of his tubercular disease ran the development of his sexual imagination, again intensified by the disease itself, but otherwise not inappropriate to the age he had reached. Since he was so much attracted to sexual themes, some consideration must be given to the nature of the mind that pursued them.

Beardsley has often been referred to as homosexual.* His aggressive-looking Messalinas are said to represent a morbid interest in dominating women. What was felt to be his degradation of feminine attractions; his obsession with phalluses and their sizes; his many delineations of hermaphrodite creatures and a pederastic episode in his unfinished *Story of Venus and Tannhäuser* are supposed to be evidence of homosexual inclination. To these symptoms can be added his graphic references to transvestism, flagellation, lesbianism and sexual symbolism of all kinds, revealing a mental erethism, to which one key might be the supposed homosexual strain. All this is doubtless orthodox, but it is also unsatisfactory.

Given the mental erethism, and this is sufficiently pronounced, we might look for the

* A recent exponent of this view is Armand Bitoun, in his interesting article 'Aubrey Beardsley et l'esthétisme homosexuel' in *Les Lettres Nouvelles,* Mars – Avril, 1967.

origins of this in Beardsley's upbringing and to his first knowledge, suggested by his early story published in *Tit-Bits* in 1889, where the subject of breach-of-promise occurs, that his father had a misadventure which ended in the selling of all the inherited Beardsley property to buy off a breach-of-promise threat soon after his marriage with Mrs Beardsley in 1870. This seems to have been something the family, remarkably broad-minded as it was, made little attempt to conceal, and something also perhaps that started in Beardsley a lifelong curiosity about what sexual relationships were, or what they could be.

A point to emphasize is that just when homosexual developments might have been expected in his life, in the school years for instance, there is no evidence of them; in fact it was during those years that an autobiographical incident recorded in the manuscript of *Venus and Tannhäuser,* but scored out, shows the author as a heterosexual voyeur; while such a passive attitude agrees with the legend, and with his own boasts to the same effect,* that his chief erotic experiences were incestuous and that his sister Mabel led the way in this, as in much else. It was she, as we have already noted, who took up acting as a profession, her sick brother, equally keen though he was on the stage, having to fall back on the sedentary art of drawing. Both Mabel and Aubrey liked on occasions to dress in the clothes of the opposite sex, but transvestism is usually its own reward, and not by any means a necessary phase of homosexuality. This tendency in Aubrey ran alongside his resignation to an art, as it were, of the voyeur, and with obscure attempts to identify himself perhaps with the sex of the only two beings he might be said to have loved.

Passive and non-aggressive heterosexual males are vulnerable to advances from either sex, which condition may explain not only the narcissism of Tannhäuser in the story, but the whole tone of this composition, not to mention a passage in which the hero invites seduction from Venus: it suggests also how Beardsley could attract Oscar Wilde's friend, Ada Leverson, to make an attempt at seducing him;** and on the other hand, it sheds light on the emotional approach to him sought by André Raffalovich, an overt homosexual, converted in 1896 to chastity and to the Roman Church, who influenced Beardsley to become another convert to the same faith, paying him £100 a quarter to keep him in reasonable comfort — far more indeed than the poor young man ever earned from the drawings he sold to Leonard Smithers.

While Beardsley had prominent painters among his friends, including William Rothenstein and Richard Sickert, and from 1895, Charles Conder, his work as an illustrator ranged up against his own literary tastes, and it was in the literary and aesthetic circles of the Nineties that he began to be noticed soon after he came to live with his family in London. The emotional pressures exerted by an interlinked minority in this very mixed group were either pro-matriarchal or candidly homosexual, pressures increased by the relay of forerunners going back through Wilde to Pater, Simeon Solomon, Oscar Browning, William Cory, Swinburne and Mulready to Beckford; and to the works, sayings and behaviour of Englishmen who had adapted an ideal of masculine beauty to women. It will have to be admitted sooner or later that a large part of English culture in the nineteenth century was underwritten not overtly, not even consciously perhaps, but none the less distinctly, by homosexual men; and the decay of this culture can be seen in the world of High Camp in the 1920s and later. Through the veils that darkened his private life and made him aloof and mysterious, Beardsley was anxious to give signs that he too was willing to please: hence the outcrop of homosexual images in *Le Morte Darthur* early in 1893, when he had adopted something of the mores of his new friends, Robert Ross and Count Eric Stenbock. When in 1896 and 1897 it was expedient to please Smithers, who was avid for women, and when it was expedient to express a revulsion of feeling towards the set which had launched him, now discredited for a year or two after the trial of Wilde, Beardsley had no qualms at all in writing to Smithers in the style of some fully-fledged mulierast. If there

---

* Information from Mr David Carr, recorded in correspondence between him and Mrs Olive Scanlan, formerly a friend of Ellen and Mabel Beardsley and their circle (1966).

**Information from Mr Vyvyan Holland.

was an overt homosexual strain in Beardsley, fomented by cultural values, it may have revealed itself in his drawings of youths and boys with their hair piled high on their heads: many examples of these appear in *Le Morte Darthur,* and there is a later example in the tall young Lacedaemonian ambassador in the last drawing for *The Lysistrata* (Plate 466). Nor should we forget the pierrots who stood for some sort of ideal rejected by the Philistine world; that they were sex-objectives is possible; they also represent, I should think, projections of his own body-image. The idea of himself as a spavin-legged dandy that was given a form in 'The Abbé' (Plate 423), was at first the Abbé Aubrey, and then on second thoughts the hero of his unfinished novel, the Abbé Fanfreluche, later changed to Tannhäuser. In the story Tannhäuser enjoys a light-hearted pederastic diversion (borrowed from Suetonius' life of the Emperor Tiberius) and is mentally stimulated by various deviations; but his objective is Venus herself, while he is the personification of the feminine anima in a masculine (not very masculine) body, so that his 'reactions' to Venus are almost like those of some type of lesbian. Beardsley's preoccupation with lesbians was marked; but this again was linked with a knowledge of his sister, whose form appears often in his drawings of women — in the frontispiece to Davidson's *Plays* for example (Plate 321) — and there seems indication enough to believe that she, like her brother in an inverse sense, was an aggressive heterosexual woman with transvestite leanings, capable moreover of lesbian emotions. If anything of a homosexual ideal goes into Beardsley's life therefore, it seems probable it was cancelled by irony, and again irony — the very tension of his art.

The fact is left that many of his drawings embody both conscious and unconscious hetero-sexual symbolism. In this one respect he was the most powerful, because the most recondite and productive, symbolist of the nineteenth century. Look for instance at the design for the front cover of *The Rape of the Lock* (Plate 404): a near-abstract design with miniature prophecies in certain details of the visual experiences we now associate with Mondrian's paintings of thirty years later. But the whole design also breaks up into symbols, with Belinda's lock of hair in a significant position surrounded by the shadows of breasts and buttocks. Beardsley's emblem itself is an emblem of coitus, despite indignant protests to the contrary from his Edwardian-minded biographer MacFall; and a phallic interpretation must be given to the adaptation of a bentwood chair on which Salome, in the published version of 1894, sits at her toilet (Plate 281). It is the constant occurrence of forms like these, disguised as linear descriptions of plausible objects, that both repels and attracts the observer according to breed. And to have achieved suggestion by a deliberately non-suggestive craft, for it would be absurd to suppose that Beardsley never knew what he was doing, was to have achieved a compromise by distortion of the Neo-Classical ideals on which his technique was based — and this may be the measure of his 'decadence'. But to reject, to dismiss, to pretend to ignore the results of an intuitive reading of his drawings is what I mean in the first paragraph of this essay by walking away from the shadow of oneself. That is what anyone does who puts Beardsley aside as a decorator; and that is what anyone does also who says with indifference 'Beardsley has nothing to do with me'.

The shadows which Beardsley never walked away from, but even tried, as it were, to embrace, became the shadows of his own inadequacy, frail as he was from the start and sensitive to all that divided him from the sheep of this world. It is from conflicts like this that arrogance emerges, and Beardsley's own arrogance was discarded finally when, as Rothenstein noticed in 1897, he accepted the fact of imminent death, and perhaps a little the consolations of his adopted faith. But years before that, in 1892 and 1893, a curious passion for the hideous declared itself, in the *Bon-Mots* grotesques most of all, but again in several drawings of those years in which a foetus or an abortion, or some other diminutive monster, appears. Just why the foetus especially meant so much to Beardsley has never been explained, or rather explained away. MacFall supposed, without going into detail, that

Beardsley was influenced by the perusal of medical books, presumably belonging to the old surgeon-major or to the surgeon-major's father who had been a doctor in Brighton. But it was not until 1892 at the earliest that foetuses came to be drawn by Beardsley, and this was long after the period when he could have pored over medical books as a child. What was the occasion, or the trauma, that suggested these foetus shapes? Had he seen one preserved in a bottle somewhere? Such experiences would seem too casual to inspire what amounted to a minor obsession. Had he witnessed a miscarriage of his sister's and one for which he himself had been responsible? She is certainly known to have had an illegitimate birth.* Whatever happened and whatever the explanation may be, Beardsley took pains to render his diminutive monsters with humour, so that their original hideousness was redeemed and they became amusing and endearing even. As with introverted humorists, and in a limited sense he was a comic artist, Beardsley's fantasies evolved from within a doubting, disturbed unconscious, and had to be justified as parts of himself. We find a similar process of humorization in Edward Lear. And just as Beardsley belongs in a way to each one of his inventions, so the foetus shapes belonged to him, and were symbols perhaps of his own despair in face of the future. How otherwise can we find any meaning in the drawing of a mother and foetus modelled remotely on an Italian Renaissance picture of the Virgin and Child and entitled 'Incipit Vita Nova' (Plate 275)? Here anyway is the expression of a cancelled ideal in a simple form.

Let us return to our word ideal. As was agreed, Beardsley, the eclectic, solitary magpie, needs no comparison with erudite academics, nor with artists of the nineteenth century who complemented the scientific programme of that age as aesthetic observers. The art of the materialist, of the impressionist, is the art of finding concepts and harmonies in the varied material he observes: the art of Beardsley, like Blake's art, was that of clothing his concepts in minimal and adequate observations and forcing these into quasi-mathematical harmonies. It is odd how many of his figures were seen in profile: he was evidently content to remain from the academic viewpoint an amateur, not much concerned with discovering how he might have drawn his figures in more complex positions. At the same time he had little of that Platonism fashionable in the 1880s, he enjoyed but he mocked the confusion of attributes favoured by homosexuals and never imposed a hieratic symbolism on what was provisionally an illustrative art. Only in the *Volpone* drawings there appeared at last signs of a retreat, or an advance, from those limits that helped him to fuse his almost auto-biographical fantasies with the act of drawing, signs that he was beginning to panic away from those flippant shades which kept him cool amidst the bustle of nineteenth-century beliefs, including the prominent superstition that there is one kind of knowledge proved by the test of function, the trend of expediency. Such is the masculine-favoured trend, making men scientific, sensible even, and incorrigible. But as Meier-Graefe has said, our utilitarianism was never rebuked in stronger or haughtier terms than in Beardsley's art, the art of a schizoid, epigraphic mind which only death could heal.

The tools of his craft were not unusual: a pencil, a pen, indian ink, water to make ink washes (which he used occasionally), a brush of 'camel' or of sable hair, and drawing paper of ordinary grades. It was customary at that date to recommend Bristol board and other smooth cards for black-and-white drawings reproduced by the line-block process; but these were never in use by Beardsley, and drawings on that type of support which bear his emblem or his name or his initials are, without question, forgeries. There are visible in some of the *Morte Darthur* drawings certain lines made by comparatively broad nibs: in the *Bon-Mots* vignettes, the lines are so fine that a Gillot crowquill, or the Gillot nib No. 1000 which came on the market before 1894, would seem to have been necessary. When he gave up the hair-line manner it is probable he gave up the use of fine nibs, and the variety of line-drawing in his later work was evidently attained by the flexible use of drawing nibs of

* See Malcolm Easton, *Aubrey and the Dying Lady: A Beardsley Riddle,* London, 1972.

average breadth. As was mentioned above, a special gold-nibbed pen fell from his hand for the last time shortly before he died. The same dandified taste was apparent in his method of work. He never, so far as we know, made preliminary studies, or took tracings from sketches, for any of his compositions, though drawings survive which are unfinished or went wrong and were abandoned. His usual practice was to begin his drawing by scribbling with a pencil, making a host of flourishes and loops and scratchy lines. Over these somewhat vague schemata he drew with pen and brush, and with a firmness of hand that led without considerable erasion to the finished result. He had the reputation of working at night by the flames of the candles in his two favourite candlesticks, and although the notion of nocturnal labours lends itself to satanic pictures of Beardsley, as if he were a lamp that shed darkness by day, it is true that frequently he worked very late, having been conditioned to do so when still a clerk, drudging from nine-thirty to five-thirty in the Guardian Life Insurance. In his last years he often drew at any hour that suited him, as he found sleeping difficult.

Beardsley's end was tragic, if mainly because he was not convinced that his achievement was sufficient. 'Destroy all copies of Lysistrata & bad drawings', he wrote pathetically to Smithers, as death approached. But Smithers knew better. And for the unprejudiced commentator his achievement was more than sufficient; it was concrete, and charged with the new meanings which independent works of art accumulate, as round them everything changes. That achievement of his varied in quality: like anyone else, Beardsley was capable of vulgarisms; also he was capable of 'daintiness', to use an irritating word beloved by Whistler. These were rare slips in the polarization of a most unusual mentality, less divisible obviously by any ideal than his so-called decadence or his bias in sexual fantasy. None the less, his mastery of dramatic and disintegrative pattern, to emphasize this apart from his mastery of line, was unique in the history of European art, and none combined as he did the matching of such gifts with an ability to fix and enlarge certain shades of dawning consciousness in works as calculated as those of a line-engraver. By comparison the relative stability, or on the other hand the fugitive dash, in the drawings of other artists, can seem sometimes oppressive. If he had worked on a larger scale, or in colour, he might have compromised the standards he set himself. For it could be said that he brought, without intending or heeding it, the craft of the jeweller, the craft, that is, of his paternal ancestors, and the craft of the silhouettist, which was that of his maternal grandmother, to the intellectual art of draughtsmanship. Indeed his best drawings have a material excellence which paintings can rarely have, like the sheer excellence of a flawless stone; and Beardsley himself can be seen united with Pater at length in his search for the condition of a hard, gem-like flame. It was impossible of course. But our metaphor seems to go often into the life and works of this exceptional youth.

Guide to the plates and the notes

The chief aim in making this survey of Beardsley's work has been to reproduce as many drawings by him as became available after the Beardsley Exhibition of 1966, and this has permitted the inclusion of a number of illustrations for *Le Morte Darthur* and for the *Bon-Mots* series which have never been published since the dates of their appearance in the original books. These early professional works of the artist have been much underrated, and the present time seems favourable to a better appreciation of them. Another advantage in making reproductions whenever possible from the actual drawings and not from existing reproductions, is that Beardsley's skill as a draughtsman is brought closer to the eye, and in some instances where there are abrasions or erasions or traces of pencil sketching, these have been reproduced by using half-tone methods for the plates, although the drawings may have been made for line-blocks in which such details would never have appeared.

A comprehensive selection of Beardsley's works could scarcely be arranged however without adding to the reproductions of surviving drawings many other plates, either, for example, of books to show stamped covers after his designs, or from existing reproductions when the drawings for these are not to be found. In such cases the plates have been made from the earliest line-blocks or half-tones after the drawings, as for *The Yellow Book, The Savoy,* and other publications during Beardsley's lifetime.

The dimensions of the present volume have not enabled me to keep the plates in the second class always separate from those in the first class, but each plate is annotated, and in these notes will be found measurements in inches for almost all of the drawings; and when media other than indian ink have been employed, this is stated: when, as in the majority of the notes, no medium is stated, indian ink is all that is readily visible in the drawing described.

Reproductions of Beardsley's posters have been included, and of his two paintings in oil. The quantity of juvenile drawings published by John Lane in *The Uncollected Work of Aubrey Beardsley* in 1925 records so much similar material of limited interest that only a small but relevant proportion of it has been thought suitable for representation in this book. Otherwise the selection covers all the most important of Beardsley's designs and illustrations, including many not reproduced in the standard books on the subject, and several drawings never before published in any form.

References to the authors Vallance and Gallatin indicate the following works of reference:
Robert Ross, *Aubrey Beardsley,* with revised iconography by Aymer Vallance, London, 1909.
A.E. Gallatin, *Aubrey Beardsley,* Catalogue of Drawings and Bibliography, New York, The Grolier Club, 1945.
There are also references to the following, sometimes abbreviated:
The Early Work of Aubrey Beardsley, with prefatory note by H.C. Marillier, John Lane, London and New York, 1899.
The Later Work of Aubrey Beardsley, John Lane, London and New York, 1901.
The last two books have been frequently republished and the plates were re-arranged in the later editions. Unless otherwise stated, the letters from Beardsley referred to will be found in *The Letters of Aubrey Beardsley,* edited by Henry Maas, J.L. Duncan and W.G. Good, Cassell, London, 1971. Other works connected with the subject have been referred to fully, when occasion has arisen.   B.R.

The notes following the illustration plates are arranged chronologically or in groups to maintain a logical sequence through Beardsley's work. The illustrations, because of problems caused by the layout, do not exactly follow this sequence. They are cross-referenced to the notes by bracketed figures after the captions.

1 Drawing done at the age of eleven (1)

2 Drawing done at the age of eleven (2)

3 La discourse (3)

4 La lecture (4)

5 La chymist (5)

6 Flavouring the apple tart (6)

7 A little chamber music (7)

8 The Jubilee Cricket Analysis (8)

9 Sketches of violinists (9)

10 Illustrations to *The Pay of the Pied Piper* (10)

11 Paganini (11)

12 Sarah Bernhardt (12)

13 Holywell Street, London (13)

15 The Jolly Mashers (15)

16 Songs (16)

17 Dante in Exile (17)

18 A scene in Ibsen's play *Ghosts* (18)

19 Tannhäuser (19)

20 The Litany of Mary Magdalen (20)

22 Hail Mary (21)

21 Hamlet Patris Manem Sequitur (22)

23 Self-Portrait (23)

24 Professor Fred Brown (24)

25 Die Götterdämmerung (25)

26 Perseus (26)

27 Withered Spring (27)

28 Katharina Klavsky (28)

29 Max Alvary (32)

30 Carl Maria von Weber (29)   31 Raphael Sanzio (30)

32 Le Dèbris [*sic*] d'un Poète (31)

33 The Achieving of the Sangreal, from *Le Morte Darthur* (33)

34 Front cover of *Evelina* (34)

35 Title-page of *Evelina* (35)

37 Title-page design (37)

36 Evelina and her Guardian (36)

38 A little girl seated on a sand castle (38)

39 Caricature of Whistler's signature (39)

40 Caricature of Walter Crane's socialist opinions (40)

41 Caricature of Queen Victoria as a ballet dancer (41)

42 Master Leo (Master Leo Byrne as Godfrey) (43)

43 Margery (Kate Phillips) (44)

44 The Composer (Sir Charles Villiers Stanford) (45)

45 The King makes a move on the Board (William Terriss) (46)

46 Caricature of Arthur Cecil (50)

MR ARTHUR CECIL

BARON STEIN

L'ACADÉMIE FR-

MISS TERRY

Beardsley

47 Miss Terry (42)

48 The Disappointment of Émile Zola (47)

49 Caricature of Forbes Robertson (49)

50 Pope Leo XIII's Jubilee (48)

51 'The Bullet-Proof Uniform: Tommy Atkins thinks it rather fun' (51)

52 Becket (52)

53 Caricatures of Norman O'Neill (53)

54 Caricature of Norman O'Neill (54)

55 Projected design for covers of the parts of *Le Morte Darthur* (55)

56 How King Arthur saw the Questing Beast, for *Le Morte Darthur* (56)

57 For the title-page of *Le Morte Darthur* (57)

58 For the preface of *Le Morte Darthur* (58)

59 Merlin in *Le Morte Darthur* (59)

60 Chapter-heading for *Le Morte Darthur* (60)

61 Chapter-heading for *Le Morte Darthur* (63)

62 Chapter-heading for *Le Morte Darthur* (64)

63 Chapter-heading for *Le Morte Darthur* (61)

64 Chapter-heading for
   Le Morte Darthur (62)

65 Chapter-heading for
   Le Morte Darthur (65)

66 Chapter-heading for *Le Morte Darthur* (66)

67 Chapter-heading for *Le Morte Darthur* (67)

68 Chapter-heading for *Le Morte Darthur* (68)

69 Initial A for *Le Morte Darthur* (69)

Book ij.   Chapter j.

OF A DAMOSEL WHICH CAME GIRT WITH
A SWORD FOR TO FIND A MAN OF SUCH
VIRTUE TO DRAW IT OUT OF THE SCABBARD.

AFTER the death of Uther Pendragon reigned Arthur his son, the which had great war in his days for to get all England into his hand. For there were many kings within the realm of England, and in Wales, Scotland, and Cornwall. So it befell on a time when King Arthur was at London, there came a knight and told the king tidings how that the King Rience of North Wales had reared a great number of people, and were entered into the land, and burnt and slew the king's true liege people. If this be true, said Arthur, it were great shame unto mine estate but that he were mightily withstood. It is truth, said the knight, for I saw the host myself. Well, said the king, let make a cry, that all the lords, knights, and

70 Border and Initial A with text from *Le Morte Darthur* (70)

71 Full page border for *Le Morte Darthur* (72)

72 Chapter-heading for *Le Morte Darthur* (75)

73 Chapter-heading for *Le Morte Darthur* (73)

74 Chapter-heading for
Le Morte Darthur (74)

75 Chapter-heading for *Le Morte Darthur* (71)

76 Chapter-heading for *Le Morte Darthur* (77)

77 Chapter-heading for
Le Morte Darthur (78)

78 Merlin and Nimue, from *Le Morte Darthur* (76)

79 Chapter-heading for *Le Morte Darthur* (83)

80 Chapter-heading for *Le Morte Darthur* (81)

81 Chapter-heading from *Le Morte Darthur* (80)

82 Chapter-heading for *Le Morte Darthur* (82)

ARTHVR AND
THE STRANGE
MANTLE

83 Full-page illustration for *Le Morte Darthur* (79)

84 Chapter-heading from *Le Morte Darthur* (85)

85 Chapter-heading for *Le Morte Darthur* (84)

87 Chapter-heading for *Le Morte Darthur* (87)

86 Chapter-heading for *Le Morte Darthur* (86)

88 Full-page border for *Le Morte Darthur*, 89 Initial S for *Le Morte Darthur* (88, 89)

The illustration contains the lettered text:

HOW. FOVR. QVEENS.
FOVND. LAVNCELOT.
SLEEPING.

90 How Four Queens Found Launcelot Sleeping, for *Le Morte Darthur* (90)

91 Chapter-heading from *Le Morte Darthur* (91)

92 Chapter-heading for *Le Morte Darthur* (92)

93 Sir Launcelot and the Witch Hellawes, for *Le Morte Darthur* (93)

94 Chapter-heading for *Le Morte Darthur* (97)

95 Chapter-heading from *Le Morte Darthur* (96)

96 Chapter-heading from *Le Morte Darthur* (94)

97 Chapter-heading for
Le Morte Darthur (98)

98 Chapter-heading for *Le Morte Darthur* (95)

𝔅𝔬𝔬𝔨 𝔳𝔦𝔦𝔧. 𝔠𝔥𝔞𝔭𝔱𝔢𝔯 𝔧.

HOW SIR TRISTRAM DE LIONES WAS BORN, AND HOW HIS MOTHER DIED AT HIS BIRTH, WHEREFORE SHE NAMED HIM TRISTRAM.

IT was a king that hight Meliodas, and he was lord and king of the country of Liones, and this Meliodas was a likely knight as any was that time living. And by fortune he wedded King Mark's sister of Cornwall; and she was called Elizabeth, that was called both good and fair. And at that time King Arthur reigned, and he was whole king of England, Wales, and Scotland, and of many other realms: howbeit there were many kings that were lords of many countries, but all they held their lands of King Arthur; for in Wales were two kings, and in the north were many kings; and in Cornwall and in the west were two kings; also in Ireland were two or three kings, and all were under the obeissance of King Arthur. So was the King of France, and the King of Brittany, and all the lordships unto Rome. So when this King Meliodas had been with his wife, within a while she waxed great with child, and she was a full meek lady, and well she loved her lord, and he her again, so there was great joy betwixt them. Then there was a lady in that country that had loved King Meliodas long, and by no mean she never could get his love;

HOW LA BEALE
ISOVD NVRSED
SIR TRISTRAM

100 How La Beale Ysoud Nursed Sir Tristram, for *Le Morte Darthur* (100)

102 Chapter-heading for *Le Morte Darthur* (102)

101 Chapter-heading for *Le Morte Darthur* (101)

Chap.
rrriiij.

103 Chapter-heading for *Le Morte Darthur* (103)

104 Chapter-heading from *Le Morte Darthur* (105)

105 How Sir Tristram Drank of the Love Drink, for *Le Morte Darthur* (104)

HOW LA BEALE
ISOVD WROTETO
SIR TRISTRAM

106 How La Beale Isoud Wrote to Sir Tristram, for *Le Morte Darthur* (108)

Book ix. Chapter j.

HOW A YOUNG MAN CAME INTO THE COURT OF KING ARTHUR, AND HOW SIR KAY CALLED HIM IN SCORN LA COTE MALE TAILE.

T the court of King Arthur there came a young man and bigly made, and he was richly bisene; and he desired to be made knight of the king, but his over-garment sat over-thwartly, howbeit it was rich cloth of gold. What is your name? said King Arthur. Sir, said he, my name is Breunor le Noire, and within short space ye shall know that I am of good kin. It may well be, said Sir Kay the Seneschal, but in mockage ye shall be called La Cote Male Taile, that is as much to say the evil-shapen coat. It is a great thing that thou askest, said the king; and for what cause wearest thou that rich coat? tell me, for I can well think for some cause it is. Sir, he answered, I had a father a noble knight, and as he rode on hunting upon a day it happed him to lay him down to sleep; and there came a knight that had been long his enemy, and when he saw he was

107 Border and initial A with text from *Le Morte Darthur* (107)

108 Chapter-heading for *Le Morte Darthur* (109)

109 Chapter-heading for *Le Morte Darthur* (106)

110 Chapter-heading for *Le Morte Darthur* (112)

111 Chapter-heading from *Le Morte Darthur* (111)

112 How King Mark found Sir Tristram sleeping, for *Le Morte Darthur* (110)

113 La Beale Isoud at Joyous Gard, for *Le Mort Darthur* (114)

114 Chapter-heading for *Le Morte Darthur* (116)

115 Chapter-heading for *Le Morte Darthur* (115)

116 Chapter-heading for *Le Morte Darthur* (120)

117 Chapter-heading from *Le Morte Darthur* (118)

118 How Morgan le Fay Gave a Shield to Sir Tristram, for *Le Morte Darthur* (113)

Book xj. Chapter j.

HOW SIR LAUNCELOT RODE ON HIS ADVEN-
TURE, AND HOW HE HOLPE A DOLOROUS
LADY FROM HER PAIN, AND HOW THAT HE
FOUGHT WITH A DRAGON.

OW leave we Sir Tristram de Liones, and speak we of Sir Launcelot du Lake and of Sir Galahad, Sir Launcelot's son, how he was gotten, and in what manner, as the book of French rehearseth. Afore the time that Sir Galahad was gotten or born, there came in an hermit unto King Arthur upon Whitsunday, as the knights sat at the Table Round. And when the hermit saw the siege perilous, he asked the king and all the knights why that siege was void. Sir Arthur and all the knights answered, There shall never none sit in that siege but one, but if he be destroyed. Then said the hermit, Wot ye what is he? Nay, said Arthur and all the knights, we wot not who is he that shall sit therein. Then wot I, said the hermit, for he that shall sit there is unborn and ungotten, and this same year

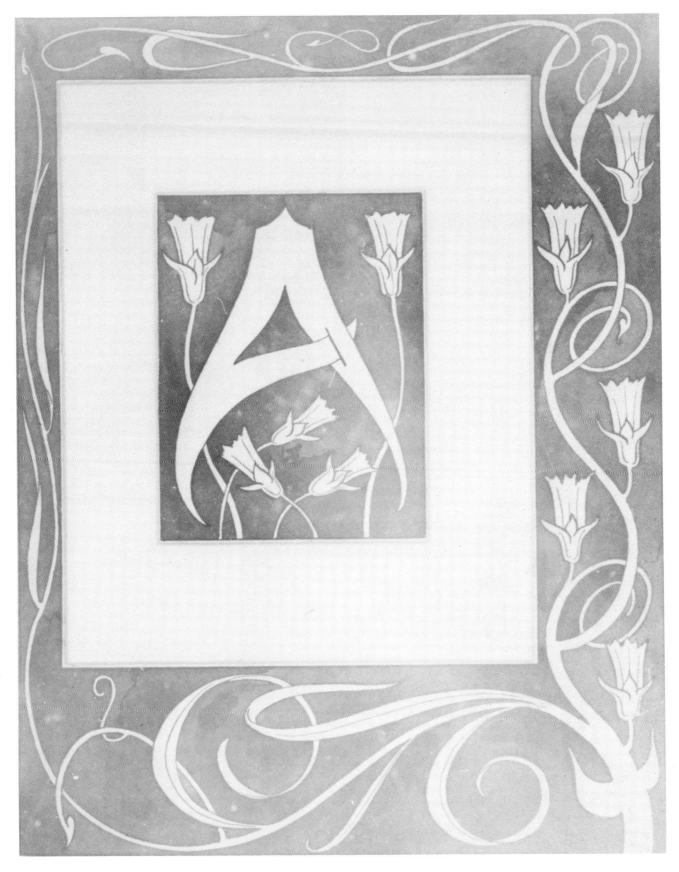

120 Full-page border with the initial A, for *Le Morte Darthur* (119)

Book xiij. Chapter j.

HOW AT THE VIGIL OF THE FEAST OF PENTECOST ENTERED INTO THE HALL BEFORE KING ARTHUR A DAMOSEL, AND DESIRED SIR LAUNCELOT FOR TO COME AND DUB A KNIGHT, AND HOW HE WENT WITH HER.

A T the vigil of Pentecost, when all the fellowship of the Round Table were come unto Camelot, and there heard their service, and the tables were set ready to the meat, right so entered into the hall a full fair gentlewoman on horseback, that had ridden full fast, for her horse was all besweated. Then she there alit, and came before the king and saluted him; and he said, Damosel, God thee bless. Sir, said she, for God's sake say me where Sir Launcelot is. Yonder ye may see him, said the king. Then she went unto Launcelot and said, Sir Launcelot, I salute you on King Pelles' behalf, and I require you come on with me hereby into a forest. Then Sir Launcelot asked her with whom she dwelled. I dwell, said she, with King Pelles. What will ye with me? said Launcelot. Ye shall know, said she, when ye come thither. Well, said he, I will

122 Border and initial A, with text from *Le Morte Darthur* (123)

Book xiv. Chapter j.

HOW SIR PERCIVALE CAME TO A RECLUSE
AND ASKED COUNSEL, AND HOW SHE TOLD
HIM THAT SHE WAS HIS AUNT.

OW saith the tale, that when Sir Launcelot was ridden after Sir Galahad, the which had all these adventures above said, Sir Percivale turned again unto the recluse, where he deemed to have tidings of that knight that Launcelot followed. And so he kneeled at her window, and the recluse opened it and asked Sir Percivale what he would. Madam, he said, I am a knight of King Arthur's court, and my name is Sir Percivale de Galis. When the recluse heard his name she had great joy of him, for mickle she had loved him tofore any other knight, for she ought to do so, for she was his aunt. And then she commanded the gates to be opened, and there he had all the cheer that she might make him, and all that

123 Initial N and full-page border from *Le Morte Darthur* (125)

125 Chapter-heading for *Le Morte Darthur* (126)

126 Chapter-heading for *Le Morte Darthur* (124)

127 Chapter-heading from *Le Morte Darthur* (127)

128 Chapter-heading for *Le Morte Darthur* (130)

129 Chapter-heading from *Le Morte Darthur* (128)

Book xb. Chapter j.

HOW SIR LAUNCELOT CAME TO A CHAPEL, WHERE HE FOUND DEAD, IN A WHITE SHIRT, A MAN OF RELIGION, OF AN HUNDRED WINTER OLD.

HEN the hermit had kept Sir Launcelot three days, the hermit gat him an horse, an helm, and a sword. And then he departed about the hour of noon. And then he saw a little house. And when he came near he saw a chapel, and there beside he saw an old man that was clothed all in white full richly; and then Sir Launcelot said, God save you. God keep you, said the good man, and make you a good knight. Then Sir Launcelot alit and entered into the chapel, and there he saw an old man dead, in a white shirt of passing fine cloth. Sir, said the good man, this man that is dead ought not to be in such clothing as ye see him in, for in that he brake the oath of his order, for he hath been more

131 How a Devil in a Woman's likeness would have tempted Sir Bors, for *Le Morte Darthur* (131)

132 Chapter-heading for *Le Morte Darthur* (134)

133 Chapter-heading from *Le Morte Darthur* (133)

134 Border and initial N for *Le Morte Darthur* (132)

135 Chapter-heading for *Le Morte Darthur* (135)

Book xviij. Chapter j.

OF THE JOY OF KING ARTHUR AND THE QUEEN HAD OF THE ACHIEVEMENT OF THE SANGREAL; AND HOW LAUNCELOT FELL TO HIS OLD LOVE AGAIN.

SO after the quest of the Sangreal was fulfilled, and all knights that were left on live were come again unto the Table Round, as the book of the Sangreal maketh mention, then was there great joy in the court; and in especial King Arthur and Queen Guenever made great joy of the remnant that were come home, and passing glad was the king and the queen of Sir Launcelot and of Sir Bors, for they had been passing long away in the quest of the Sangreal. Then, as the book saith, Sir Launcelot began to resort unto Queen Guenever again, and forgat the promise and the perfection that he made in the quest. For, as the book saith, had not Sir Launcelot been in his privy thoughts and in his mind so set inwardly

136 Border and initial S with text from *Le Morte Darthur* (136)

137 How Queen Guenever rode
on Maying, for *Le Morte Darthur* (141)

138 Chapter-heading for *Le Morte Darthur* (140)

139 Chapter-heading for
Le Morte Darthur (138)

140 Chapter-heading from
Le Morte Darthur (137)

141 Chapter-heading from *Le Morte Darthur* (139)

142 Chapter-heading for *Le Morte Darthur* (145)

143 Chapter-heading from *Le Morte Darthur* (143)

144 Chapter-heading for *Le Morte Darthur* (148)

145 Chapter-heading for *Le Morte Darthur* (144)

146 Chapter-heading for *Le Morte Darthur* (142)

147 Chapter-heading for *Le Morte Darthur* (147)

148 Chapter-heading for *Le Morte Darthur* (146)

149 How Sir Belvidere cast the sword Excalibur into the water, for *Le Morte Darthur* (149)

150 How Queen Guenever Made Her a Nun, from *Le Morte Darthur* (150)

151 Front cover design on the bound volumes of *Le Morte Darthur* (151)

153 Chapter-heading for
Le Morte Darthur (1909) (155)

152 Front cover and spine of *Le Morte Darthur* (152)

154 Chapter-heading for *Le Morte Darthur* (1909) (154)

155 Chapter-heading for *Le Morte Darthur* (1909) (153)

156 Chapter-heading for *Le Morte Darthur* (1927) (158)

157 Grotesque figure of a man
wearing a monocle (163)

158 Unfinished drawing for border for *Le Morte Darthur* (161)

159 Chapter-heading for *Le Morte Darthur* (1909) (156)

160 Initial J ascribed to Beardsley (160)

161 Chapter-heading (not used) for *Le Morte Darthur* (159)

162 Chapter-heading for *Le Morte Darthur* (1909) (157)

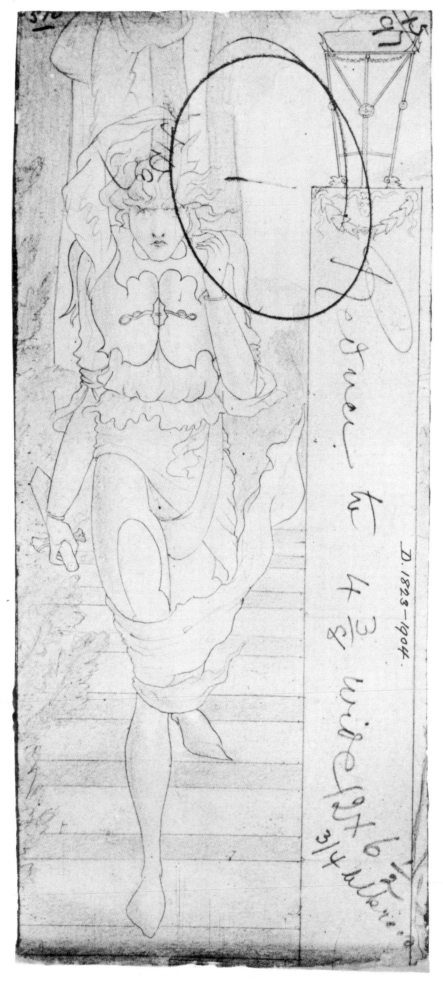

163 A male figure holding a dagger and descending a staircase (162)

164 Siegfried, Act II (164)

Bon=Mots

OF

SYDNEY SMITH

AND

R. BRINSLEY SHERIDAN

EDITED BY

WALTER JERROLD

WITH GROTESQUES BY

AUBREY BEARDSLEY

LONDON Published by J. M. DENT and COMPANY
at ALDINE HOUSE in Great Eastern Street, E.C.
MDCCCXCIII

165 Title-page of *Bon-Mots* of Smith and Sheridan (165)

166 Vignette in *Bon-Mots* of Smith and Sheridan (167)

167 Vignette in *Bon-Mots* of Smith and Sheridan (166)

168 Vignette in *Bon-Mots* of Smith and Sheridan (168)

169 Vignette in *Bon-Mots* of Smith and Sheridan (169)

171 Vignette in *Bon-Mots* of Smith and Sheridan (173)

170 Vignette in *Bon-Mots* of Smith and Sheridan (170)

172 Vignette in *Bon-Mots* of Smith and Sheridan (171)

173 Vignette in *Bon-Mots* of Smith and Sheridan (172)

174 Vignette in *Bon-Mots* of Smith and Sheridan (176)

175 Vignette in *Bon-Mots* of Smith and Sheridan (175)

176 Vignette in *Bon-Mots* of Smith and Sheridan (174)

177 Vignette in *Bon-Mots* of Smith and Sheridan (177)

179 Vignette in *Bon-Mots* of Smith and Sheridan (179)

178 Vignette in *Bon-Mots* of Smith and Sheridan (184)

180 Vignette in *Bon-Mots* of Smith and Sheridan (182)

181 Vignette in *Bon-Mots* of Smith and Sheridan (185)

182 Vignette in *Bon-Mots* of Smith and Sheridan (183)

183 Vignette in *Bon-Mots* of Smith and Sheridan (181)

184 Vignette in *Bon-Mots* of Smith and Sheridan (178)

185 Vignette in *Bon-Mots* of Smith and Sheridan (180)

186 Vignettes in *Bon-Mots* of Smith and Sheridan (188)

187 Vignette in *Bon-Mots* of Smith and Sheridan (186)

188 Vignette in *Bon-Mots* of Smith and Sheridan (189)

189 Vignette in *Bon-Mots* of Smith and Sheridan (195)

190 Vignette in *Bon-Mots* of Smith and Sheridan (187)

191 Vignette in *Bon-Mots* of Smith and Sheridan (194)   192 Vignette in *Bon-Mots* of Smith and Sheridan (193)

193 Vignette in *Bon-Mots* of Smith and Sheridan (191)

194 Vignette in *Bon-Mots* of Smith and Sheridan (192)   195 Vignette in *Bon-Mots* of Smith and Sheridan (190)

197 Vignette in *Bon-Mots* of Smith and Sheridan (197)

196 Vignette in *Bon-Mots* of Smith and Sheridan (196)

198 Vignette in *Bon-Mots* of Smith and Sheridan (199)

199 Vignette in *Bon-Mots* of Smith and Sheridan (201)

200 Vignette in *Bon-Mots* of Smith and Sheridan (198)

201 Vignette in *Bon-Mots* of Smith and Sheridan (203)

202 Vignette in *Bon-Mots* of Smith and Sheridan (202)

203 Vignette in *Bon-Mots* of Smith and Sheridan (200)

204 Vignette in *Bon-Mots* of Smith and Sheridan (204)

205 Vignette in *Bon-Mots* of Smith and Sheridan (205)

206 Vignette in *Bon-Mots* of Smith and Sheridan (208)

207 Vignette in *Bon-Mots* of Smith and Sheridan (209)

208 Vignette in *Bon-Mots* of Smith and Sheridan (207)

209 Vignette in *Bon-Mots* of Smith and Sheridan (206)

210 Vignette in *Bon-Mots* of Smith and Sheridan (214)

211 Vignette in *Bon-Mots* of Lamb and Jerrold (216)

212 Vignette in *Bon-Mots* of Smith and Sheridan (215)

213 Vignette in *Bon-Mots* of Smith and Sheridan (211)

214 Vignette in *Bon-Mots* of Smith and Sheridan (210)

215 Vignette in *Bon-Mots* of Smith and Sheridan (212)

216 Vignette in *Bon-Mots* of Smith and Sheridan (213)

217 Vignette in *Bon-Mots* of Lamb and Jerrold (219)

218 Vignette in *Bon-Mots* of Lamb and Jerrold (221)

220 Vignette in *Bon-Mots* of Lamb and Jerrold (218)

219 Vignette in *Bon-Mots* of Lamb and Jerrold (217)

221 Vignette in *Bon-Mots* of Lamb and Jerrold (220)

222 Vignette in *Bon-Mots* of Lamb and Jerrold (225)

223 Vignette in *Bon-Mots* of Lamb and Jerrold (224)

224 Vignette in *Bon-Mots* of Lamb and Jerrold (222)

225 Vignette in *Bon-Mots* of Lamb and Jerrold (223)

226 Vignette in *Bon-Mots* of Lamb and Jerrold (229)

227 Vignette in *Bon-Mots* of Lamb and Jerrold (228)

228 Vignette in *Bon-Mots* of Lamb and Jerrold (226)

229 Vignette in *Bon-Mots* of Lamb and Jerrold (230)

230 Vignette in *Bon-Mots* of Lamb and Jerrold (231)

231 Vignette in *Bon-Mots* of Foote and Hook (233)

232 Grotesque with half-title in
Bon-Mots of Foote and Hook (232)

233 Grotesque in *Bon-Mots* of Foote and Hook (234)

234 Grotesque in *Bon-Mots* of Lamb and Jerrold (227)

235 Vignette in *Bon-Mots* of Foote and Hook (237)

236 Vignette in *Bon-Mots* of Foote and Hook (244)

237 Vignette in *Bon-Mots* of Foote and Hook (235)

238 Echo of Venice (236)

239 Grotesque in *Bon-Mots* of Foote and Hook (239)

240 Vignette in *Bon-Mots* of Foote and Hook (243)

241 Grotesque in *Bon-Mots* of Foote and Hook (240)

242 Vignette in *Bon-Mots*
of Foote and Hook (238)

243 Vignette in *Bon-Mots* of Foote and Hook (242)

244 Vignette in *Bon-Mots* of Foote and Hook (241)

245 Grotesque in *Bon-Mots* of Foote and Hook (245)

246 Vignette in *Bon-Mots* of Foote and Hook (246)

247 Grotesque in *Bon-Mots* of Foote and Hook (247)

248 Vignette in *Bon-Mots* of Foote and Hook (248)

249 Vignette in *Bon-Mots* of Foote and Hook (250)

250 Vignette intended for the *Bon-Mots* series (not used) (251)

251 Grotesque in *Bon-Mots* of Foote and Hook (249)

252 A Snare of Vintage, for *Lucian's True History* (254)

253 A Snare of Vintage, from *Lucian's True History* (255)

254 Dreams, for *Lucian's True History* (256)

255 Birth from the Calf of the Leg, for *Lucian's True History* (not used) (258)

256 Lucian's Strange Creatures, for *Lucian's True History* (not used) (257)

257 La Femme Incomprise (252)

258 Design for a book-marker (253)

259 The Birthday of Madame Cigale (260)

OF A NEOPHYTE
AND HOW THE
BLACK ART WAS
REVEALED UNTO
HIM BY THE
FIEND ASOMVEL

260 Of a Neophyte and how the Black Art was revealed unto him, from *The Pall Mall Magazine* (262)

261 The Kiss of Judas, illustration for *The Pall Mall Magazine* (263)

262 Frontispiece to *The Wonderful History of Virgilius the Sorcerer of Rome* (267)

263 Frontispiece (The Landslide) to *Pastor Sang* (264)

VOL. I. NO. 1.

APRIL, 1893.

THE STUDIO

AN ILLVSTRATED MAGAZINE OF FINE AND APPLIED ART.

Artists as Craftsmen. No. I.
Sir Frederic Leighton as a Modeller.

The Growth of Recent Art.
By R. A. M. STEVENSON.

A New Illustrator : Aubrey Beardsley. By JOSEPH PENNELL.

Spitalfields Brocades.
By LASENBY LIBERTY.

Designing for Book-plates.

Spain as a Sketching Ground.
By FRANK BRANGWYN.

The Newlyn Point of View.

The Grafton Gallery.
By C. W. FURSE.

News of the Month. Reviews. &c. &c.

———

With Auto-lithograph (33 × 15),
" *WEED BURNERS IN THE FENS.* "
By R. W. MACBETH, A.R.A.

SIXPENCE

OFFICES : 16 HENRIETTA ST., COVENT GARDEN, LONDON

MONTHLY

Annual Subscription, Seven Shillings and Sixpence, Post Free.

265 Réjane (265)

266 Réjane (266)

267 Title-page to *Pagan Papers* (268)

268 Drawings on the cover of *Tristan und Isolde* (270)

269 The Playgoers' Club Menu (271)

270 Front cover of *Salome* (not used for 1894 edition) (272)

271 Front cover of *Salome* (273)

272 J'ai Baisé Ta Bouche Iokanaan (261)

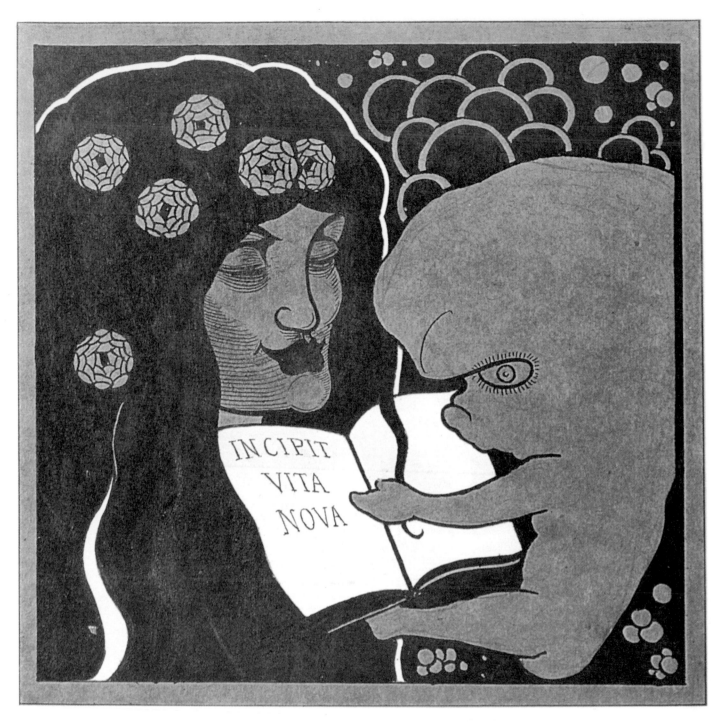

273 Incipit Vita Nova (269)

274 Title-page (274)

275 The Woman in the Moon (Frontispiece) (275)

276 Border for the List of Pictures (276)

277 The Peacock Skirt (277)

278 The Black Cape (278)

279 The Eyes of Herod (279)

280 The Stomach Dance (280)

281 The Toilet of Salome (281)

282 The Dancer's Reward (282)

283 The Burial of Salome (cul-de-lampe) (283)

284 A Platonic Lament from *Salome* (284)

285 Enter Herodias. Proof of an illustration for *Salome* (285)

286 The Climax, from *Salome* (286)

287 The Toilet of Salome. First Version (287)

288 The Toilet of Salome. Working proof of a line-block for *Salome* (288)

289 Salome on Settle, or Maitresse d'Orchestre (289)

290 John and Salome (290)

291 Pierrot and cat, from *St Paul's* (294)

292 Music, from *St Paul's* (291)

293 The Man that holds the Watering Pot, for *St Paul's* (293)

294 Design for *St Paul's* (292)

295 Design for front cover and title-page of *Keynotes* (295)

THE

PSEUDONYM

AND

AUTONYM

Libraries.

Published
Monthly
Price
Paper, 1/6
Cloth, 2/-

*May be had at all the Booksellers
and Bookstalls.*

PSEUDONYM.—1. Mademoiselle Ixe. 2. Story of Eleanor Lambert. 3. Mystery of the Campagna. 4. The School of Art. 5. Amaryllis. 6. Hôtel D'Angleterre. 7. A Russian Priest. 8. Some Emotions and a Moral. 9. European Relations. 10. John Sherman. 11. Through the Red-Litten Windows. 12. Green Tea. 13. Heavy Laden. 14. Makar's Dream. 15. New England Cactus. 16. The Herb of Love. 17. The General's Daughter. 18. Saghalien Convict. 19. Gentleman Upcott's Daughter. 20. A Splendid Cousin. 21. Colette. 22. Ottilie. 23. A Study in Temptations. 24. The Cruise of the "Wild Duck." 25. Squire Hellman. 26. A Father of Six. 27. The Two Countesses. 28. The Sinner's Comedy. 29. Cavalleria Rusticana. 30. The Passing of a Mood. 31. God's Will. 32. Dream Life and Real Life. 33. The Home of the Dragon. 34. A Bundle of Life. 35. Mimi's Marriage. 36. The Rousing of Mrs. Potter. 37. A Study in Colour. 38. The Hon. Stanbury, and Others. 39. The Shen's Pigtail. 40. Young Sam and Sabina. 41. The Silver Christ, by "Ouida."

AUTONYM.—1 The Upper Berth, by Marion Crawford. 2. Mad Sir Uchtred, by S. R. Crockett, author of "The Raiders." 3. By Reef and Palm, by Louis Becke.

LANOE FALCONER

——

MADEMOISELLE IXE

TENTH EDITION

LONDON
T. FISHER UNWIN
PATERNOSTER SQUARE

PSEUDONYM LIBRARY

The Upper
Berth, by
F. Marion
Crawford

LONDON: T. FISHER
UNWIN, PATERNOSTER
SQUARE. MDCCCXCIV

AVBREY
BEARDSLEY

T. FISHER UNWIN,

Paternoster Square, London.

296 Poster advertising The Pseudonym and Autonym Libraries (333)

297 Poster advertising *A Comedy of Sighs* (319)

The

Dancing
Faun

by

Florence
Farr

London
Elkin Mathews
and John Lane
———
Roberts Brothers
Boston
1894

Poor Folk

translated
from
the Russian
of
F. Dostoievsky
by
Lena Milman
with an
Introduction
by
George Moore

London
Elkin Mathews
and John Lane
———
Roberts Brothers
Boston
1894

298 Title-page of *The Dancing Faun* (296)   299 Title-page of *Poor Folk* (297)

301 Design for front cover and title-page
of *The Great God Pan and The Inmost Light* (299)

302 Unfinished and unused design for *The Great God and The Inmost Light* (300)

303 Design for front cover
and title-page of *Discords* (301)

304 Design for front cover
and title-page of *Grey Roses* (302)

At the First Corner

AND OTHER STORIES BY

H. B. Marriott Watson

AUTHOR OF
'DIOGENES OF LONDON'

London : John Lane, Vigo St.
Boston : Roberts Bros., 1895

305 Title-page of *At The First Corner and Other Stories* (303)

MONOCHROMES

BY ELLA D'ARCY

LONDON : JOHN LANE, VIGO ST.
BOSTON : ROBERTS BROS., 1895

306 Title-page of *Monochromes* (304)

307 Designs for front cover, title-page
and key monogram of *The Mountain Lovers* (309)

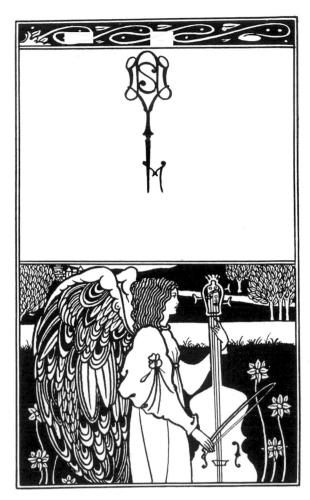

308 Designs for front cover, and title-page
and key monogram of *The Mirror of Music* (307)

309 Title-page of *At The Relton Arms* (305)

310 Title-page of *The Girl from the Farm* (306)

311 Eight designs in the *Keynotes* series (313)

312 Six designs in the *Keynotes* series, and one for *The Barbarous Britishers* (314)

NOBODY'S FAULT
BY NETTA SYRETT

LONDON : JOHN LANE, VIGO ST
BOSTON : ROBERTS BROS., 1896

313 Title-page of *Nobody's Fault* (310)

314 Designs for front cover and title-page of *Yellow and Whi*
and key monogram for *The Three Impostors* (308)

315 Design for front cover
   and title-page of *The British Barbarians* (311)

316 Design for front cover
   and title-page of *Platonic Affections* (312)

YOUNG OFEG'S DITTIES

BY OLA HANSSON

TRANSLATED FROM
THE SWEDISH BY
GEORGE EGERTON

LONDON: JOHN LANE, VIGO ST
BOSTON: ROBERTS BROS., 1895

317 Title-page of *Young Ofeg's Ditties* (315)

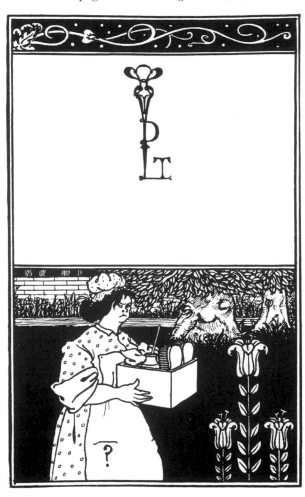

318 Design for front cover and title-page,
   and key monogram of *The Barbarous Britishers* (316)

319 Masked Pierrot in black from *Plays*
by John Davidson (318)

320 Girl and a Bookshop (334)

321 Frontispiece to *Plays* by John Davidson (317)

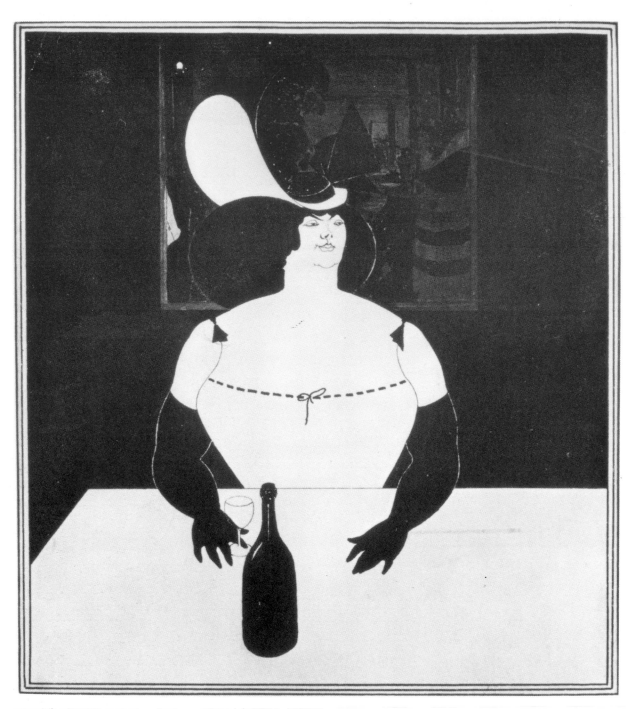

322 The Fat Woman (325)

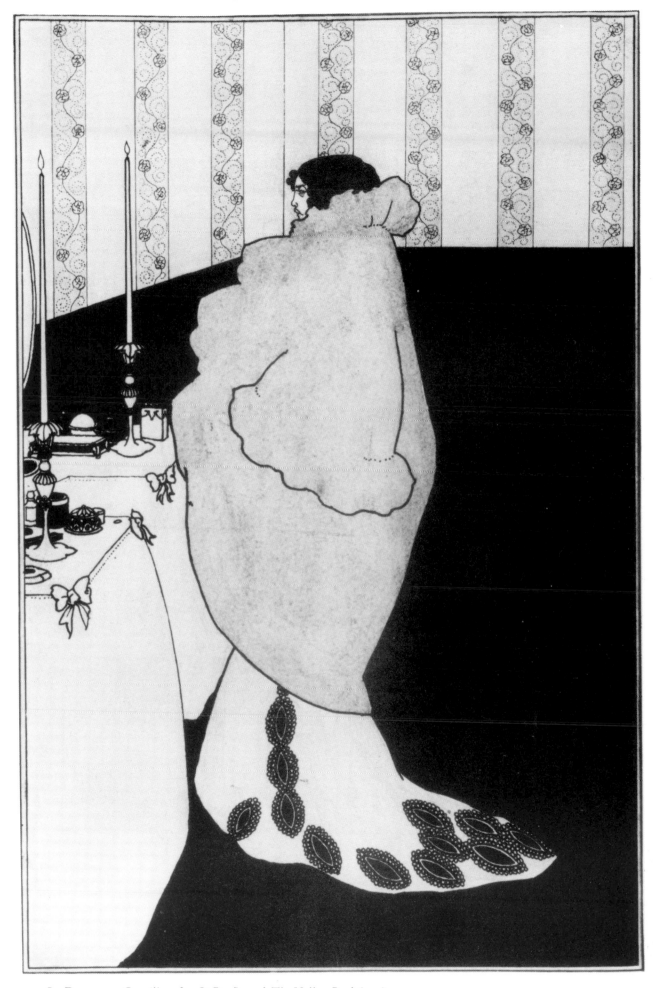

323 La Dame aux Camélias, for *St Paul's* and *The Yellow Book* (322)

AVBREY BEARDSLEY

PUBLISHER.

CHILDREN'S BOOKS.

Topsys and Turvys.

Vols. I & II. By P. S. NEWELL. Coloured Illustrations.
Oblong, size 9 by 7 in. Paper Boards, each 3s. 6d. net.

WORKS BY PALMER COX.

Quarto, 10¼ by 9 inches. Illustrated.

The Brownies Around the World. Cloth, 6s.

The Brownies at Home. Cloth, 6s.

The Brownies, their Book. Paper Boards, 3s. 6d.

Another Brownie Book. Paper Boards, 3s. 6d.

THE CHILDREN'S LIBRARY.

Illustrated, post 8vo., Pinafore Cloth Binding, floral edges, 2s. 6d. each.

1. The Brown Owl.
2. The China Cup.
3. Stories from Fairyland
4. The Story of a Puppet
5. The Little Princess.
6. Tales from the Mabinogion.
7. Irish Fairy Tales.
8. An Enchanted Garden
9. La Belle Nivernaise.
10. The Feather.
11. Finn and His Companions.
12. Nutcracker & Mouse King.
13. Once upon a Time.
14. The Pentamerone.
15. Finnish Legends.
16. The Pope's Mule.
17. The Little Glass Man.
18. Robinson Crusoe.
19. The Magic Oak Tree.

The Land of Pluck.

By MARY MAPES DODGE. Illustrated.
Crown 8vo., Cloth Gilt, 5s.

ST. NICHOLAS

For YOUNG FOLKS.

An Illustrated Monthly Magazine for Boys and Girls, price 1s.

Bound Half-Yearly Volumes, 5s.

The Volumes for 1894 contain Four "Jungle Stories," by
RUDYARD KIPLING: "Tom Sawyer Abroad," by MARK
TWAIN: Stories by MARY WILKINS, KATE WIGGIN,
MARY MAPES DODGE, &c.

BOOKSELLERS.

324 Poster advertising *Children's Books* (335)

325 Chopin Ballade III (320)

326 Invitation card to the opening of the Prince's Ladies Golf Club (329)

The Cambridge A.B.C.
No. 1.   June 8, 1894.

Cambridge: Elijah Johnson

PRICE SIXPENCE

328 Front Wrapper of *The Cambridge A.B.C.* (326)

327 Frontispiece to *Baron Verdigris.*
    A Romance of the Reversed Direction (328)

329 A Caprice (323)

330 A masked woman (324)

331 Caricature of Beardsley (379)

332 Rejane [*sic*] (327)

333 Caricature of Whistler (336)

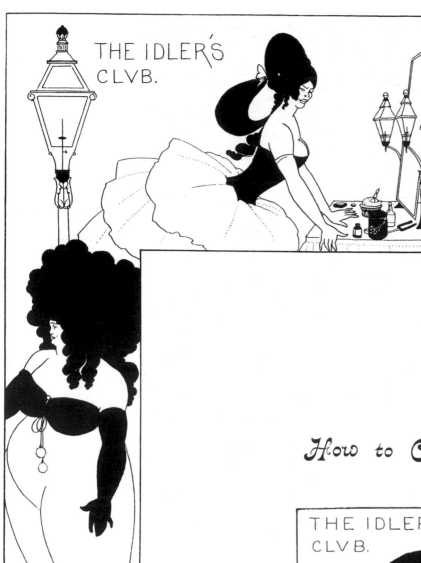

334 The Idler's Club (331)

How to Court the "Advanced Woman."

335 Headpiece from *The Idler* (330)

THE DEVELOPMENT OF THE "EMANCIPATED."

ANGUS EVAN ABBOTT.

THE development of the Emancipated Woman has been a gradual development, and, step by step, as emancipation has proceeded on its way to consummation, the conditions of courtship have undergone proportionate change. Looking into the subject, it will be found that originally women were Spoil. In earliest days, Man went courting with a club. He thirled the wood, and lurked in ambush

336 Les Passades, from *To-Day* (332)

337 The Murders in the Rue Morgue (337)

338 The Black Cat (338)

339 The Fall of the House of Usher (339)

340 The Mask of the Red Death (340)

341 Design for a poster advertising *The Yellow Book* (341)

342 Poster advertising Singer sewing machines (321)

343 Design for the prospectus of *The Yellow Book* (342)

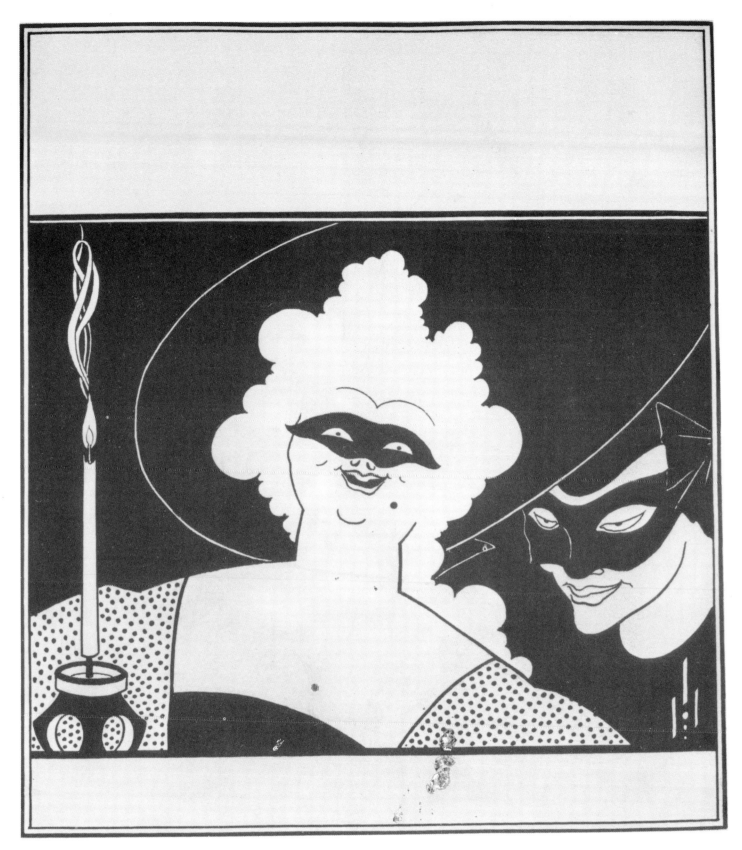

344 Design for front cover of *The Yellow Book*, Vol. I (343)

The Yellow Book

An Illustrated Quarterly

Volume I   April 1894

London : Elkin Mathews
& John Lane
Boston : Copeland &
Day

345 Title-page of *The Yellow Book*, Vol. I (345)

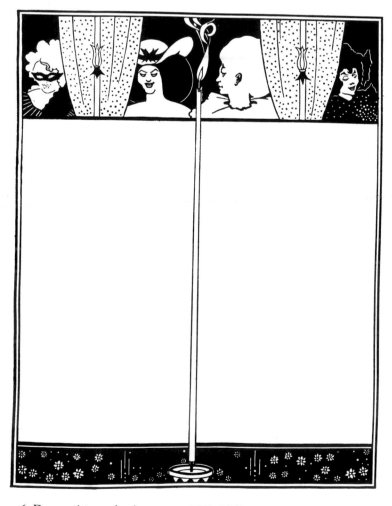

346 Decoration on back covers of *The Yellow Book* (344)

347 Mrs Patrick Campbell (349)

348 Part of the drawing 'L'Éducation Sentimentale' (347)

349 L'Éducation Sentimentale (346)

350 Bookplate of John Lumsden Propert (350)

351 A Night Piece (348)

352 Design for title-page of
The Yellow Book, Vol. II (352)

353 Design for front cover of *The Yellow Book*, Vol. II (351)

355 The Slippers of Cinderella (358)

356 No. I of 'The Comedy Ballet of Marionettes' (353)

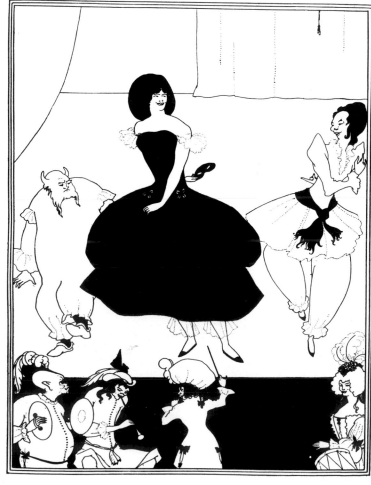

357 No. III of 'The Comedy Ballet of Marionettes' (355)

358 No. II of 'The Comedy Ballet of Marionettes' (354)

359 The Dancer (356)

360 Madame Réjane (359)

The Yellow Book

An Illustrated Quarterly

Volume III   October, 1894

London : John Lane, The Bodley Head, Vigo Street
Boston : Copeland & Day
Agents for the Colonies : Robt. A. Thompson & Co.

361 Design for front cover of *The Yellow Book*, Vol. III (360)

362 Title-page of *The Yellow Book*, Vol. III (361)

363 Portrait of Himself (362)

364 Lady Gold's Escort (363)

366 The Wagnerites (364)

367 The Mysterious Rose Garden (366)

368 Discarded drawing for 'The Mysterious Rose Garden' (367)

THE REPENTANCE
OF Mᴿˢ ....

369 The Repentance of Mrs . . . (368)

370 Portrait of Winifred Emery (369)

371 Frontispiece of Juvenal (370)

372 Atalanta in Calydon (372)

373 Design for the prospectus and the front cover of *The Yellow Book*, Vol. V (371)

374 Portrait of Miss Letty Lind (373)

375 A Nocturne of Chopin (374)

376 Design for a poster advertising *The Yellow Book* (not used) (375)

378 Design for a front cover of *The Yellow Book* (not used) (376)

377 Madame Réjane (378)

379 A title-page ornament (377)

380 Poster advertising *The Spinster's Scrip* (380)

381 Frontispiece to *A Full and True Account of the Wonderful Mission of Earl Lavender* (383)

382 Front cover of *Sappho* (385)

383 Invitation card for John Lane's 'Sette of Odd Volumes Smoke' (382)

384 The Scarlet Pastorale (384)

385 The Mirror of Love (386)

VENUS.

386 Venus between Terminal Gods (387)

387 Design for a frontispiece to *The Story of Venus and Tannhäuser* (389)

388 Venus (388)

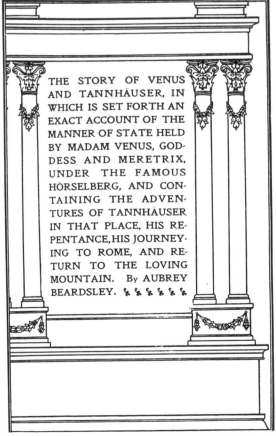

THE STORY OF VENUS
AND TANNHÄUSER, IN
WHICH IS SET FORTH AN
EXACT ACCOUNT OF THE
MANNER OF STATE HELD
BY MADAM VENUS, GOD-
DESS AND MERETRIX,
UNDER THE FAMOUS
HÖRSELBERG, AND CON-
TAINING THE ADVEN-
TURES OF TANNHÄUSER
IN THAT PLACE, HIS RE-
PENTANCE, HIS JOURNEY-
ING TO ROME, AND RE-
TURN TO THE LOVING
MOUNTAIN. By AUBREY
BEARDSLEY.

389 *The Story of Venus and Tannhäuser* (390)

390 The Return of Tannhäuser to the Venusberg (391)

ISOLDE

391 Isolde (392)

392 Messalina returning home (393)

393 First frontispiece to *An Evil Motherhood* (394)

394 Second frontispiece to *An Evil Motherhood* (395)

395 Illustration to 'At a Distance' (396)

396 Autumn (381)

397 Designs for volumes in the 'Pierrot's Library' (397)

398 Title-pages in the 'Pierrot's Library' (399)

399 Back covers of volumes in the 'Pierrot's Library' (398)

400 Front end-papers of volumes in the 'Pierrot's Library' (400)

401 Back end-papers of volumes in the 'Pierrot's Library' (401)

No. 6   1896

CATALOGUE OF RARE BOOKS

OFFERED FOR SALE BY

LEONARD SMITHERS

EFFINGHAM HOUSE ARUNDEL STREET STRAND

LONDON W.C.

PRICE ONE SHILLING

402   Front wrapper of *Catalogue of Rare Books* (402)

403   The Billet-Doux, from *The Rape of the Lock* (405)

404 Design for front cover of *The Rape of the Lock* (403)

405 The Dream, for *The Rape of the Lock* (404)

406 The Toilet, for *The Rape of the Lock* (406)

407 The Baron's Prayer, for *The Rape of the Lock* (407)

408 The Barge, from *The Rape of the Lock* (408)

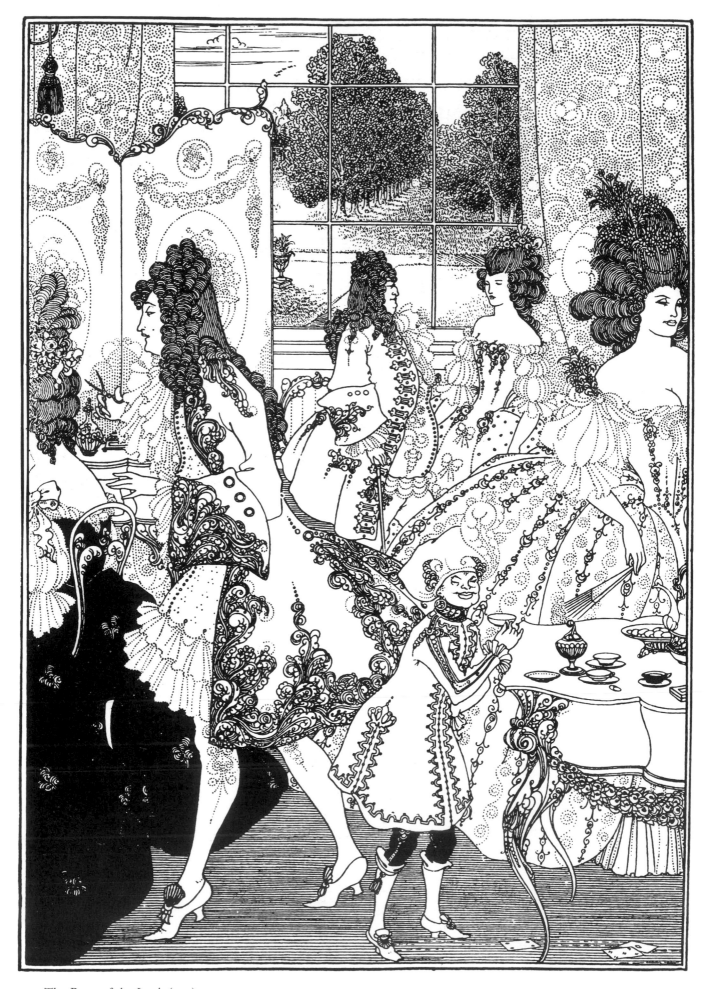

409 The Rape of the Lock (409)

410 The Battle of the Beaux and the Belles, for *The Rape of the Lock* (411)

411 The Cave of Spleen, for *The Rape of the Lock* (410)

AB.

412 The New Star, for *The Rape of the Lock* (412)

413 Front cover of the bijou edition of *The Rape of the Lock* (413)

AUBREY BEARDSLEY.

414 Design for front cover of prospectus of *The Savoy*, NO. I (414)

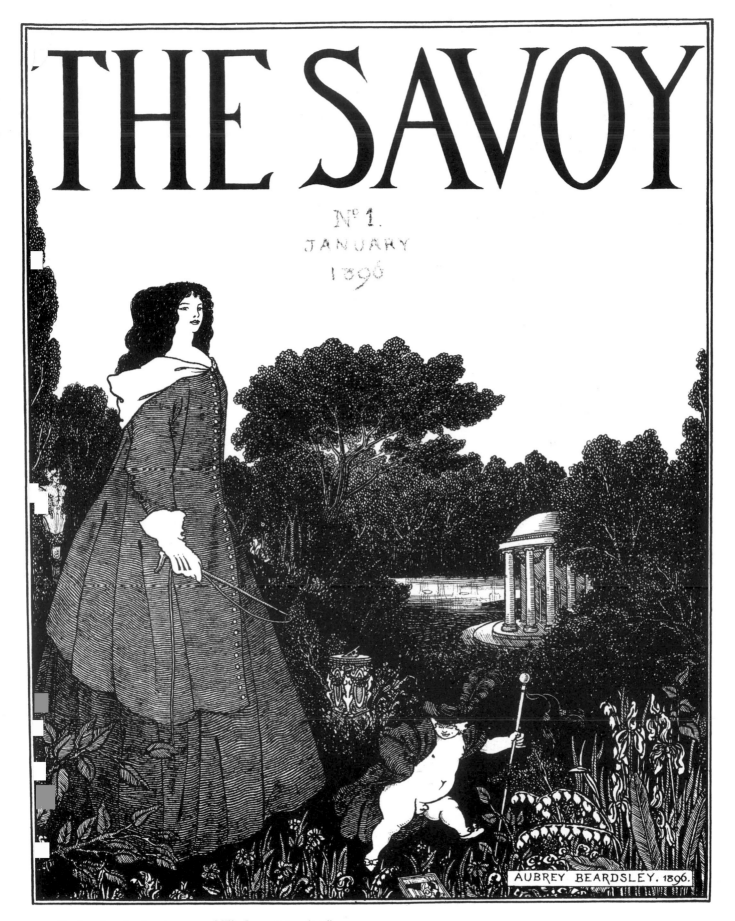

THE SAVOY

Nº 1.
JANUARY
1896

AUBREY BEARDSLEY. 1896.

415 Design for the front cover of *The Savoy*, NO. I (416)

416 Design for title-page of *The Savoy*, NO. I (417)

418 Design for page preceding contents list in *The Savoy*, NO. 1 (418)

419 The Three Musicians
(not used for poem in *Savoy*) (419)

420 The Three Musicians (420)

MOSKA

421 Moska (422)

422 The Bathers (421)

423 The Abbé (423)

424 The Toilet (424)

425 The Fruit Bearers (425)

426 The Ascension of Saint Rose of Lima (429)

427 Choosing the New Hat. Front cover of *The Savoy*, NO. 2 (427)

429 A Large Christmas Card (426)

428 A Footnote (428)

430 The Third Tableau of Das Rheingold (430)

431 The Driving of Cupid from the Garden. Design for the front wrapper of *The Savoy*, NO. 3 (431)

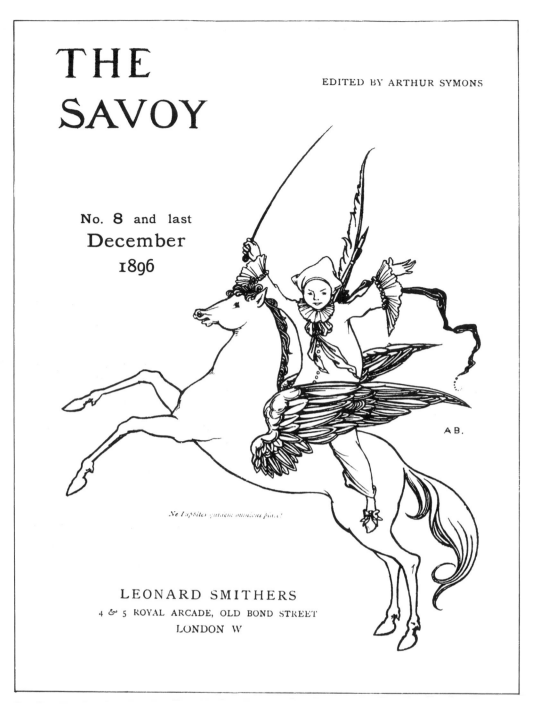

THE
SAVOY

EDITED BY ARTHUR SYMONS

No. **8** and last
December
1896

LEONARD SMITHERS
4 & 5 ROYAL ARCADE, OLD BOND STREET
LONDON W

432 Puck on Pegasus (432)

AUBREY BEARDSLEY.

433 Design for the front wrapper of *The Savoy*, NO. 4 (435)

AUBREY BEARDSLEY.

434 The Coiffing, illustrating Beardsley's poem 'The Ballad of a Barber' (433)

435 The Death of Pierrot (439)

436 *Cul-de-lampe* illustrating Beardsley's poem 'The Ballad of a Barber' (434)

437 The Woman in White (437)

438 Front wrapper of *The Savoy*, NO. 5 (436)

THE SAVOY

AN ILLUSTRATED MONTHLY

No. 7   November 1896   Price **2/-**

EDITED BY ARTHUR SYMONS

439 First page of *The Savoy*, NO. 7 (440)

440 The Fourth Tableau of 'Das Rheingold'. Design for the front wrapper of *The Savoy*, NO. 6 (438)

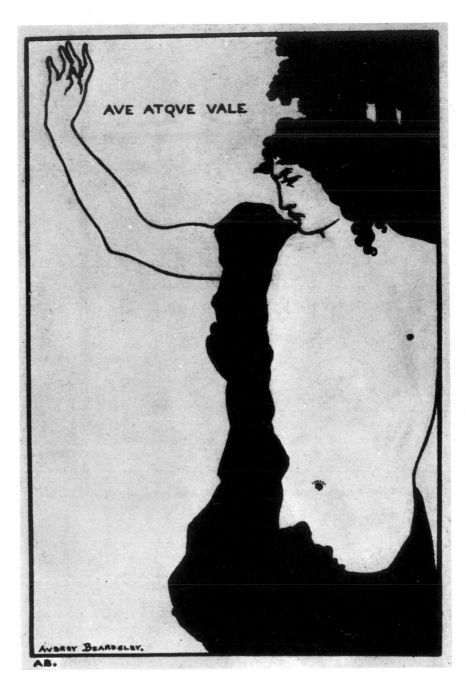

441 Ave atque Vale (441)

442 First page of *The Savoy*, NO. 8 (442)

443 Mrs Pinchwife, from Wycherley's *Country Wife* (443)

444 A Repetition of 'Tristan und Isolde' (444)

445 Don Juan Sganarelle, and the Beggar (445)

446 Flosshilde (447)

447 Erda (449)

449 Et in Arcadia Ego (452)

450 Frontispiece to
The Comedy of the Rhinegold (446)

THE
COMEDY
OF
THE
RHINEGOLD

ALBERICH

451 Alberich (448)

453 Poster for *The Savoy* (453)

454 Sketch of a young girl (454)

455 Apollo pursuing Daphne (455)

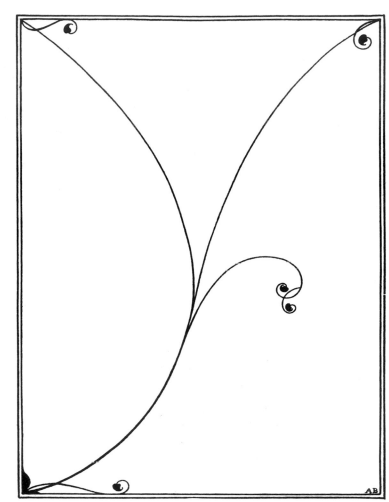

457 Design for front cover of *Verses* by Ernest Dowson (457)

456 Design for front cover of *The Life and Times of Madame Du Barry* (456)

458 Ali Baba (458)

459 Ali Baba in the Wood (459)

LYSISTRATA.

460 Lysistrata shielding her Coynte (460)

AVBREY BEARDSLEY.

461 The Toilet of Lampito (461)

462 Lysistrata Haranguing the Athenian Women (462)

AVBREY
BEARDSLEY

467 Two Athenian Women in Distress (467)

AVBREY BEARDSLEY. MDCCCXCVI.

468 Juvenal Scourging Woman (468)

469 Bathyllus in the Swan Dance (469)

470 Bathyllus Posturing (470)

472 Self-portrait (472)

471 Design for the artist's bookplate, used by Pollitt (471)

473 Design for front cover of *A Book of Fifty Drawings by Aubrey Beardsley* (473)

THE PARADE
AN ILLUSTRATED
GIFT BOOK FOR
BOYS AND GIRLS
1897

LONDON H. HENRY AND CO. LTD.
93 ST. MARTIN'S LANE W.C.   1897

475 Frontispiece to *A Book of Bargains* (475)

476 Design for front cover of *The Pierrot of the Minute* (476)

477 Frontispiece to *The Pierrot of the Minute* (477)

478 Headpiece and the initial letter P in *The Pierrot of the Minute* (478)

479 *Cul-de-lampe* in *The Pierrot of the Minute* (479)

480 Head of Balzac for front covers of *Scenes of Parisian Life* (480)

481 For spines of *Scenes of Parisian Life* (481)

482 Atalanta in Calydon, with the hound (482)

MESSALINA.

483 Messalina returning from the bath (483)

484 La Dame aux Camélias (484)

485 Front cover of *The Houses of Sin* (485)

486 Front cover of *The Souvenirs of Léonard,
Hairdresser to Queen Marie Antoinette* (486)

488 D'Albert (488)

487 Mademoiselle de Maupin (487)

489 D'Albert in Search of His Ideals (489)

490 The Lady at the Dressing Table (490)

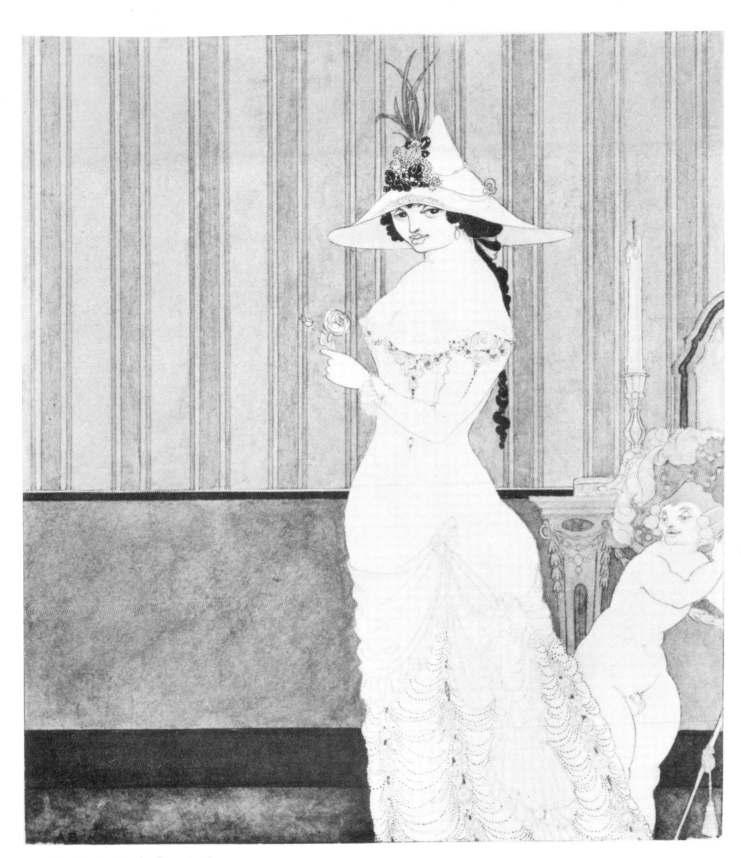

491 The Lady with the Rose (491)

492 The Lady with the Monkey (492)

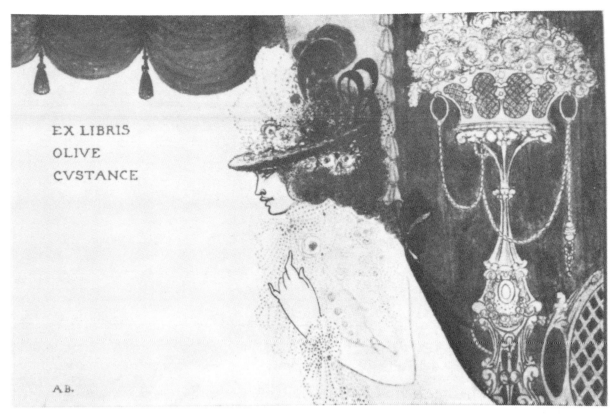

EX LIBRIS
OLIVE
CVSTANCE

A.B.

493 Book-plate of
the poetess Olive Custance (493)

494 Arbuscula (494)

495 Design for the front cover of *Ben Jonson His Volpone* (495)

VOLPONE

496 Volpone Adoring his Treasure (496)

497 Initial V for *Ben Jonson his Volpone* (497)

498 Initial V for *Ben Jonson his Volpone* (498)

499 Initial S for *Ben Jonson his Volpone* (499)

500 Sketch for a variant of initial S for *Ben Jonson his Volpone* (500)

501 Initial M for *Ben Jonson his Volpone* (501)

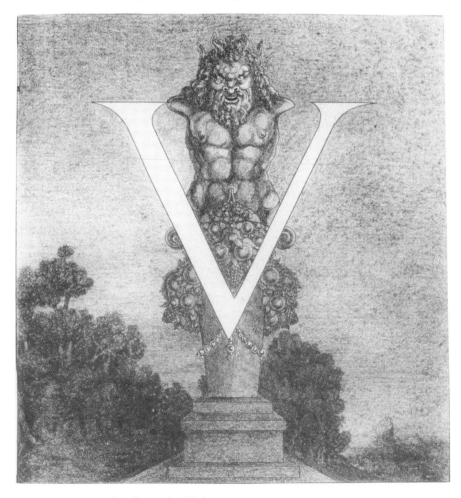

502 Initial V for *Ben Jonson his Volpone* (502)

Notes

In the notes, references to plate numbers are given at the end of the first paragraph. References to other notes are given in brackets.

1 Drawing based on an illustration by Kate Greenaway. Done by Beardsley at the age of eleven, 1884. Pl. 1
Pen and crayon, $3\frac{1}{2} \times 2\frac{1}{8}$ inches
Rosenwald Collection, National Gallery of Art, Washington

This coloured drawing and the one reproduced at No. 2 were mounted in an album containing thirteen other drawings of the same kind, and a letter from 'Aubrey V. Beardsley' dated 1 February [1884], in which it is stated that all the drawings were copied from different books sent to him by Lady Henrietta Pelham, for whom the drawings were made. Another letter, hinged into the album, is from Sir Edmund Gosse, dated 20 March 1928, and explains that the drawings were the earliest known to be by Beardsley. He says therein that Lady Henrietta Pelham helped Beardsley's parents, who were at the time 'in destitute circumstances', and that she paid for Aubrey Beardsley's music lessons.

2 Drawing based on an illustration by Kate Greenaway. Done by Beardsley at the age of eleven, 1884. Pl. 2
Pen and crayon, $2\frac{5}{8} \times 3\frac{3}{4}$ inches
Rosenwald Collection, National Gallery of Art, Washington

The drawing is a companion to No. 1 and is mounted in the same album.

3 La discourse. A caricature of Mr Marshall, Beardsley's headmaster at Brighton Grammar School, c. 1885–1888. Pl. 3
Pen and violet ink, $8\frac{1}{4} \times 6\frac{3}{8}$ inches
Princeton University Library

4 La lecture. A caricature of Mr Marshall, Beardsley's headmaster at Brighton Grammar School, c. 1885–1888. Pl. 4
Pen and violet ink, $8 \times 6\frac{1}{4}$ inches
Princeton University Library

5 La chymist. A caricature of Mr Marshall, Beardsley's headmaster at Brighton Grammar School, c. 1885–1888. Pl. 5
Pen and violet ink, $7\frac{3}{4} \times 6\frac{1}{4}$ inches
Princeton University Library

6 Flavouring the apple tart. A caricature of Mr Marshall, Beardsley's headmaster at Brighton Grammar School, c. 1885–1888. Pl. 6
Pen and violet ink, $7\frac{3}{4} \times 6\frac{1}{4}$ inches
Princeton University Library

7 A little chamber music. Drawing with a caricature of Mr Marshall (on the left), Beardsley's headmaster at Brighton Grammar School, c. 1885–1888. Pl. 7
Size of sheet $6\frac{1}{4} \times 7$ inches
Princeton University Library

8 The Jubilee Cricket Analysis. Reproduction facing p. 48 in *Past and Present,* Vol. XII, NO. 2, June 1887, 8vo. Signed A. V. Beardsley. Pl. 8
From the line-block
Brighton and Hove Grammar School, England

Past and Present was the Brighton Grammar School magazine, and this plate was the first reproduction of any drawing by Beardsley. He attended the school from the end of 1884 until the summer of 1888. The eleven sketches illustrate visual puns on cricketing terms.

9 Sketches (four on one sheet) of violinists, c. 1885–1888. Pl. 9
Size of sheet $7\frac{3}{8} \times 10\frac{3}{4}$ inches
Princeton University Library

Beardsley's taste for music developed early. As a child he sang, recited and gave piano performances to his mother's friends; and since she taught the piano as well as French, her son's interest in music must be accredited partly to her.

10 Illustrations to *The Pay of the Pied Piper,* A Legend of Hamelin Town, written by Fred Edmonds, composed by C. T. West: representing the first syllable of the Charade, invented and arranged by Mr C. T. West for the Dome Entertainment of the Brighton Grammar School, Christmas 1888. Reprinted in *Past and Present,* the magazine of the School, February 1889, Vol. XIV, NO. 1. Pl. 10
Line-blocks
Brighton and Hove Grammar School, England

Beardsley produced eleven drawings illustrating the text of *The Pay of the Pied Piper,* of which two are here reproduced. He also designed the costumes, acted the part of Herr Kirschwasser in this comic opera, and appeared too as Mercury in the Prologue by his house-master, A. W. King. The entertainment was held at the Dome on 19 December 1888; Beardsley had left the School at the end of the Michaelmas term of that year, and he was therefore by Christmas time an Old Boy.

11 Paganini. Sketch in pen and pencil made in 1888. Reproduced as NO. 50 in *The Uncollected Work of Aubrey Beardsley,* John Lane, London, 1925. Pl. 11
From the half-tone plate

At the time when this sketch was made, Beardsley had evolved a style of grotesque drawing quite distinct from his comic style, and somewhat sinister, as in this conception of Paganini.

12 Sarah Bernhardt. Head and shoulders. Drawing made by Beardsley c. 1888 in a scrap-album belonging to his family. Pl. 12
Pencil, $9\frac{1}{2} \times 7\frac{1}{4}$ inches
Princeton University Library

13 Holywell Street, London. Sketch in ink wash reproduced as NO.4 in *The Early Work of Aubrey Beardsley,* John Lane, London, 1899. Pl.13
From the half-tone plate

This early drawing was reproduced first on a small scale as an illustration on p. 104 in an article by Charles B. Cochran in *The Poster,* Vol. I, August–September 1898, pp. 102–105, entitled 'Aubrey Beardsley at School'. There the drawing is said to have been done when Beardsley was sixteen, that is in 1888. It is one of his very few and immature attempts to draw in an Impressionist style—an attempt which has a certain crude merit.

14 The Cambridge Theatre of Varieties. Drawing for the programme of an amateur theatrical performance by Mabel and Aubrey Beardsley, *c.*1888–1889. Pl.14
Pen, ink and wash, $7 \times 4\frac{1}{2}$ inches
Princeton University Library

The name of the 'Theatre' was taken from the address, 32 Cambridge Street, Pimlico, London, where the Beardsleys were living at the time. Madame 'Mâbélè' was Mabel Beardsley and 'André' was of course her brother, the artist himself.

15 The Jolly Mashers. Drawing for the programme of an amateur theatrical performance by Mabel and Aubrey Beardsley, *c.*1888–1889. Pl.15
Pen, ink and wash, $7 \times 4\frac{1}{2}$ inches
Princeton University Library

These burlesque drawings, NOS.14–16, have something of the spidery character of the manner of George Cruikshank, and of the silhouette images in optical toys of the mid-nineteenth century.

16 Songs. Drawing for the programme of an amateur theatrical performance by Mabel and Aubrey Beardsley, *c.*1888–1889. Pl.16
Pen, ink, wash and water-colour, $7 \times 4\frac{1}{2}$ inches
Princeton University Library

17 Dante in Exile. Reproduced from a pen, ink and wash drawing as NO.6 in *The Later Work of Aubrey Beardsley,* John Lane, 1901. Signed with the initials A.V.B. Pl.17
From the half-tone plate

This 'illuminated' sonnet dates probably from 1890, when Beardsley was drawn towards the study of Dante by A. H. Pargeter, a fellow clerk at the Guardian Fire and Life Insurance offices. The script used for writing out the poem and the rustic-romantic style of the surrounding ornament are in the manner of William Blake's illustrated works; but not the trailing wisps, which are Beardsley's own.

18 Drawing illustrating a scene in Ibsen's play *Ghosts,* Act I, *c.*1890. In a scrap-book which belonged to the Beardsley family. Pl.18
Pencil, pen and ink, $8 \times 8\frac{1}{2}$ inches
Princeton University Library

19 Tannhäuser. 1891. Inscribed with title. Pl.19
Indian ink and wash
Rosenwald Collection, National Gallery of Art, Washington

The theme of Tannhäuser had a fascination for Beardsley. The composition of this amateur drawing became the basis for one of his finest designs (NO.391).

20 The Litany of Mary Magdalen. 1891. Inscribed with title. Pl.20
Pencil, 8×6 inches
Chicago Institute of Art

This was one of the drawings made by Beardsley shortly after his visit to Burne-Jones on 12 July 1891. It reveals that the young amateur artist had studied the figure of St John in Mantegna's engraving *The Entombment* (Armand-Durand, No. 3) for the kneeling figure of Mary Magdalen. A similar kneeling figure, linked in form to the Mary Magdalen and the St John, occurs in Beardsley's *Repentance of Mrs . . .* published in *The Yellow Book,* Vol. IV, October 1894 (NO.368)

21 Hail Mary. Head in profile to the left with a lily, *c.*1891. Pl.22
Pencil, $5\frac{7}{16} \times 4\frac{5}{8}$ inches
Princeton University Library

In 1891 Beardsley was a clerk in the Guardian Life Insurance Company, near which stood the bookshop of Jones and Evans in Queen Street. Having visited the shop often in his lunch-hours and made friends with Frederick H. Evans, Beardsley presented him with this drawing in 1891. At the end of the following year Evans showed it to John Dent, who was sufficiently impressed by it, and others by Beardsley, to commission the young man to illustrate *Le Morte Darthur.*

22 Hamlet Patris Manem Sequitur. Drawing reproduced by lithography in light red as a frontispiece to *The Bee,* the journal of the Blackburn Technical Institute, Vol. II, Part 2, November 1891. Inscribed with title. Pl.21
Pencil, $11\frac{1}{2} \times 5\frac{3}{8}$ inches
British Museum

Beardsley's design was redrawn professionally on the lithographic stone for the frontispiece. A. W. King, who had been his housemaster at Brighton Grammar School, and in 1890 had become Secretary of the Institute, arranged for the frontispiece to be made and wrote a notice of it in the same number of the journal. Beardsley met Burne-Jones for the first time on 12 July 1891, and the present drawing is an example of how at this date he chose to borrow certain mannerisms of the painter, giving them a twist of his own. The subject is Hamlet following the ghost of his Father.

23 Self-portrait. Head and shoulders, full face, *c.*1892. Pl.23
$9\frac{3}{4} \times 3\frac{1}{2}$ inches
British Museum

Beardsley's own idea of his appearance in the year he made the acquaintance of Robert Ross, to whom he gave the drawing.

24 Professor Fred Brown. Signed with monogram (AVB) and inscribed 'Fred Brown N.E.A.C.', 1892. Pl. 24
Pencil, pen and ink, 10 × 10 inches
Tate Gallery, London

Professor Brown was a founder-member of the New English Art Club, which explains the initials in the drawing. He also taught at the Westminster School of Art where Beardsley went to evening classes from the autumn of 1891 for a year. The drawing is intended to be in the manner of an etching by Whistler.

25 Die Götterdämmerung. Lettered with title, 1892. On the back, rough sketch in pencil and indian ink of Siegfried, Act II ($14\frac{11}{16}$ × 12 inches). Pl. 25
Pen, ink wash and chinese white, $12\frac{1}{8}$ × $20\frac{1}{4}$ inches
Princeton University Library

The generalized forms in this drawing have a sculpturesque quality not to be seen in any other work of Beardsley. It was executed in a manner employed by Burne-Jones in sketches for metalwork.

26 Perseus. Design for a panel. Above the standing nude figure of Perseus is a frieze of small figures. On the back, a pencil sketch of two unfinished figures, c. 1892. Pl. 26
Indian ink and pencil, $17\frac{1}{2}$ × $6\frac{1}{5}$ inches
Mrs Pierre Matisse, New York

In 1891 Beardsley had made an inferior drawing, 'Perseus and the Monstre', in pencil, showing the kneeling figure of a horrified Perseus with draperies burlesquing the style of Burne-Jones, holding out the head of Medusa.

27 Withered Spring. Inscribed with title and (on the gate) 'Ars Longa', c. 1892. Pl. 27
Rosenwald Collection, National Gallery of Art, Washington

Among the earliest designs for chapter headings in *Le Morte Darthur* is one for Book I, Chapter VI, p. 10, adapted from this drawing. The allegory expresses half-consciously perhaps the tragedy of Beardsley's own life. Walter Crane's influence in the somewhat heavy style of the drawn lines is discernible here.

28 Klafsky [*sic*]. Representation of Katharina Klavsky, full-length, as Isolde in Wagner's opera *Tristan und Isolde*. Inscribed 'Klafsky' and 'Isolde', c. 1892. Pl. 28
Pen, ink and water-colour, $12\frac{1}{2}$ × $4\frac{3}{8}$ inches
Princeton University Library

Katharina Klavsky (1855–1896) appeared in the part of Isolde in London in 1892. The opera was to remain a favourite with Beardsley.

29 Carl Maria von Weber. c. 1892. Pl. 30
11 × $4\frac{3}{8}$ inches
Princeton University Library
One of Beardsley's earliest drawings in the personal manner which distinguished him later.

30 Raphael Sanzio. Inscribed with title, c. 1892. Pl. 31
$11\frac{1}{16}$ × $4\frac{3}{16}$ inches
Princeton University Library

During 1892 Beardsley evolved what he called his 'Japonesque' style. The dramatic and decorative use of black areas was arrived at, it appears, by means of experiments with blots of indian ink, and the value of asymmetry in the placing of these areas of black was observed by him in the works of the Japanese print-makers. In his earliest drawings in the 'Japonesque' manner Beardsley lightened the areas of black ink by scratching and rubbing the dried surfaces, so that, as in this case and also in the following drawing, the areas have a richness of texture especially when descriptive of textiles, which is not at all Japanese. In time Beardsley abandoned the practice of varying the texture of his blacks by abrasions.

31 Le Débris [*sic*] d'un Poète. c. 1892. The wreck of a poet. Pl. 32
Pen, indian ink and wash, 13 × $4\frac{7}{8}$ inches
Victoria and Albert Museum, London

An early example of Beardsley's 'Japonesque' style which was evolved by him during 1892. The drawing commemorates his disgust with the life which at this date he was obliged to lead as a clerk in the Guardian Life Insurance Company. The title is quoted from a sentence near the end of Flaubert's *Madame Bovary* meaning that in many a notary there is the débris of a poet.

32 Max Alvary. Portrait of Alvary, half-length in profile to the left. Signed with monogram and inscribed 'Alvary'. Pl. 29
Indian ink on brown paper, $9\frac{1}{2}$ × 5 inches
Princeton University Library

Max Alvary (1856–1898) appeared in the roles of Tristan and Tannhäuser at Covent Garden during 1892 (see *Catalogue of Aubrey Beardsley Exhibition at the Victoria and Albert Museum*, 1966, NO. 132).

33 The Achieving of the Sangreal. Drawing for the frontispiece to Vol. II of *Le Morte Darthur*, 1893–4. Pl. 33
Indian ink and wash, $14\frac{1}{4}$ × $11\frac{1}{4}$ inches
Mr F. J. Martin Dent, London

After his introduction by Frederick Evans to John Dent in the bookshop of Jones and Evans, Beardsley was commissioned to illustrate *Le Morte Darthur*, which Dent was planning to publish with line-block embellishments instead of ornaments and illustrations from hand-engraved wood-blocks as used at the Kelmscott Press by William Morris. Before actually confirming this decision to employ Beardsley for the work, Dent required a sample illustration by him of a theme in the book. The drawing of the 'Sangreal' was the sample Dent received in the autumn of 1892. In it Beardsley has not freed himself from the conventional illusionism of a line-and-wash technique, and the drawing therefore had to be reproduced by photogravure and not by line-block. 'How King Arthur saw the Questing Beast' (56) was the only other drawing for *Le Morte Darthur* to be reproduced by this method. Paintings by Crivelli, Pollaiuolo and Burne-Jones were the chief sources of details in this drawing.

34 Front cover of *Evelina* by Frances Burney, as edited by R. Brimley Johnson, illustrated by W. Cubitt Cooke and published in two volumes by J. M. Dent and Company, London, 1893, 8vo. (Small paper edition.) Pl. 34
Buff cloth boards stamped with title in gold
Mr W. G. Good, England

Writing to André Raffalovich in November 1896, Beardsley

says 'Thank you so much for the volumes of Miss Burney. I was so amused to find that they had covers and title-pages of my own early designing'. (J. Gray [ed.], *Last Letters of Aubrey Beardsley*, London, 1904, No. LI.) The decoration on the spine too was undoubtedly his work.

35 Title-page of *Evelina* by Frances Burney, as edited by R. Brimley Johnson, illustrated by W. Cubitt Cooke and published in two volumes by J. M. Dent and Company, London, 1893, 8vo. Signed with the artist's monogram. Pl. 35

From the lineblock and letterpress
Mr W. G. Good, England

Both the large and small-paper volumes of this edition had the same title-page design, which has features of late Regency and early Victorian ornament, decorated with hair-line arabesques.

36 Evelina and her Guardian. Illustration in pen, ink and wash intended for *Evelina* as published in two volumes by J. M. Dent in 1893, but not used. Reproduced on p. 81 in *Aubrey Beardsley* by Arthur Symons, London, 1905 (large paper edition only), 4to. Pl. 36
From the photogravure
Victoria and Albert Museum, London

The carpet is in Beardsley's 'Japonesque' style 'invented' by him during 1892; but in the rest of the drawing he has made an effort to compete with the conventional book-illustrations of his period, using ink wash for smooth tone transitions. An early example of a recurrent motif in his work can be seen in the flight of birds outside the window. These always symbolized open air.

He was commissioned by Dent to illustrate *Evelina* at the end of 1892, but had so much else to do by the beginning of the following year that he made only the designs for the title-page, front cover and spine of this edition, and the illustrations were done finally by W. Cubitt Cooke.

37 Title-page design. Reproduced for the title-page of *The Early Work of Aubrey Beardsley*, with a prefatory note by H. C. Marillier, published by John Lane, The Bodley Head, London and New York, 1899, 4to. Pl. 37
From the half-tone plate

In certain regions of Brighton, in Oriental Place for example, the architectural adornments in stucco have an assertive baroque quality that is at the same time entirely of the early nineteenth century and not to be seen elsewhere. Something of this quality, and of the almost brutal eclecticism of the decorations in the Royal Pavilion, seem to have been absorbed by Beardsley and intensified by his own grotesque fantasies in this design. It is similar in principle to the published title-page of *Evelina* (NO. 35), except that the drawing is not calligraphic but 'solid', and the effect is of a record of some actual architectural feature. It represents a deviation, albeit a convincing one, from Beardsley's natural form as an artist, to be encountered again in his last work, the initial letters for *Volpone* (NOS. 497–502), where at the end of his life he strived, so it seems, to make tangible in the *trompe l'oeil* idiom of the seventeenth century the conceptions of his brain.

The present design was described in *The Early Work* as unpublished and it is neither signed nor dated. It seems likely that it was made at about the same time as the title-page for *Evelina*.

38–40 Three caricatures from a series of four entitled 'The New Coinage. Four designs which were not sent in for competition'. Reproduced as illustrations on p. 154 of *The Pall Mall Budget*, 9 February 1893. Inscribed with simulated signatures and in pencil with notes. (See also NO. 41.)
Indian ink and pencil, diameter 4 inches
Victoria and Albert Museum, London

38 A little girl seated on a sand castle in the style of a painting by Sir John Millais, R.A. Pl. 38
39 Caricature of Whistler's signature. Pl. 39
40 Caricature of Walter Crane's socialist opinions. Pl. 40
The fourth of these caricatures, of which the original drawing is not available for reproduction here, is shown in No. 141 of *The Early Work of Aubrey Beardsley*, 1899. It caricatures Britannia and has the simulated signature BURNE JONES A R A.

41 Caricature of Queen Victoria as a ballet dancer in the form of a design for a coin. One of the suppressed designs for 'The New Coinage . . .' intended for reproduction in *The Pall Mall Budget*, 9 February 1893. Pl. 41

Indian ink and pencil, diameter 4 inches
Victoria and Albert Museum, London

Beardsley worked for a short time early in 1893 making journalist drawings for *The Pall Mall Budget*, of which Lewis Hind had become the editor. In search of topical subjects both men amused themselves by visiting the Mint to inspect the plaster casts for the new coinage, and Beardsley made a series of caricatures of the designs. Four of these caricatures were published in *The Pall Mall Budget*. The rest were considered too provocative: 'I suppressed them', Hind recorded, 'because Aubrey made them comic, and I think I tore them up', (See *The Uncollected Work of Aubrey Beardsley*, 1925, p. XX.) This drawing however survived (See also NOS. 38–40.)

42 Miss Terry. Caricature of Ellen Terry as Rosamund in Tennyson's *Becket*, produced by Henry Irving at the Lyceum Theatre, London, 6 February 1893. Published in *The Pall Mall Budget*, 9 February 1893, p. 188. Signed A. Beardsley and inscribed with title. Pl. 47
$7\frac{3}{8} \times 3\frac{3}{8}$ inches
Mr Vyvyan Holland OBE, London

43–46 Caricatures of C. V. Stanford, composer of the music for Tennyson's *Becket*, and of three actors in the production of the play by Henry Irving at the Lyceum Theatre, London, 6 February 1893. Published on pp. 188 and 190 of *The Pall Mall Budget*, 9 February 1893. Signed with initials in ink and inscribed in ink with titles and in pencil with notes.
Pen and indian ink over pencil, $4\frac{1}{2} \times 3$ inches
Victoria and Albert Museum, London

43 Master Leo (Master Leo Byrne as Godfrey). Pl. 42
44 Margery (Kate Phillips). Pl. 43
45 The Composer (Sir Charles Villiers Stanford). Pl. 44
46 The King makes a move on the Board (William Terriss). Pl. 45

47 The Disappointment of Émile Zola. Caricature published in *The Pall Mall Budget*, 9 February 1893, p. 202. Signed A V Beardsley. Pl. 48
$8\frac{3}{4} \times 4\frac{1}{4}$ inches
Mr Vyvyan Holland, OBE, London

Marillier in his preface to *The Early Works of Aubrey Beardsley*, London, 1899, regarded this and the sketches for 'The New Coinage' (see NOS. 38–41) as the only successful journalistic drawings made by Beardsley for *The Pall Mall Budget*.

48 Pope Leo XIII's Jubilee. The Pilgrim (Old Style); and The Pilgrim (New Style). Illustration on p. 270 of *The Pall Mall Budget*, 23 February 1893. Signed with the monogram AVB. Inscribed in pencil and pen. Stamped 'Ronald Searle' (collection). Pl. 50
Indian ink over pencil, together 6×7 inches
Mr R. A. Harari, London

49 Caricature of Forbes Robertson as Julian Beauclerc in *Diplomacy*, a play by B.C. Stephenson and Clement Scott, adapted from *Dora* by Victorien Sardou and produced at the Garrick Theatre, London, 18 February 1893. Reproduced with similar caricatures on p. 281 of *The Pall Mall Budget*. 23 February 1893. Inscribed with title and in pencil with notes. Pl. 49
$3\frac{1}{8} \times 2\frac{3}{8}$ inches
Victoria and Albert Museum, London

50 Caricature of Arthur Cecil as Baron Stein in *Diplomacy* (see previous caption). Reproduced with similar caricatures on p. 281 of *The Pall Mall Budget*, 23 February 1893. Inscribed with title and in pencil with notes. Pl. 46
$4\frac{3}{8} \times 3$ inches
Victoria and Albert Museum, London

51 'The Bullet-Proof Uniform: Tommy Atkins thinks it rather fun.' Drawing reproduced in *The Pall Mall Budget*, 30 March 1893, p. 491. Inscribed in ink 'What our military artist saw in a dream after reading an account of the uniform'. Pl. 51
$7\frac{1}{8} \times 10\frac{1}{2}$ inches
Present owner unknown

52 Becket. Henry Irving as Becket in Tennyson's play of that name produced by Irving at the Lyceum Theatre, London, 6 February 1893. Proof from steel-faced copperplate. Signed A Beardsley. Pl. 52
Etching and aquatint, $8\frac{1}{2} \times 5\frac{1}{4}$ inches
Mr W. G. Good, England

In an undated letter of 1893 Beardsley told Robert Ross that 'This morning Pennell has been giving me Lessons in Etching'. This pull, with the copperplate from which it was taken by Beardsley, seems to be the only known etching by him. A reproduction of his wash drawing of the same subject was published in *The Pall Mall Budget*, 9 February 1893.

53 Caricature of Norman O'Neill. 1. N begs from Mayor permission to play golf. 2. N the Masher. Inscribed with titles by Count Eric Stenbock, *c.* 1893. Pl. 53
$4\frac{1}{4} \times 6\frac{1}{4}$ inches
Mrs Derek Hudson, London

Norman O'Neill was a young friend of Eric Stenbock, a Count of Swedish origin who had been for a short time at Oxford and later lived in Campden Hill, London. W. B. Yeats called him 'scholar, connoisseur, drunkard, poet, pervert, most charming of men'. He was a friend of More Adey and of Robert Ross, and made Beardsley's acquaintance through Ross in 1892. O'Neill (1875–1934), later well-known as a theatre composer, studied music at the Hoch Conservatorium at Frankfurt from 1893 to 1897. Soon after he went to Frankfurt, Stenbock persuaded Beardsley to make these caricatures, which were inscribed by Stenbock and sent with a covering note from Beardsley (see also NO. 54).

54 Caricature of Norman O'Neill. The English flower in the German Conservatory. Inscribed with title by Count Eric Stenbock, *c.* 1893. Pl. 54
$4\frac{1}{8} \times 6\frac{3}{8}$ inches
Mrs Derek Hudson, London

See note to NO. 53. The word 'Conservatory' here alludes to the Hoch Conservatorium at Frankfurt where O'Neill was studying music. There was a fourth caricature showing O'Neill masked and fighting a students' duel in the German style (see Derek Hudson, *Norman O'Neill*, London, 1945).

55 Projected design for the front wrappers of the parts of *Le Morte Darthur*, published by J. M. Dent, London, 1893–4. Pl. 55
Platinotype, $8\frac{1}{2} \times 7$ inches
Mr W. G. Good, England

The original drawing was in yellowish-green water-colour on white paper. The platinotype was made by Frederick H. Evans, partner in the bookshop of Jones and Evans where Beardsley spent his lunch hours when he was a clerk at the Guardian Life Insurance Company nearby. The naïveté of the design, with its Burne-Jones brambles, its Botticelli lilies, its Japanese ground rendered in wavy lines and its childish lettering was superseded by the more complicated design that was actually used for the same purpose and which had the character of a thicket of vegetation somewhat in the style of the *Studio* wrapper and poster (see NO. 259).

56 How King Arthur saw the Questing Beast, and thereof had great marvel. Drawing for the frontispiece to Vol. I of *Le Morte Darthur*, 1893–4. Signed on the trees with the artist's name and dated 8 March 1893; also with the artist's emblem. Pl. 56
Pen, ink and wash, $14 \times 10\frac{5}{8}$ inches
Mr R. A. Harari, London

This is the most elaborate of Beardsley's drawings in the hair-line manner, which was used also for 'Siegfried' (NO. 164) and for many of the *Bon-Mots* vignettes. There is a strange profusion of what amounts almost to automatic drawing in the details that decorate every part of the landscape: these include a treble clef, a signature, a spider's web, a phallus and calligraphic flourishes in the manner of the seventeenth-century writing masters. The Beast is a pseudo-Japanese dragon, with overlapping discs representing scales, but in fact memorized from the scale-like feathers in Whistler's decorations in the Peacock Room (1878). The lines defining

Arthur's garments imitate the gougings of the burin on the copperplate reproduced in the lines of a fifteenth-century engraving. The beautifully precise castle in the distance reveals, apart from the rest of the work, how in March 1893 Beardsley was still entranced a little by the legend he was illustrating.

57 Drawing for the headpiece on the title-page of *Le Morte Darthur*, 1893–4. The support was extended by extra strips at each end to accommodate the design. Pl. 57
$4\frac{1}{2} \times 13\frac{3}{8}$ inches
Mr F. J. Martin Dent, London

In *Le Livre et l'Image*, Vol. XII, March 1894, this design was reproduced as the headpiece of an article in which Beardsley was mentioned and his drawings described as a 'mélange de germanisme et de japonisme', alongside those of Granville Fell, which were said to have been influenced by Walter Crane. The convoluted design here is certainly Beardsley's greatest advance on the type of foliated ornament he adapted from Morris and Burne-Jones.

58 Design for the headpiece of the preface (p. xi of Vol. I) in *Le Morte Darthur*, 1893–4. On the back, part of a design showing a male figure holding a dagger, etc. (see NO. 162). Pl. 58
$3\frac{7}{16} \times 8\frac{11}{16}$ inches
Victoria and Albert Museum, London

59 Merlin. Drawing for the roundel on the verso of the contents page in *Le Morte Darthur*, Vol. I, 1893–4. Pl. 59
Diameter 6 inches
Rosenwald Collection, Library of Congress, Washington

60 Design for the chapter-heading of Chapter III, Book I (p. 5 of Vol. I) in *Le Morte Darthur*, 1893–4. Repeated elsewhere in the book. Pl. 60
$4\frac{3}{8} \times 3\frac{1}{4}$ inches
Western Australian Art Gallery, Perth, Western Australia

One of the earliest drawings made for the book, appearing in Part I.

61 Design showing figures in a sailing vessel, for the chapter-heading of Chapter IV, Book I (p. 6 of Vol. I) in *Le Morte Darthur*, 1893–4. Repeated elsewhere in the book. Pl. 63
$2\frac{7}{16} \times 1\frac{13}{16}$ inches
Mr W. G. Good, England

An example of the smallest type of chapter-heading, reproduced in two sizes. It was one of the earliest drawings made for the book, appearing in Part I.

62 Design for a small chapter-heading in *Le Morte Darthur*, 1893–4; appearing in Vols. I and II, on pp. 7, 138, 359, 715, 818, 891 and 905. Pl. 64
$2\frac{1}{8} \times 1\frac{11}{16}$ inches
Mr Draper Hill, Worcester, Massachusetts

One of the earliest drawings made for the book, appearing in Part I.

63 Design for the chapter-heading of Chapter VIII, Book I (p. 13 of Vol. I) in *Le Morte Darthur*, 1893–4. Repeated elsewhere in the book. Pl. 61
$3\frac{1}{4} \times 3$ inches
The Rosenwald Collection, Library of Congress, Washington

64 Design for the chapter-heading of Chapter XI, Book I (p. 19 of Vol. I) in *Le Morte Darthur*, 1893–4. Repeated elsewhere in the book. Pl. 62
$3\frac{1}{4} \times 2\frac{1}{4}$ inches
Victoria and Albert Museum, London

The tail of the mermaid is composed of forms derived from the short feathers in Whistler's Peacock Room (1878). Similar groups of overlapping discs were adapted by Beardsley to various formulae, in the *Salome* illustrations, for instance, and in other drawings of 1893. The water is conventionalized after the fashion of water-forms in Japanese art, but the varying and complicated undulations of the lines forecast the macaroni lines in *art nouveau*—usually associated with hair, as in Toorop's poster *Delfsche Slaolie* (1895).

65 Design for a small chapter-heading in *Le Morte Darthur*, 1893–4; appearing in Vols. I and II on pp. 22, 474 and 857. Pl. 65
$2\frac{1}{4} \times 1\frac{1}{2}$ inches
Mr Anthony d'Offay, London

66 Design for the chapter-heading of Chapter XIV, Book I (p. 23 of Vol. I) in *Le Morte Darthur*, 1893–4. Repeated elsewhere in the book. Pl. 66
$5\frac{1}{4} \times 3\frac{1}{4}$ inches
Rosenwald Collection, Library of Congress, Washington

The figure of the piper was recalled from the piper in Beardsley's illustrations to *The Pay of the Pied Piper* in the programme and book of words of the comic opera so-named, performed at the Dome in Brighton as part of the Brighton Grammar School's Christmas entertainment on 19 December 1888. The design appeared in Part I.

67 Design for the chapter-heading of Chapter XIX, Book I (p. 36 of Vol. I) in *Le Morte Darthur*, 1893–4. Signed with monogram. Repeated elsewhere in the book. Pl. 67
$4\frac{11}{16} \times 3\frac{3}{8}$ inches
Western Australian Art Gallery, Perth, Western Australia

This drawing was executed apparently in the style of an early woodcut. It was published in Part I and must have been among the earliest ones made for the book. It was not long before Beardsley gave up such archaisms. The twigs in the rectangle were replaced in the line-block by chapter numerals.

68 Design for the chapter-heading of Chapter XXI, Book I (p. 40 in Vol. I) of *Le Morte Darthur*, 1893–4. Repeated elsewhere in the book. Pl. 68
Measurements not known
Formerly the property of Mr Godfrey Pilkington, Piccadilly Gallery, London

One of the earliest of the smaller designs for headings in

Le Morte Darthur, appearing first in Part I, and frequently in the later Parts. The winged, heraldic beast surmounts the recumbent body of a fallen angel, who supports his head with his hands and looks forward with a flippant expression of resigned worry. It is hard to think of anyone but Beardsley who would have deliberately given such an expression to the angel. The background is filled in with the knotted tail of the beast, and disconnected dots, leaves, scales and enlacements which have been put into the drawing in order to produce the dense effect of a design by Morris or Burne-Jones. But this was really a juvenile evasion of Beardsley's true nature: for if there was one dominant trait that Beardsley lacked, it was the *horror vacui* of these other artists.

69 Initial A of Chapter I, Book II (p. 51 of Vol. I) in *Le Morte Darthur*, 1893–4. Pl. 69
$3\frac{5}{8} \times 2\frac{5}{8}$ inches
Victoria and Albert Museum, London

An early contribution to *Le Morte Darthur*, following the *horror vacui* principles of William Morris, but using the briar motif of Burne-Jones transformed by bentwood lines and Celtic interlacings.

70 Border and initial A with the text of the opening of Chapter I, Book II (p. 51 of Vol. I) in *Le Morte Darthur*, 1893–4. Pl. 70
From the line-block and letterpress

See also NO. 69 which reproduces the original drawing for the initial. The dense twisting briars show what Beardsley had learned in the way of decoration from Morris and Burne-Jones. But the restless feeling transmitted to this decoration, and the idea of female fauna climbing in and out of it, suggest a conflict in Beardsley between what he admired and what he was.

71 Design for the chapter-heading of Chapter III, Book II (p. 55 of Vol. I) in *Le Morte Darthur*, 1893–4. Repeated elsewhere in the book. Pl. 75
$5 \times 3\frac{1}{2}$ inches
Rosenwald Collection, Library of Congress, Washington

72 Drawing for a full-page border for the beginning of Chapter I, Book III (p. 81 of Vol. I) in *Le Morte Darthur*, 1893–4. Pl. 71
$11\frac{1}{4} \times 9\frac{1}{4}$ inches
Princeton University Library

In 1891 the artist visited the room decorated by Whistler in 1878 at 49 Prince's Gate. The stylized peacock feathers which are so prominent in these decorations made a deep impression on Beardsley, who by 1893 was introducing his own versions of them in *Le Morte Darthur* and *Salome*. Those motifs can be seen here, alongside the figures of knights in the manner of Burne-Jones, but reduced to simple terms.

73 Drawing for the chapter-heading of Chapter III, Book III (p. 84 of Vol. I) in *Le Morte Darthur*, 1893–4. Repeated elsewhere in the book. Pl. 73
$5\frac{1}{16} \times 2\frac{1}{2}$ inches
Rosenwald Collection, Library of Congress, Washington

74 Design for the chapter-heading of Chapter VII, Book III (p. 90 of Vol. I) in *Le Morte Darthur*, 1893–4. Repeated elsewhere in the book. Pl. 74
$5\frac{7}{16} \times 3\frac{1}{4}$ inches
Mr Brian Reade, London

The drawing appeared in Part I and would date from late 1892 or early 1893. The influence of Burne-Jones is generally evident, though the features of the face have an added glowering expression typical of Beardsley's heads. The breeze-blown curves of the scarf reflect certain *art nouveau* trends.

75 Design for the chapter-heading of Chapter XII, Book III (p. 98 of Vol. I) in *Le Morte Darthur*, 1893–4. Pl. 72
$5\frac{3}{4} \times 2\frac{1}{2}$ inches
Mrs B. S. Clauson, England

76 Merlin and Nimue. Full-page illustration facing p. 106 (Chapter I, Book IV) of *Le Morte Darthur*, Vol. I, 1893–4. Pl. 78
From the line-block

The figure of Merlin seems quite likely to have been based on a reminiscence of the pilgrim in the picture *Love Leading the Pilgrim* by Burne-Jones, though the form of Merlin is also influenced by the style of early woodcuts. Other elements in the composition have a Burne-Jones iconographical history, but are rendered more broadly and boldly. The honeysuckle border on the right has as much of the rigidity of art-school anthemion as Beardsley could reconcile with an essentially serpentine instinct, which pervaded his art always, and particularly during this period. The illustration was published in Part II.

77 Design for the chapter-heading of Chapter V, Book IV (p. 112 of Vol. I) in *Le Morte Darthur*, 1893–4. Pl. 76
$6\frac{1}{4} \times 3\frac{1}{2}$ inches
Rosenwald Collection, Library of Congress, Washington

An early drawing for the book, containing more detail than those produced in the later stages, as the work got wearisome. It appeared in Part II.

78 Design for the chapter-heading of Chapter X, Book IV (p. 121 of Vol. I) in *Le Morte Darthur*, 1893–4. Repeated elsewhere in the book. Pl. 77
$5\frac{5}{8} \times 2\frac{3}{4}$ inches
Victoria and Albert Museum, London

An example of one of the earlier drawings for the book, showing the strong influence of Burne-Jones. It appeared in Part II.

79 Drawing for a full-page illustration facing p. 132, Chapter XVI, Book IV, Vol. I of *Le Morte Darthur*, 1893–4. Pl. 83
$11\frac{1}{2} \times 9$ inches
Mr John Hay Whitney, New York

It is typical of Beardsley that the heroic face of King Arthur should be conceived as a refined profile, emphasized by heavy Medusan locks. The bat's-wing forms in his armour surpass in idiosyncrasy the equivalent inventions of Burne-Jones. This page illustrates a passage in Chapter XVI, where it is related how the lady represented by the artist as gentle, sleek and pious-looking, was in fact a sinister messenger, and when King Arthur ordered her first to put on the mantle which she had brought, she put it over herself and was burnt to a cinder. In the distance is the Wagnerian castle, as it were, another Neuschwanstein built by the mad king Ludwig II of Bavaria.

80   Heading of Chapter XIX, Book IV (p. 137 of Vol. I) in *Le Morte Darthur*, 1893–4. Repeated elsewhere in the book. Pl. 81
From the line-block

The woman is shown playing what is evidently a bass-viol, in which case her hand is holding the bow the wrong way. A less rigid version of the subject, with an angel in place of a woman, was adopted by Beardsley for the title and front-cover design of *The Mirror of Music* by Stanley Makower in the *Keynotes* series (see NO. 307). This design, which appeared in Part II of *Le Morte Darthur*, is an early example of Beardsley's use of white silhouettes against a flat black background.

81   Design for the chapter-heading of Chapter XXVII, Book IV (p. 152 of Vol. I) in *Le Morte Darthur*, 1893–4. Pl. 80
$3\frac{7}{8} \times 2\frac{3}{4}$ inches
Rosenwald Collection, Library of Congress, Washington

82   Design for the chapter-heading of Chapter IV, Book V (p. 161 of Vol. I) in *Le Morte Darthur*, 1893–4. Pl. 82
$5\frac{7}{8} \times 2\frac{5}{8}$ inches
Scofield Thayer Collection, Fogg Art Museum, Harvard University, Massachusetts

83   Design for the chapter-heading of Chapter V, Book V (p. 162 of Vol. I) in *Le Morte Darthur*, 1893–4. Inscribed on the back in pencil 'Reduce by $\frac{1}{3}$' etc. Repeated elsewhere in the book. Pl. 79
$4\frac{11}{16} \times 3\frac{3}{8}$ inches
Mr F. M. Gross, London

84   Design for the chapter-heading of Chapter VI, Book V (p. 166 of Vol. I) in *Le Morte Darthur*, 1893–4. Pl. 85
$4\frac{13}{16} \times 3\frac{3}{8}$ inches
Scofield Thayer Collection, Fogg Art Museum, Harvard University, Massachusetts

85   Heading of Chapter VIII, Book V (p. 170 of Vol. I) in *Le Morte Darthur*, 1893–4. Pl. 84
From the line-block

The twining briars and vertical trees are bold simplifications, qualified by Beardsley's organic energy, of familiar Burne-Jones features. The exaggerated length of the wings, and the convention for the hair, based on the artist's own forward-brushed fringe, are essentially Beardsleyesque.

86   Design for the chapter-heading of Chapter X, Book V (p. 175 of Vol. I) in *Le Morte Darthur*, 1893–4. Pl. 86
$5 \times 3\frac{3}{8}$ inches
Mr John Hay Whitney, New York

Japanese stylization of water somewhat in this fashion occurs in prints by Hiroshige and in lacquer work: similar in principle is the stylization of water by Burne-Jones in his Karlsefne and Gudrida cartoons of 1883 for stained glass (at Newport, Rhode Island, U.S.A. See Malcolm Bell, *Sir Edward Burne-Jones*, London, reprint of 1901, after p. 82). Beardsley used these serpentine ribbons for other purposes, sometimes decorative, as in the border of 'Merlin and Nimue' (NO. 76). The rectangle for letterpress has been blacked out.

87   Design for the chapter-heading of Chapter XI, Book V (p. 178 of Vol. I) in *Le Morte Darthur*, 1893–4. Inscribed on the back in pencil 'Reduce by $\frac{1}{3}$' and with measurements etc. Repeated elsewhere in the book. Pl. 87
$4\frac{5}{8} \times 3\frac{3}{8}$ inches
Mr F. M. Gross, London

88   Drawing for a full-page border for the beginning of Chapter I, Book VI (p. 183 of Vol. I) in *Le Morte Darthur*, 1893–4. Pl. 88
$11 \times 8\frac{7}{8}$ inches
Mr Draper Hill, Worcester, Massachusetts

The drawing for the initial S within this border is reproduced at NO. 89.

89   Design for an initial S for Chapter I, Book VI (p. 183 of Vol. I) in *Le Morte Darthur*, 1893–4. Pl. 89
$3\frac{13}{16} \times 2\frac{7}{8}$ inches
Victoria and Albert Museum, London

The initial was used for the word 'Soon' with which Book VI began and was set inside the border reproduced at NO. 88.

90   How Four Queens Found Launcelot Sleeping. Full-page illustration facing p. 18, Chapter I, Book VI (Vol. I) in *Le Morte Darthur*, 1893–4. Lettered with title. Pl. 90
$12 \times 9\frac{5}{16}$ inches
Scofield Thayer Collection, Fogg Art Museum, Harvard University, Massachusetts

91   Heading of Chapter V, Book VI (p. 190 of Vol. I) in *Le Morte Darthur*, 1893–4. Pl. 91
From the line-block

The figure seems to have been based on a study of a living female nude, possibly at the Westminster School of Art, which Beardsley had attended in the evenings from the autumn of 1891 to the same season in 1892; or it may possibly have been based on a study or memory of his sister Mabel. The figure is in fact facing a dado and what looks like a Morris wallpaper in a typical modern room of 1890.

92   Design for the chapter-heading of Chapter XIV, Book VI (p. 209 of Vol. I) in *Le Morte Darthur*, 1893–4. Repeated elsewhere in the book. Pl. 92
$4\frac{5}{8} \times 4$ inches
The Rosenwald Collection, Library of Congress, Washington

93   Sir Launcelot and the Witch Hellawes. Drawing for the full-

page illustration facing p. 212, Chapter XV, Book VI (Vol. I) in *Le Morte Darthur*, 1893–4. Pl. 93
12 × 9¼ inches
Princeton University Library

4 Heading of Chapter VI, Book VII (p. 228 of Vol. I) in *Le Morte Darthur*, 1893–4. Repeated elsewhere in the book. Pl. 96
From the line-block.

The strange trees with their flat tops and visible roots sway in counterpoint to the pose of the woman, which is taken from a reminiscence of some Japanese print. The design is strikingly *proto-art nouveau;* but the boldness of conception and touch, and the occasional over-refinement of detail, as in the face, are Beardsley's hallmarks.

5 Design for the chapter-heading of Chapter IX, Book VII (p. 234 of Vol. I) in *Le Morte Darthur*, 1893–4. Pl. 98
5¼ × 4 inches
Mrs Steven Cohen, Cambridge, Massachusetts

The lines across the drapery represent folds, in the flat mural style of Puvis de Chavannes. It is possible Beardsley memorized something of the work of Puvis, whom he went to see in Paris with an introduction from Burne-Jones in the middle of 1892. The conventionalized treatment of the valley in the distance is very odd, but similar features are to be seen in other designs for *Le Morte Darthur*. The design appeared in Part III.

6 Heading of Chapter XIV, Book VII (p. 244 of Vol. I) in *Le Morte Darthur*, 1893–4. Pl. 95
From the line-block

At first glance this figure appears to be that of a boy; at second glance a female breast will be noticed. The person is therefore hermaphrodite. The twining rose-bush is descended from the ones in *The Briar Rose* by Burne-Jones, but bleakly and capriciously stylized.

7 Design for the chapter-heading of Chapter XIX, Book VII (p. 254 of Vol. I) in *Le Morte Darthur*, 1893–4. On the back a pencil drawing of nude figures surrounded by a one-line border in pen and ink; also various inscriptions in pencil. Pl. 94
6 1/16 × 3⅜ inches
Mr R. A. Harari, London

The blue-grey mount window preserved with the drawing dates from Beardsley's lifetime and was inscribed by him, 'To Miss Mallam from Aubrey Beardsley'.

8 Design for the chapter-heading of Chapter XXXI, Book VII (p. 280 of Vol. I) in *Le Morte Darthur*, 1893–4. Repeated elsewhere in the book. Pl. 97
6⅜ × 2 11/16 inches
Mr R. A. Harari, London

9 Page 291 in Vol. I of *Le Morte Darthur*, 1893–4. Pl. 99
From the line-block and letterpress

To compare these designs for an initial and a border with

equivalent designs by William Morris is to note at once that Beardsley's lines conveyed an energy that Morris's dense and tranquil drawings lacked. The difference in temperament between the two men was so great that after one meeting neither could be induced to see the other again.

100 How La Beale Isoud Nursed Sir Tristram. Full-page illustration facing p. 306 (Chapter IX, Book VIII) of *Le Morte Darthur*, Vol. I, 1893–4. Pl. 100
11 × 8¾ inches
Scofield Thayer Collection, Fogg Art Museum, Harvard University, Massachusetts

The concept of ruled lines for the bed and curtain, making a rectangular frame for the figures, has perhaps a distant relationship to the rectilinear furniture and backgrounds in certain Japanese prints. The grotesque shape of the molten wax at the top of the candle and the singular emphasis given to the candlestick are pure Beardsley features, often to be found in his later designs.

101 Design for the chapter-heading of Chapter X, Book VIII (p. 307 of Vol. I) in *Le Morte Darthur*, 1893–4. Repeated elsewhere in the book. Pl. 101
4¼ × 2⅞ inches
Princeton University Library

102 Design with a motif of conventional veronica for the chapter-heading of Chapter XIII, Book VIII (p. 313 of Vol. I) in *Le Morte Darthur*, 1893–4. Repeated elsewhere in the book. Pl. 102
2½ × 2½ inches
Mr W. G. Good, England

Beardsley designed chapter-headings of varying sizes for the book. This is of the medium size, and is one of a minority without any human, bird or animal figures.

103 Design for the chapter-heading of Chapter XIX, Book VIII (p. 324 of Vol. I) in *Le Morte Darthur*, 1893–4. Repeated elsewhere in the book. Pl. 103
4⅛ × 2⅜ inches
Victoria and Albert Museum, London

The rectangle cut in the top right corner to leave a white space for the chapter number in letterpress has been enlarged by pasting over it an oblong piece of white paper.

104 How Sir Tristram Drank of the Love Drink. Illustration to a passage in Chapter XXIV, Book VIII (facing p. 334 in Vol. I) of *Le Morte Darthur*, 1893–4. Pl. 105
11 × 8 inches
Scofield Thayer Collection, Fogg Art Museum, Harvard University, Massachusetts

One of the boldest of Beardsley's drawings for *Le Morte Darthur*, or indeed of his whole career. The long worm-like stem of Beardsley's symbolic flower, which seems to have been derived from the passion-flower, the *Clematis viticella* or Bush Bower, and the tulip, makes the border more restless than any of the others in the book, while this quality is counteracted by the delicate tensed-up petals of the blossoms growing out of it. Symbolic roses of the diagrammatic form that was to be so popular as an *art nouveau* motif are seen, detached from any support, alongside. In the pictorial panel two curtains, treated like Japanese screens, nearly shut out the distant view, again stylized in a Japanese fashion. Across each curtain, with a curious parallel emphasis, a clematis flower with a harshly arabesque stalk sways rightwards. The passion-flower-tulip appears again stylized with great assurance on what is a simplified version of the peacock skirt in the illustration of that name for *Salome*, made probably not so very long afterwards. The hair of Isolde is in the Medusan style much favoured by Beardsley throughout *Le Morte Darthur* and taken up with relish by *art-nouveau* designers like Privat-Livemont. The strong perspective of the floorboards gives dramatic support to the tension of this scene of idealized love, which became one of Beardsley's obsessions. Isolde's high-shouldered reaction to Sir Tristram's gesture is, from the standpoint of the Wagnerian opera, which Beardsley knew so well, psychologically accurate. A smaller version of this composition was published in *The Savoy*, No. 7, November 1896, p. 91.

105 Heading of Chapter XXXIII, Book VIII (p. 348 of Vol. I) in *Le Morte Darthur*, 1893–4. Repeated elsewhere in the book. Pl. 104
From the line-block

The hair fetichism, which we can discern in the art of Frederick Sandys, and of Rossetti, is symbolized and mocked in this design by quantities of lines undulating on one plane. Beardsley's weakness for sensationalism, which he later refined away, is shown in the eyes of the lower head. The design was published in Part IV.

106 Design for the chapter-heading of Chapter XXXV, Book VIII (p. 353 of Vol. I) in *Le Morte Darthur*, 1893–4. Repeated elsewhere in the book. Pl. 109
$4\frac{1}{8} \times 3\frac{1}{8}$ inches
Mrs B. S. Clauson, England

107 Border and initial A with the text of the opening of Chapter I, Book IX (p. 367 of Vol. I) in *Le Morte Darthur*, 1893–4. Pl. 107
From the line-block and letterpress

It is instructive to compare this initial A with the one at NO. 70. Already Beardsley has given up aiming to make a rich thicket of decorative foliage as in the earlier example, and has asserted, de-naturalized and silhouetted the forms of the plants, while the restlessness has become frankly dramatic. The flower motif in the bottom margin was used again in the title-page and front cover design for *The Woman Who Did*, by Grant Allen, Vol. VIII in the *Keynotes* series, 1895.

108 How La Beale Isoud Wrote to Sir Tristram. Drawing for a full-page illustration facing p. 384 in Vol. I, Chapter X, Book IX in *Le Morte Darthur*, 1893–4. Pl. 106
$10\frac{13}{16} \times 8\frac{7}{16}$ inches
In private possession, England

The table, although at a different angle from the table in Dürer's engraving 'St Jerome in his Study', is probably based on it. But the construction of it has been misunder-

stood by the artist. The drawing shows that the hair was originally delineated in heavy waves, but was blacked over before reproduction.

109 Drawing for the chapter-heading of Chapter XVI, Book IX (p. 396 of Vol. I) in *Le Morte Darthur*, 1893–4. Pl. 108
$4\frac{3}{8} \times 2\frac{15}{16}$ inches
Rosenwald Collection, Library of Congress, Washington

A white rectangle was left by Beardsley for the chapter numerals and these were put in, but the rectangle was later blacked over to match the background above the wall.

110 How King Mark found Sir Tristram sleeping. Drawing for the full-page illustration facing p. 404, Chapter XX, Book IX (Vol. I) in *Le Morte Darthur*, 1893–4. Lettered with title, which omits the word 'sleeping'. Pl. 112
$8\frac{1}{8} \times 6\frac{5}{8}$ inches
Mr F. J. Martin Dent, London

111 Heading of Chapter XXIV, Book IX (p. 413 of Vol. I) in *Le Morte Darthur*, 1893–4. Pl. 111
From the line-block

For the figure Beardsley was indebted to Whistler's 'Princess from the Land of Porcelain', painted in 1864, an early milestone of the Aesthetic movement, which Beardsley saw hanging in 49 Prince's Gate in July 1891.

112 Design for the chapter-heading of Chapter XXXIX, Book IX (p. 446 of Vol. I) in *Le Morte Darthur*, 1893–4. Pl. 110
$4\frac{3}{8} \times 2\frac{7}{8}$ inches
Princeton University Library

This design was published in Part VI, by which time Beardsley had given up bothering with details in backgrounds or archaistic forms. The figure of the rushing girl seems neither mediaeval nor of the Nineties, but of the middle of the twentieth century; one of Beardsley's strange anticipations of the styles and the features of future women.

113 How Morgan le Fay Gave a Shield to Sir Tristram. Drawing for a full-page illustration facing p. 450 in Chapter XL, Book IX (Vol. I) in *Le Morte Darthur*, 1893–4. Inscribed on the back with numerals in pencil and pen. Pl. 118
$10\frac{5}{8} \times 8\frac{5}{16}$ inches
Fitzwilliam Museum, Cambridge, England

114 La Beale Isoud at Joyous Gard. Drawing on one sheet for a double-page illustration between pp. 556 and 557, Chapter LII, Book X (Vol. II) in *Le Morte Darthur*, 1893–4. On the back are slight scribbles, a sketch of part of the border, a caricature and an inscription, all in pencil by the artist. Pl. 113
$10\frac{5}{16} \times 17\frac{1}{8}$ inches
In private possession, England

The drawing was reproduced on one sheet of paper and the margin between the two halves was taken up as the sheet was sewn in with the rest of the volume when the twelve parts were bound in separate cases. This brought the two halves closer together and the train of La Beale Isoud's garment continued on either side more convincingly –all of which was evidently calculated by the artist. Between the sundial and the larger tree on the lawn in the right-hand picture, there are traces of another figure which was blacked over by Beardsley. The pears, it will be noted, have unconscious, or perhaps even deliberate, sexual symbols in their orifices and breast-like features.

115 Design for the chapter-heading of Chapter LXXI, Book X (p. 600 of Vol. II) in *Le Morte Darthur*, 1893–4. Pl. 115
$4\frac{7}{16} \times 3\frac{3}{8}$ inches
Western Australian Art Gallery, Perth, Western Australia

116 Design for the chapter-heading of Chapter LXXXV, Book X (p. 630 of Vol. II) in *Le Morte Darthur*, 1893–4. Pl. 114
$4\frac{1}{8} \times 3$ inches
Mr and Mrs W. M. Schwab, London

There are very few chapter-headings in *Le Morte Darthur* which have no massed blacks in their designs. This is one without any mass of black, in the thick-line style typical of the later drawings for the book: another example is to be seen at Chapter LXXXII, Book X (p. 603 of Vol. II). Beardsley here makes use of linear formulae for land which were also adopted by Burne-Jones, but were derived originally from Japanese art.

117 Page 639 in Vol. II of *Le Morte Darthur*, 1893–4. Pl. 119
From the line-block and letterpress

There are several chapter-headings in *Le Morte Darthur* showing figures emerging out of flowers, as in this border. The idea goes back to early herbals, such as the *Ortis Sanitatis* of 1491 in which superstitions about semi-human plants are illustrated as facts. It is possible that Beardsley saw books of this kind at the bookshop of Evans and Jones in Queen Street.

118 Heading of Chapter VI, Book XI (p. 649 of Vol. II) in *Le Morte Darthur*, 1893–4. Pl. 117
From the line-block

The idea of the fence stylized in this way comes from Burne-Jones's 'L'Amant' in the 'Romaunt of the Rose' series, and Beardsley used it again, reversing the elements of the original composition, in his heading of Chapter II, Book XX, p. 909 (NO. 142). The relation between the absurdly elongated white beard and the hood, which is opposed in tone and direction, yet a similar shape, is typical of Beardsley's optical wit.

119 Design for a full-page border with the initial A for the beginning of Chapter I, Book XII (p. 665 of Vol. II) in *Le Morte Darthur*, 1893–4. Pl. 120
Indian ink wash, 11×8 inches
Princeton University Library

120 Design for the chapter-heading of Chapter IV, Book XII (p. 670 of Vol. II) in *Le Morte Darthur*, 1893–4. Pl. 116
$4\frac{1}{16} \times 3\frac{1}{16}$ inches
Mrs B. S. Clauson, England

A clear example of Beardsley's pen-line treatment of the heavy Pre-Raphaelite hair, which has become in his hands a self-sufficient optical invention. Also a good example of the soft-nosed, large-lipped, anti-genteel profile which at this date Beardsley gave to his women's heads.

121 Double-page illustration between pp. 670 and 671 (Vol. II), Chapter IV, Book XII in *Le Morte Darthur*, 1893–4. Pl. 121
From the line-block

The stems of the lilies-of-the-valley have pronounced *art nouveau* lines, long curves with short returns; and for once the two halves of the border are symmetrical. The trees in the illustration have the characteristic plumage of stylized leaves, and the trunks have the usual breast-like boles. The clothes of the women seem either to be partly Japanese or partly Victorian.

122 Heading of Chapter XI, Book XII (p. 681 of Vol. II) in *Le Morte Darthur*, 1893–4. Pl. 124
from the line-block

Published in Part IX. The design is unique in the *Morte Darthur* series, being all in diagrammatic outlines, with one small area of massed black. The curves of the raised arm are generalized in contradiction to the known form, with reference to the looseness of the woman's sleeve. Such curious swervings will be found often in Beardsley's later work, as in the cut-away figure on the right in *The Repentance of Mrs...* (see NO. 368). The drawing for this design, formerly in the Pickford Waller Collection, was sold by Christie, London, on 12 November 1965.

123 Border and initial A, with the text of the opening of Chapter I, Book XIII (p. 689 of Vol. II) in *Le Morte Darthur*, 1893–4. Pl. 122
From the line-block and letterpress

Compared with the other borders designed by Beardsley for the book, this one is the least flamboyant and reflects very little of the *art nouveau* spirit already moving in the rest. The simplified pattern of conventionalized flowers is nearest perhaps to the domestic embroidery of the time (and later) based on the principles of William Morris.

124 Design for the chapter-heading of Chapter XVII, Book XIII (p. 718 of Vol. II) in *Le Morte Darthur*, 1893–4. Pl. 126
$4\frac{15}{16} \times 3\frac{3}{8}$ inches
Victoria and Albert Museum, London

The simple form and the somewhat thick line are characteristic of Beardsley's later drawings for the book. This appeared in Part IX.

125 Initial N and full-page border of Chapter I, Book XIV (p. 725 of Vol. II) in *Le Morte Darthur*, 1893–4. Pl. 123
From the line-block

The design has a restless quality which separates it from anything of the kind produced in this period by other artists. Behind the perversely shaped initial N the four stems rise together in the rhythm of a wave, the six Canterbury Bells are blown in a backward direction, and the barren ends twine in *art nouveau* enlacements. As usual in *Le Morte Darthur*, the border is a little too dramatic for the letterpress.

126 Design for the chapter-heading of Chapter III, Book XIV (p. 728 of Vol. II) in *Le Morte Darthur*, 1893–4. Pl. 125
$4\frac{3}{8} \times 3\frac{7}{16}$ inches
Mr R. A. Harari, London

One of the later drawings for *Le Morte Darthur*, in which Beardsley has simplified the design to white silhouettes against a plain black background. It appeared in Part IX.

127 Heading of Chapter VI, Book X (p. 733 of Vol. II) in *Le Morte Darthur*, 1893–4. Pl. 127
From the line-block

Beardsley's immaturity is revealed by his journalistic debasement of a Rossetti head, added to the body of a female faun; but all is redeemed by his mastery of black and white and the careless force of the drawing.

128 Heading of Chapter IX, Book XIV (p. 738 of Vol. II) in *Le Morte Darthur*, 1893–4. Repeated elsewhere in the book. Pl. 129
From the line-block

Appearing first on p. 738 in Part X on a small scale, this heading was repeated on a larger scale for Chapter XXII, Book XX (p. 953 in Vol. II) which came out in Part XII. The subject seems to have been inspired by representations of the drowned Ophelia, but the idea of the dead and severed head was clearly transferred from the head of John the Baptist in 'The Dancer's Reward' of *Salome*, on which Beardsley was working at about the time when this late contribution to *Le Morte Darthur* was made. The unrelieved black of the background above the water, unrelieved, that is, except for an attenuated tree-trunk, is the kind of dramatic excess that was soon copied by graphic artists in every field, to become one of the recognition features of design between the Nineties and the 1914 War.

129 Border and initial W with the text of the opening of Chapter I, Book XV (p. 741 of Vol. II) in *Le Morte Darthur*, 1893–4. Pl. 130
From the line-block and letterpress

This shows Beardsley getting into his stride as an *art nouveau* designer. By comparison with the book decorations of Morris and Burne-Jones, the border is meagre and unbalanced, and the initial eccentric. The element of wildness in the poppies and their foliage is not an element in the character of these plants, so much as a passion in the mind of the draughtsman.

130 Design for the chapter-heading of Chapter III, Book XVI (p. 755 of Vol. II) in *Le Morte Darthur*, 1893–4. Pl. 128
Measurements not known
J. S. Maas and Company, London

A black background typical of the later drawings made for *Le Morte Darthur*. Beardsley was becoming tired of his work for the book, his designs tended to bold simplifications, and the clothes of his figures, as here, began to have the characteristics of the late nineteenth century instead of the Middle Ages.

131 How a Devil in a Woman's likeness would have tempted Sir Bors. Two drawings together forming a design for a double-page illustration in Chapter XII, Book XVI (between pp. 768 and 769, Vol. II) in *Le Morte Darthur*, 1893–4. Pl. 131
$10\frac{3}{16} \times 7\frac{5}{8}$ inches: $10\frac{3}{8} \times 7\frac{1}{2}$ inches
The Art Institute of Chicago

132 Drawing for a full-page border with the initial N for the beginning of Chapter I, Book XVII (p. 779 of Vol. II) in *Le Morte Darthur*, 1893–4. Pl. 134
$8\frac{5}{16} \times 6\frac{1}{2}$ inches
Princeton University Library

The foliated ornament springing from one corner is derived in principle from the border ornaments by William Morris in the books of the Kelmscott Press, but is bolder and less erudite.

133 Heading of Chapter XVI, Book XVII (p. 807 of Vol. II) in *Le Morte Darthur*, 1893–4. Pl. 133
From the line-block

This extraordinary scene through a gully, from the sides of which trees grow to form a roof of leaves, is one of Beardsley's most original developments of the idea of a stylized valley which he presents in such designs as that at NO. 95.

134 Design for the chapter-heading of Chapter XIX, Book XVII (p. 812 of Vol. II) in *Le Morte Darthur*, 1893–4. Pl. 132
$4 \times 3\frac{3}{8}$ inches
The Cooper Union Museum, New York

The design appeared in Part IX.

135 Design for the chapter-heading of Chapter XX, Book XVII (p. 814 of Vol. II) in *Le Morte Darthur*, 1893–4. Pl. 135
$5\frac{3}{4} \times 3\frac{3}{8}$ inches
The Hon. Christopher Lennox-Boyd, London

136 Border and initial S with the text of the opening of Chapter I, Book XVIII (p. 823 of Vol. II) in *Le Morte Darthur*, 1893–4. Pl. 136
From the line-block and letterpress

It was typical of Beardsley that he did not avoid, he grasped, the opportunity of identifying leaves with the feathers in angels' wings. The angels' heads with their folded wings were based presumably on memories of Burne-Jones's 'Angels of Creation', originally designed for stained glass in Tamworth church and begun in 1872. It so happened that these six panels were exhibited for the third time in 1893, at the New Gallery in London. Beardsley's design has none of their complexity and is the work of a different type of mind, having the direct shock of an epigram.

137 Heading of Chapter III, Book XVIII (p. 827 of Vol. II) in *Le Morte Darthur*, 1893–4. Pl. 140
From the line-block

Half a woman, clipped away vertically, and half a child clipped off horizontally, as in the manner of a snapshot photograph, and a not very successful one at that. This of course burlesques in a distant way the camera-style impressionism which attracted Degas and others from the 1870s onward.

8 Design for the chapter-heading of Chapter IX, Book XVIII (p. 839 of Vol. II) in *Le Morte Darthur*, 1893–4. Pl. 139
$3\frac{3}{4} \times 3\frac{1}{8}$ inches
Rosenwald Collection, Library of Congress, Washington

9 Heading of Chapter XIV, Book XVIII (p. 851 of Vol. II) in *Le Morte Darthur*, 1893–4. Pl. 141
From the line-block

The drawing for this chapter-heading was until recently in the possession of Dr Catherine Boelcke, Wiesbaden.

o Design for the chapter-heading of Chapter XXI, Book XVIII (p. 867 of Vol. II) in *Le Morte Darthur*, 1893–4. Pl. 138
$5\frac{1}{4} \times 3\frac{1}{4}$ inches
National Gallery of Canada, Ottawa

This drawing appeared first in Part XI of the book and must have been one of the last Beardsley made for it. By that time he had almost given up the attempt to clothe his figures in a mediaeval fashion. His boredom with the work of producing so many drawings for *Le Morte Darthur* is shown by his indifference to the fact that he has drawn the woman leaning against the apple tree as if she were of his own period.

How Queen Guenever rode on Maying. Two drawings together forming a design for a double-page illustration in Chapter I, Book XIX (between pp. 880 and 881 of Vol. II) in *Le Morte Darthur*, 1893–4. Pl. 137
$8\frac{1}{8} \times 6\frac{5}{8}$ inches: $8\frac{1}{8} \times 6\frac{5}{8}$ inches
Mr R. A. Harari, London

Beardsley's interpretation of this scene, with all the figures in full profile, is very much in the manner of a pageant.

2 Design for the chapter-heading of Chapter II, Book XX (p. 909 of Vol. II) in *Le Morte Darthur*, 1893–4. Pl. 146
Measurements not recorded
Present owner unknown

This is a very loose, freehand drawing for Beardsley. It has a certain charm; but apart from the well, the imagery has been plagiarized from 'L'Amant' in the series 'The Romaunt of the Rose' by Burne-Jones, even to the gesture of the figure. The rose-bush and the figure are the other way round in 'L'Amant' and of course very much more elaborate, while Beardsley's figure is behind the fence, not in front of it, and the face in the large rose in 'L'Amant' has not been imitated. The drawing appeared in Part XII and may have been among the last done for *Le Morte Darthur*.

Heading of Chapter IV, Book XX (p. 913 of Vol. II) in *Le Morte Darthur*, 1893–4. Pl. 143
From the line-block

144 Design for the chapter-heading of Chapter VI, Book XX (p. 918 of Vol. II) in *Le Morte Darthur*, 1893–4. Pl. 145
$6\frac{3}{4} \times 2\frac{1}{8}$ inches
Victoria and Albert Museum, London

145 Design for the chapter-heading of Chapter X, Book XX (p. 926 of Vol. II) in *Le Morte Darthur*, 1893–4. Pl. 142
$4\frac{3}{8} \times 2\frac{7}{8}$ inches
Princeton University Library

This design appeared in Part XII, the last part of the book.

146 Design for the chapter-heading of Chapter XII, Book XX (p. 931 of Vol. II) in *Le Morte Darthur*, 1893–4. Pl. 148
$5\frac{1}{4} \times 3\frac{1}{2}$ inches
Victoria and Albert Museum, London

This design appeared in Part XII, the last part of the book.

147 Design for the chapter-heading of Chapter XVIII, Book XX (p. 945 of Vol. II) in *Le Morte Darthur*, 1893–4. Pl. 147
$4\frac{13}{16} \times 3\frac{3}{8}$ inches
Victoria and Albert Museum, London

This design appeared in Part XII, the last part of the book.

148 Design for the chapter-heading of Chapter XX, Book XX (p. 949 of Vol. II) in *Le Morte Darthur*, 1893–4. Pl. 144
$4\frac{1}{4} \times 3$ inches
Mrs B. S. Clauson, England

The drawing of the hair shows uncertainty, and Beardsley's technique of leaving white forms in reserve has failed him in the detail of the hand. The tree in a rectangular tub and the topiary work in the background remind one of his preference for extremes of artificiality, even in gardens.

149 How Sir Belvidere cast the sword Excalibur into the water. Drawing for the full-page illustration facing p. 967, Chapter V, Book XII (Vol. II) in *Le Morte Darthur*, 1893–4. Pl. 149
$8\frac{3}{8} \times 6\frac{1}{2}$ inches
Mr F. J. Martin Dent, London

150 How Queen Guenever Made Her a Nun. Illustration facing p. 975 in Chapter IX, Book XXI, Vol. II, in *Le Morte Darthur*, 1893–4. Pl. 150
From the line-block

Probably the best early example of the mysterious massed blacks that later constituted a feature of Beardsley's style.

151 Drawing for the front cover design stamped in gold on the bound volumes of *Le Morte Darthur*, published by J. M. Dent and Company in parts, 1893–4. Pl. 151
$10\frac{3}{4} \times 8$ inches
Mr Brian Reade, London

This design has ingeniously thought-out serpentine lines which symbolize twisting leaves and stems moving in unison, contrasted with the hard and horizontal clematis flowers that recur as a theme in the *Morte Darthur* illustrations. The masterful simplicity of it, which had a considerable influence on *art nouveau* artists, suggests that it was made by Beardsley towards the end of the period when he was working on this book and had developed away from the kind of design he made for the wrappers of the parts. See also NO. 152.

The plant forms are Beardsley hybrids, part passion-flower, part *Clematis viticella*, part tulip—perhaps.

152 Front cover and spine of Vol. I of *Le Morte Darthur*. From one of three volumes specially bound in vellum cases. No. 117 of 300 copies printed on Dutch hand-made paper, with publisher's imprint on the title-page and initials in the text printed in red. Published by J. M. Dent and Company, London, 1893–4, 4to. Pl. 152
Designs stamped in gold on vellum
Mr R. A. Harari, London

The small paper issue of the first edition of *Le Morte Darthur* was limited to 1500 copies published in parts at 2s 6d each, having green wrappers with a front cover design by Beardsley. The large paper edition, limited to 300 copies, was published in parts at 6s 6d each, with grey wrappers bearing the same design. Cases for the small paper issue were of cream cloth with the design as shown here stamped in gold: these were supplied by the publishers at 3s per volume, with binding costs for two volumes at 4s 6d per volume. The large paper edition was divided for binding into three sections instead of two, and cases were supplied at 3s 6d per volume, with binding costs at 5s per volume. Vellum was recommended for the large paper edition, but the cases of this material were not supplied, the binding costs of it being 8s 6d per volume.

The original drawing for the front cover of the bound volumes is reproduced at NO. 151. The dramatic effect of the swaying clematis stems points to a date either late in 1893 or in early 1894. The design for the wrappers was less masterly and more in the style of *The Studio* poster and cover.

153 Design for a chapter-heading, used for Chapter VII, Book IV, p. 75 in the edition of 1909 of *Le Morte Darthur*. Repeated elsewhere in the book. Pl. 155
$4\frac{3}{4} \times 3\frac{1}{2}$ inches
Victoria and Albert Museum, London

This was one of the ten designs omitted from the first edition of *Le Morte Darthur* as published in 1893–4, and included in Dent's one-volume edition of 1909. It may have been rejected because the chapter-heading rectangle obliterated the top of the largest of the female figures.

154 Design for a chapter-heading, used for Chapter IX, Book VI, p. 128 in the edition of 1909 of *Le Morte Darthur*. Repeated elsewhere in the book. Pl. 154
$4\frac{3}{4} \times 3\frac{5}{8}$ inches
Victoria and Albert Museum, London

This was one of ten designs omitted, possibly by mistake, from the first edition of *Le Morte Darthur* as published in 1893–4, and included in Dent's one-volume edition of 1909. Like many of the later drawings for the book it has little relevance to the text, while the scene and details are anachronistic.

155 Design for a chapter-heading, used for Chapter XII, Book VI, p. 133 and elsewhere in the edition of 1909 of *Le Morte Darthur*. Pl. 153
$2\frac{3}{16} \times 1\frac{5}{8}$ inches
Princeton University Library

This was one of the ten designs omitted from the first edition of 1893–4 and first published in the edition of 1909.

156 Design for a chapter-heading, used for Chapter XXXI, Book IX, p. 276 in the edition of 1909 of *Le Morte Darthur*. Pl. 159
$6\frac{1}{8} \times 3\frac{3}{8}$ inches
Mr F. J. Martin Dent, London

This design was omitted from the first edition of 1893–4 and not published until it was included in the one-volume edition of 1909. The blue-grey mount-window, which has been preserved with it, dates from Beardsley's lifetime and is the same size as that referred to at NO. 97.

157 Design for a chapter-heading, used for Chapter VIII, Book X, p. 302 in the edition of 1909 of *Le Morte Darthur*. Pl. 162
$4\frac{1}{4} \times 2\frac{1}{2}$ inches
Mrs B. S. Clauson, England

This was one of the ten designs omitted from the first edition of 1893–4 and first published in the edition of 1909.

158 Chapter-heading for *Le Morte Darthur*, used in Book XII, chapter XI, p. 368 in the edition of 1927. Pl. 156
$7\frac{1}{4} \times 4\frac{3}{8}$ inches
Princeton University Library

This design, which dates from *c.* 1893, was omitted from the editions of 1893–4 and 1909, possibly because the foliage spread into the margin in a way out of keeping with the other ornaments in the book.

159 Design for a chapter-heading in *Le Morte Darthur*, 1893–4, but not used. Pl. 161
$4\frac{3}{4} \times 3\frac{3}{8}$ inches
The Cooper Union Museum, New York

160 Design for an initial J possibly intended for *Le Morte Darthur*, 1893–4, but not used. Pl. 160
$5\frac{7}{16} \times 3\frac{9}{16}$ inches
Princeton University Library

R. A. Walker did not consider this drawing to be by Beardsley. Certainly the adaptation of Celtic ornament is rare in his work, but it is recorded in Aymer Vallance's Iconography at the bottom of p. 202 in *A Book of Fifty Drawings by Aubrey Beardsley*, 1897. It belonged then to Frederick H. Evans.

161 Unfinished drawing for a border intended for a page in *Le Morte Darthur*, 1893–4. Pl. 158
Pencil, pen and ink, $11\frac{7}{16} \times 8\frac{3}{16}$ inches
Princeton University Library

At some time in 1893 the artist gave this drawing to his ex-schoolfriend, George Scotson-Clark, who was born in the same year as himself, and had gone to the United States to work there first as an actor and then as an illustrator. Scotson-Clark returned to England in 1897 and died in 1927.

162 A male figure holding a dagger and descending a staircase, with a chafing dish on a tripod supported by a column on the right. Inscribed in pencil with an oval flourish and instructions for reduction. On the back, a design for *Le Morte Darthur* in pen (see NO. 58). Pl. 163
$9\frac{1}{16} \times 5\frac{5}{8}$ inches
Victoria and Albert Museum, London

This drawing is unusual in that it shows Beardsley using a pencil to make the sort of firm outline he generally reserved for penwork over rough pencil lines. It is not clear what the subject represents, and the instructions for reduction would refer to the drawing on the other side.

163 Grotesque figure of a man wearing a monocle. On the reverse side of the drawing 'La Beale Isoud at Joyous Gard' for *Le Morte Darthur* (see NO. 114). Pl. 157
Pencil
In private possession, England

This little grotesque has not been published before, or even been seen, since the back of the drawing on the recto side was detached in 1967 from the remains of an old mount. It is in the style of the vignettes in the *Bon-Mots* series: these were done concurrently with the work for *Le Morte Darthur* and furnished Beardsley with an outlet for his comic fantasies. On other parts of the verso of 'La Beale Isoud at Joyous Gard' are some sketches for the border of pears which decorate that illustration.

164 Siegfried, Act II. Drawing illustrating Wagner's lyric drama. Signed AVB. Pl. 164
Indian ink and wash, $15\frac{3}{4} \times 11\frac{1}{4}$ inches
Victoria and Albert Museum, London

This drawing was given by the artist to Burne-Jones, after whose death in 1898 Lady Burne-Jones gave it to Beardsley's mother. It is in the hairline style cultivated by Beardsley in 1892-3 and belongs to the group that includes 'How King Arthur saw the Questing Beast' (see NO. 56) and, on a smaller scale, many of the *Bon-Mots* drawings. The distant riverscape has been translated from similar details in Pollaiuolo's *Martyrdom of St Sebastian* in the National Gallery, London. Siegfried's figure is notable for its feminine spavin-legged posture, to be seen again in Beardsley's caricature of himself (NO. 428) and in his drawing 'The Abbé' (NO. 423). There is little attempt at recession: most of the forms are decorated and most of the details seem to be on the same plane; and the tree-trunk on the right is stylized in the pole-shape soon to become a formula of *art nouveau* decoration.

165 Title-page of *Bon-Mots* of Sydney Smith and R. Brinsley Sheridan, edited by Walter Jerrold and published by J. M. Dent and Company, London, 1893, 8vo. Pl. 165
From the line-block and letterpress (in black and red)
Mr Brian Reade, London

A design with motifs extended in linear scrolls. Among the motifs is Whistler's butterfly emblem, and a figure with a floral headdress in the manner of Grandville's *Les Fleurs*

Animées (1847), though Beardsley is more likely to have found this idea in *Flora's Feast* (1889) or some other book illustrated by Walter Crane.

166 Vignette on p. 7 in *Bon-Mots* of Sydney Smith and R. Brinsley Sheridan, edited by Walter Jerrold and published by J. M. Dent and Company, London, 1893. Repeated on p. 84 in *Bon-Mots* of Charles Lamb and Douglas Jerrold, etc., 1893. Pl. 167
From the line-block

Beardsley has represented the cat on two legs: the other two legs would have confused the design, he must have thought. There are other instances of this economy (see NO. 294). The cat's hair on end and its tail in a brush with excitement are wittily stylized in a way that was entirely Beardsley's own.

167 Vignette for p. 13 in *Bon-Mots* of Sydney Smith and R. Brinsley Sheridan, edited by Walter Jerrold and published by J. M. Dent and Company, London, 1893. Signed with the artist's emblem. Pl. 166
$1\frac{3}{8} \times 3\frac{1}{8}$ inches
Mr Brian Reade, London

These heads, Beardsley's own head amongst them, with a fringe, may have been suggested by the somewhat ghostly heads drawn by Simeon Solomon in his later years.

168 Vignette for p. 15 in *Bon-Mots* of Sydney Smith and R. Brinsley Sheridan, edited by Walter Jerrold and published by J. M. Dent and Company, London, 1893. Repeated on p. 80 in *Bon-Mots* of Samuel Foote and Theodore Hook, etc., 1894. Pl. 168
$2\frac{1}{8} \times 1\frac{3}{4}$ inches
Mr Charles Alan, New York

169 Vignette for p. 17 in *Bon-Mots* of Sydney Smith and R. Brinsley Sheridan, edited by Walter Jerrold and published by J. M. Dent and Company, London, 1893. Repeated on p. 120 in *Bon-Mots* of Charles Lamb and Douglas Jerrold, etc., 1893. Signed with the artist's emblem. Pl. 169
$2\frac{1}{2} \times 4\frac{5}{8}$ inches
Mr M. H. Schwab, Maidenhead, England

The extraction of teeth in the nineteenth century was simply a matter of drawing them out roughly with pincers. An assistant pulling the dentist to add to his drawing power was one of the bizarre elements in this operation. The idea of the patient's eye coming out on stalks is akin to similar ideas expressed by Cocteau in his illustrations to *Opium* (1930).

170 Vignette for p. 19 (small) in *Bon-Mots* of Sydney Smith and R. Brinsley Sheridan, edited by Walter Jerrold and published by J. M. Dent and Company, London, 1893; and for p. 117 (large) in *Bon-Mots* of Charles Lamb and Douglas Jerrold, etc., 1893. Pl. 170
$2\frac{3}{8} \times 1\frac{13}{16}$ inches
Grenville L. Winthrop Bequest, Fogg Art Museum, Harvard University, Massachusetts

In this excellently drawn fantasy the black plaits of the Dark Angel, which Lionel Johnson had only just invented (1893) and certainly not published, look like a wing. Or is it perhaps a wing that looks like plaits?

171   Vignette on p. 23 in *Bon-Mots* of Sydney Smith and R. Brinsley Sheridan, edited by Walter Jerrold and published by J. M. Dent and Company, London, 1893. Repeated on p. 29 in a smaller version in *Bon-Mots* of Charles Lamb and Douglas Jerrold, etc., 1893. Pl. 172
From the line-block

172   Vignette for p. 26 in *Bon-Mots* of Sydney Smith and R. Brinsley Sheridan, edited by Walter Jerrold and published by J. M. Dent and Company, London, 1893. Repeated on p. 151, and as full-page illustration facing p. 122, in *Bon-Mots* of Charles Lamb and Douglas Jerrold, etc., 1893; and on p. 165 in *Bon-Mots* of Samuel Foote and Theodore Hook, etc., 1894. Signed with the artist's emblem. Pl. 173
$2\frac{1}{8} \times 3\frac{7}{8}$ inches
Mr R. A. Harari, London

In 1892 or 1893 Beardsley may have seen either an actual foetus or some representation of one: in which case the experience made a strong impression. The obsessional foetus is seen here pointing to the creature in a fur-lined cloak, who puts out a dark hand with long finger-nails to give it to its mother – or is it the mother giving it to him? The object in the pocket of the cloak is perhaps an abortionist's instrument, but also a displaced phallic symbol, likewise the guttering candle with the flame pointing towards the woman.

173   Vignette for p. 27 in *Bon-Mots* of Sydney Smith and R. Brinsley Sheridan, edited by Walter Jerrold and published by J. M. Dent and Company, London, 1893. Pl. 171
$1\frac{15}{16} \times 1\frac{13}{16}$ inches
Mr R. A. Harari, London

174   Vignette on p. 30 in *Bon-Mots* of Sydney Smith and R. Brinsley Sheridan, edited by Walter Jerrold and published by J. M. Dent and Company, London, 1893. Pl. 176
From the line-block
The gallows-tree is alive and looking at the cat, whose extremities are attenuated in hair-line whorls. The more macabre etchings of Callot and of Cruikshank come to mind, but it is doubtful whether Beardsley could be said to have imitated them here.

175   Vignette for p. 40 in *Bon-Mots* of Sydney Smith and R. Brinsley Sheridan, edited by Walter Jerrold and published by J. M. Dent and Company, London, 1893. Pl. 175
$2\frac{1}{8} \times 2\frac{1}{4}$ inches
Mr Joseph T. Butler, New York

176   Vignette for p. 41 in *Bon-Mots* of Sydney Smith and R. Brinsley Sheridan, edited by Walter Jerrold and published by J. M. Dent and Company, London, 1893. Repeated on a smaller scale on p. 13 in *Bon-Mots* of Charles Lamb and Douglas Jerrold, etc., 1893. Pl. 174
$3\frac{1}{8} \times 2\frac{3}{4}$ inches
Mr F. J. Martin Dent, London

In the *Bon-Mots* of Smith this design is switched so that the beetle appears on the left. In the Lamb *Bon-Mots* the beetle is in the same position as here. The idea of a round-shaped spider with a human eye may well have been suggested to Beardsley by Odilon Redon's lithograph 'Araignée' (Mellerio, 72), which shows a spider with a grotesque semi-human face and two wide-open eyes. For another version of this possible link with Redon's spider, see NO. 208. Several other *Bon-Mots* vignettes show probable memorizations of lithographs by Redon, which Beardsley could have seen either at the Jones and Evans bookshop in London, or during his visit to Paris in 1892.

177   Vignette for p. 44 in *Bon-Mots* of Sydney Smith and R. Brinsley Sheridan, edited by Walter Jerrold and published by J. M. Dent and Company, London, 1893. Repeated on p. 174 of *Bon-Mots* of Samuel Foote and Theodore Hook, etc., 1894. Pl. 177
$2\frac{7}{16} \times 1\frac{3}{4}$ inches
Princeton University Library

178   Vignette on p. 47 in *Bon-Mots* of Sydney Smith and R. Brinsley Sheridan, edited by Walter Jerrold and published by J. M. Dent and Company, London, 1893. Signed with the artist's emblem. Pl. 183
From the line-block

179   Vignette for p. 50 in *Bon-Mots* of Sydney Smith and R. Brinsley Sheridan, edited by Walter Jerrold and published by J. M. Dent and Company, London, 1893. Repeated on p. 57 of *Bon-Mots* of Charles Lamb and Douglas Jerrold, etc., 1893. Pl. 179
$1\frac{9}{16} \times 1$ inches
Mr R. A. Harari, London

180   Vignette for p. 55 in *Bon-Mots* of Sydney Smith and R. Brinsley Sheridan, edited by Walter Jerrold and published by J. M. Dent and Company, London, 1893. Repeated on p. 177 and p. 132 (smaller version) in *Bon-Mots* of Charles Lamb and Douglas Jerrold, etc, 1893. Pl. 185
$2\frac{5}{8} \times 4\frac{1}{16}$ inches
Mr Brian Reade, London

181   Vignette for p. 58 in *Bon-Mots* of Sydney Smith and R. Brinsley Sheridan, edited by Walter Jerrold and published by J. M. Dent and Company, London, 1893. Repeated as a full-page grotesque facing p. 146 in *Bon-Mots* of Charles Lamb and Douglas Jerrold, etc, 1893. Pl. 183
$3\frac{3}{8} \times 3$ inches
The Art Institute of Chicago

182   Vignette for p. 61 in *Bon-Mots* of Sydney Smith and R. Brinsley Sheridan, edited by Walter Jerrold and published by J. M. Dent and Company, London, 1893. Repeated on p. 52 in *Bon-Mots* of Charles Lamb and Douglas Jerrold, etc., 1893. Signed with the artist's emblem. Pl. 180
$2\frac{1}{4} \times 1\frac{3}{4}$ inches
Princeton University Library

83 Vignette on p. 70 in *Bon-Mots* of Sydney Smith and R. Brinsley Sheridan, edited by Walter Jerrold and published by J. M. Dent and Company, London, 1893. Repeated on p. 119 in *Bon-Mots* of Samuel Foote and Theodore Hook, etc., 1894. Signed with the artist's emblem. Pl. 182
From the line-block

The large head seems to have been based on a seventeenth-century portrait (? Molière): the small heads seem to have been developed from the eyes of peacock feathers. If the head with horns represents a cuckold, the allusion is to a sex triangle, manipulated by strings as in puppetry.

84 Vignette for p. 73 in *Bon-Mots* of Sydney Smith and R. Brinsley Sheridan, edited by Walter Jerrold and published by J. M. Dent and Company, London, 1893. Repeated on a smaller scale on p. 65 of *Bon-Mots* of Charles Lamb and Douglas Jerrold, etc., 1893, and on p. 117 of *Bon-Mots* of Samuel Foote and Theodore Hook, etc., 1894. Pl. 178
$3\frac{3}{16} \times 2\frac{1}{16}$ inches
Mrs P. J. Mayer, London. Sold on 1 May 1968 at Sotheby's to Messrs Goldschmidt.

85 Vignette for p. 76 in *Bon-Mots* of Sydney Smith and R. Brinsley Sheridan, edited by Walter Jerrold and published by J. M. Dent and Company, London, 1893. Repeated on p. 46 in a smaller version in *Bon-Mots* of Charles Lamb and Douglas Jerrold, etc., 1893. Pl. 181
$3\frac{3}{8} \times 3\frac{1}{16}$ inches
Mr John Hay Whitney, New York

The form of the female figure, which seems about to be liquidated into the ground on which she is sitting, is of course inspired by Japanese prints. The twist of the wide-faced, wild-looking cat however seems to have been based upon Beardsley's own observations. The tip of the curve of the garment on the ground to the right has unfortunately been clipped away when the paper was trimmed.

86 Vignette on p. 85 in *Bon-Mots* of Sydney Smith and R. Brinsley Sheridan, edited by Walter Jerrold and published by J. M. Dent and Company, London, 1893. Repeated on p. 5, and in a smaller version on p. 36, in *Bon-Mots* of Charles Lamb and Douglas Jerrold, etc, 1893. Signed with the artist's emblem. Pl. 187
From the line-block

87 Vignette on p. 88 in *Bon-Mots* of Sydney Smith and R. Brinsley Sheridan, edited by Walter Jerrold and published by J. M. Dent and Company, London, 1893. Signed with the artist's emblem. Pl. 190
From the line-block

The foetus idea emerges here in the shape of a prawn, with a flat top to its head as though it were some kind of corbel, while over it a Whistlerian butterfly provokes a skeleton waving an Aesthetic peacock's feather. According to W. G. Good a bookplate for E. Eynor Baines was made from this drawing between 1896 and 1910.

88 Vignette on p. 96 in *Bon-Mots* of Sydney Smith and R. Brinsley Sheridan, edited by Walter Jerrold and published by J. M. Dent and Company, London, 1893. Repeated in a

smaller version on p. 153 in *Bon-Mots* of Charles Lamb and Douglas Jerrold, etc, 1893. Signed with the artist's emblem. Pl. 186
From the line-block

189 Vignette for p. 101 in *Bon-Mots* of Sydney Smith and R. Brinsley Sheridan, edited by Walter Jerrold and published by J. M. Dent and Company, London, 1893; and on p. 101 in *Bon-Mots* of Samuel Foote and Theodore Hook, etc, 1894. Signed with the artist's emblem. Pl. 188
$1\frac{15}{16} \times 1\frac{9}{16}$ inches
Mr R. A. Harari, London

Parts of the head and the whole of the hat are made up of calligraphic flourishes in the manner of seventeenth- and eighteenth-century writing masters, which Beardsley may have had opportunities of noting in the embellishments of copperplate penmanship to be seen in old manuscripts and in engraved books on handwriting. His compulsion to discover breast-forms in pears and trees (see NO. 114) sometimes took him a step further, and led to the summary indications of female breasts in odd places, as in this instance on the man's jaw, where the only possible equivalents would be ulcers.

190 Vignette for p. 107 in *Bon-Mots* of Sydney Smith and R. Brinsley Sheridan, edited by Walter Jerrold and published by J. M. Dent and Company, London, 1893. Repeated as full-page illustration facing p. 110 in *Bon-Mots* of Charles Lamb and Douglas Jerrold, etc, 1893. Signed with the artist's emblem. Pl. 195
$3\frac{3}{8} \times 3$ inches
The Art Institute of Chicago

191 Vignette for p. 109 in *Bon-Mots* of Sydney Smith and R. Brinsley Sheridan, edited by Walter Jerrold and published by J. M. Dent and Company, London, 1893. Repeated vertically on p. 142 in *Bon-Mots* of Samuel Foote and Theodore Hook, etc, 1894. Pl. 193
$1\frac{5}{16} \times 2\frac{1}{8}$ inches
Mr R. A. Harari, London

An example of one of the *Bon-Mots* drawings inspired by the pen flourishes of seventeenth-century calligraphers.

192 Vignette for p. 111 in *Bon-Mots* of Sydney Smith and R. Brinsley Sheridan, edited by Walter Jerrold and published by J. M. Dent and Company, London, 1893. Repeated on p. 60 in *Bon-Mots* of Charles Lamb and Douglas Jerrold, etc, 1893. Pl. 194
$2 \times 1\frac{3}{8}$ inches
Mr Charles Alan, New York

A miniature monster with Mephistophelian tongue, toasting-fork hand, and other endearing features.

193 Vignette on p. 119 in *Bon-Mots* of Sydney Smith and R. Brinsley Sheridan, edited by Walter Jerrold and published by J. M. Dent and Company, London, 1894. Repeated on p. 182 in *Bon-Mots* of Charles Lamb and Douglas Jerrold, etc, 1893. Signed with the artist's emblem. Pl. 192
From the line-block

Balancing on an Aesthetic feather, an apothecary and his Mephistophelian apprentice come to visit a sick person in a loose-covered Victorian armchair. A more elaborate version of the idea of the figure in the armchair appears in the second frontispiece to *An Evil Motherhood* (see NO. 395).

194 Vignette on p. 121 in *Bon-Mots* of Sydney Smith and R. Brinsley Sheridan, edited by Walter Jerrold and published by J. M. Dent and Company, London, 1893. Pl. 191
From the line-block

195 Vignette for p. 123 of *Bon-Mots* of Sydney Smith and R. Brinsley Sheridan, edited by Walter Jerrold and published by J. M. Dent and Company, London, 1893. Signed with the artist's emblem. Pl. 189
$3 \times 2\frac{3}{4}$ inches
Mr and Mrs Marvin Small, New York

196 Vignette on p. 126 in *Bon-Mots* of Sydney Smith and R. Brinsley Sheridan, edited by Walter Jerrold and published by J. M. Dent and Company, London, 1893. Repeated on p. 87 as full-page illustration in *Bon-Mots* of Charles Lamb and Douglas Jerrold, etc, 1893. Pl. 196
From the line-block

197 Vignette for p. 129 in *Bon-Mots* of Sydney Smith and R. Brinsley Sheridan, edited by Walter Jerrold and published by J. M. Dent and Company, London, 1893. Pl. 197
$2\frac{13}{16} \times 1\frac{13}{16}$ inches
Mr R. A. Harari, London

A figure almost entirely made up of pen flourishes. Pendulous breasts appear facing backwards below the hair.

198 Vignette for p. 131 of *Bon-Mots* of Sydney Smith and R. Brinsley Sheridan, edited by Walter Jerrold and published by J. M. Dent and Company, London, 1893. Repeated on p. 168 of *Bon-Mots* of Charles Lamb and Douglas Jerrold, etc, 1893. Signed with the artist's emblem. Pl. 200
$2\frac{1}{8} \times 1\frac{1}{2}$ inches
Dr and Mrs Richard W. Levy, New Orleans

199 Vignette on p. 133 in *Bon-Mots* of Sydney Smith and R. Brinsley Sheridan, edited by Walter Jerrold and published by J. M. Dent and Company, London, 1893. Pl. 198
From the line-block

A doodle on the lines of least resistance. The curious knotted goose-neck, which occurs in other *Bon-Mots* vignettes and in *Le Morte Darthur,* ends in a peacock's head. The torso is female. The single arm ends in a calligraphic version of Beardsley's initials over three dots, somewhat after the manner of his emblem. The feet are evaded and the legs end in a treble clef on the return, and in an untranslatable shape with twisted flourishes echoing the twisted neck.

200 Vignette for p. 136 in *Bon-Mots* of Sydney Smith and R. Brinsley Sheridan, edited by Walter Jerrold and published

by J. M. Dent and Company, London, 1893. Repeated on p. 113 in *Bon-Mots* of Samuel Foote and Theodore Hook, etc, 1894. Pl. 203
$2\frac{3}{4} \times 1\frac{1}{2}$ inches
Mr R. A. Harari, London

A hermaphrodite with the cut-away arms of an Antique torso, and with four legs ending in cloven hoofs.

201 Vignette for p. 139 in *Bon-Mots* of Sydney Smith and R. Brinsley Sheridan, edited by Walter Jerrold and published by J. M. Dent and Company, London, 1893. Repeated on p. 72 in *Bon-Mots* of Charles Lamb and Douglas Jerrold, etc, 1893. Pl. 199
$3\frac{7}{8} \times 2\frac{7}{8}$ inches
Mr F. J. Martin Dent, London

The showman's gesture of the pierrot was a favourite of Beardsley's, the most notable example of his use of it being in 'Enter Herodias' (see NO. 285).

202 Vignette for p. 147 in *Bon-Mots* of Sydney Smith and R. Brinsley Sheridan, edited by Walter Jerrold and published by J. M. Dent and Company, London, 1893. Signed with the artist's emblem. Pl. 202
$3\frac{1}{2} \times 2\frac{5}{8}$ inches
Victoria and Albert Museum, London

Beardsley visited Paris in the middle of 1892 and again in the middle of 1893. The first collection of *Bon-Mots* came out in June 1893, so that the influence of Chéret, which is shown perhaps in the treatment of this figure, may have been experienced during Beardsley's first visit of 1892. Compare Chéret's poster 'Olympia' of that year.

203 Vignette on p. 150 (large) in *Bon-Mots* of Sydney Smith and R. Brinsley Sheridan, and on p. 26 (small) in *Bon-Mots* of Charles Lamb and Douglas Jerrold, both edited by Walter Jerrold and published by J. M. Dent and Company, London, 1893. Pl. 201
$3\frac{15}{16} \times 3\frac{1}{2}$ inches
Grenville L. Winthrop Bequest, Fogg Art Museum, Harvard University, Massachusetts

A startling allegory perhaps of Romantic Music, whereby the grotesque 'notes' are bred in the mind of Woman by the mental energy of Man, which fecundates her aural sense by means of an ear. This is one of the most effective of Beardsley's foetal drawings, in spite of the calligraphic flourish for the sleeve, which academic draughtsmen might deprecate.

204 Vignette on p. 157 in *Bon-Mots* of Sydney Smith and R. Brinsley Sheridan, edited by Walter Jerrold and published by J. M. Dent and Company, London, 1893. Repeated on p. 21 in a smaller version in *Bon-Mots* of Charles Lamb and Douglas Jerrold, etc, 1893. Pl. 204
From the line-block

An early instance of Beardsley's manner of drawing figures which have no visible means of support—which rise out of the paper like hallucinations. A similar rendering of forms is to be seen in some of the illustrations to *Salome.*

205 Vignette for p. 160 in *Bon-Mots* of Sydney Smith and R. Brinsley Sheridan, edited by Walter Jerrold and published by J. M. Dent and Company, London, 1893. Repeated on p.

86 in *Bon-Mots* of Samuel Foote and Theodore Hook, etc, 1894. Pl. 205
$2\frac{1}{2} \times 1\frac{3}{8}$ inches
Mr R. A. Harari, London

206 Vignette for p. 162 in *Bon-Mots* of Sydney Smith and R. Brinsley Sheridan, edited by Walter Jerrold and published by J. M. Dent and Company, London, 1893. Repeated on p. 165 as full-page illustration in *Bon-Mots* of Charles Lamb and Douglas Jerrold, etc, 1893. Signed with the artist's emblem. Pl. 209
From the line-block

207 Vignette for p. 170 in *Bon-Mots* of Sydney Smith and R. Brinsley Sheridan, edited by Walter Jerrold and published by J. M. Dent and Company, London, 1893. Pl. 208
$2\frac{1}{4} \times 1\frac{13}{16}$ inches
Mr R. A. Harari, London

208 Vignette for p. 177 in *Bon-Mots* of Sydney Smith and R. Brinsley Sheridan, edited by Walter Jerrold and published by J. M. Dent and Company, London, 1893. Pl. 206
$2\frac{11}{16} \times 2\frac{5}{8}$ inches
Mr R. A. Harari, London

It would seem likely that this spider with a face and pince-nez, rather like those of Toulouse-Lautrec, was suggested by Odilon Redon's lithograph 'Araignée' (Mellerio, 72); see also NO. 176.

209 Vignette for p. 181 in *Bon-Mots* of Sydney Smith and R. Brinsley Sheridan, edited by Walter Jerrold and published by J. M. Dent and Company, London, 1893. Pl. 207
$2\frac{1}{16} \times 1\frac{1}{8}$ inches
Mr R. A. Harari, London

210 Vignette for p. 183 in *Bon-Mots* of Sydney Smith and R. Brinsley Sheridan, edited by Walter Jerrold and published by J. M. Dent and Company, London, 1893. Pl. 214
$2\frac{3}{4} \times 1\frac{1}{16}$ inches
Princeton University Library

211 Vignette for p. 185 of *Bon-Mots* of Sydney Smith and R. Brinsley Sheridan, edited by Walter Jerrold and published by J. M. Dent and Company, London, 1893. Pl. 213
$3 \times 2\frac{1}{8}$ inches
Princeton University Library

212 Vignette for p. 186 in *Bon-Mots* of Sydney Smith and R. Brinsley Sheridan, edited by Walter Jerrold and published by J. M. Dent and Company, London, 1893. Repeated on p. 98 in *Bon-Mots* of Samuel Foote and Theodore Hook, etc, 1894. Pl. 215
$2\frac{3}{16} \times 1\frac{3}{16}$ inches
Mr R. A. Harari, London

A variant of the obsessional foetus of 1893, this time with hoofs, hair fingers and arabesque tongue, drawn in a calligraphic style based on that of the seventeenth-century writing masters.

213 Vignette on p. 188 in *Bon-Mots* of Sydney Smith and R. Brinsley Sheridan, edited by Walter Jerrold and published by J. M. Dent and Company, London, 1893. Repeated on p. 105 in a smaller version in *Bon-Mots* of Charles Lamb and Douglas Jerrold, etc, 1893. Signed with the artist's emblem. Pl. 216
From the line-block

The obsessional foetus has grown here into an elegant putto on the back of a Beardsleyesque cat, being offered a quill by Pierrot—for writing or drawing, or both.

214 Vignette on p. 190 in *Bon-Mots* of Sydney Smith and R. Brinsley Sheridan, edited by Walter Jerrold and published by J. M. Dent and Company, London, 1893. Repeated on p. 145 in *Bon-Mots* of Samuel Foote and Theodore Hook, etc, 1894. Pl. 210
From the line-block

This adaptation of the form of a ragged peacock feather is a good example of Beardsley's feeling for arabesque.

215 Vignette for p. 192 in *Bon-Mots* of Sydney Smith and R. Brinsley Sheridan, edited by Walter Jerrold and published by J. M. Dent and Company, London, 1893. Repeated on p. 171 in *Bon-Mots* of Charles Lamb and Douglas Jerrold, etc, 1893. Pl. 212
$1\frac{3}{4} \times 1\frac{3}{4}$ inches
Mr Joseph T. Butler, New York

216 Vignette on p. 23 in *Bon-Mots* of Charles Lamb and Douglas Jerrold, edited by Walter Jerrold and published by J. M. Dent and Company, London, 1893. Repeated on p. 156 in *Bon-Mots* of Samuel Foote and Theodore Hook, etc, 1894. Pl. 211
From the line-block

This was supposed to be a caricature of Max Beerbohm, the shape of whose head evoked once again Beardsley's obsession with foetuses.

217 Vignette on p. 33 in *Bon-Mots* of Charles Lamb and Douglas Jerrold, edited by Walter Jerrold and published by J. M. Dent and Company, London, 1893. Pl. 219
From the line-block

The comparatively loose touch, for Beardsley, in the handling of this figure and her clothes seems to belong more to a style of fashion-drawing of the second quarter of the twentieth century than to the Nineties.

218 Vignette on p. 39 in *Bon-Mots* of Charles Lamb and Douglas Jerrold, edited by Walter Jerrold and published by J. M. Dent and Company, London, 1893. Pl. 220
From the line-block

A rare instance in Beardsley's work of loose-line realism.

219 Vignette on p. 42 in *Bon-Mots* of Charles Lamb and Douglas Jerrold, edited by Walter Jerrold and published by J. M. Dent and Company, London, 1893. Pl. 217
From the line-block

220 Vignette on p. 48 in *Bon-Mots* of Charles Lamb and Douglas Jerrold, edited by Walter Jerrold and published by J. M. Dent and Company, London, 1893. Repeated on p. 17 in *Bon-Mots* of Samuel Foote and Theodore Hook, etc, 1894. Pl. 221
From the line-block

221 Vignette for p. 69 in *Bon-Mots* of Charles Lamb and Douglas Jerrold, edited by Walter Jerrold and published by J. M. Dent and Company, London, 1893. Pl. 218
$3\frac{1}{16} \times 1\frac{5}{8}$ inches
Mr Brian Reade, London

An animated female lay-figure with horns in the form of an archaic symbol of her sex.

222 Vignette for p. 75 in *Bon-Mots* of Charles Lamb and Douglas Jerrold, edited by Walter Jerrold and published by J. M. Dent and Company, London, 1893. Pl. 224
$3\frac{1}{4} \times 1\frac{3}{4}$ inches
Mr R. A. Harari, London

The busy folds of cloth in the hat and cloak of the posturing actor are stylized in white lines left in reserve in the black masses—a technique unusual in Beardsley's work and suggestive of French influence.

223 Vignette for p. 81 in *Bon-Mots* of Charles Lamb and Douglas Jerrold, edited by Walter Jerrold and published by J. M. Dent and Company, London, 1893. Pl. 225
$3\frac{1}{2} \times 2$ inches
Mr R. A. Harari, London

224 Vignette for p. 90 of *Bon-Mots* of Charles Lamb and Douglas Jerrold, edited by Walter Jerrold and published by J. M. Dent and Company, London, 1893. Repeated on p. 139 of *Bon-Mots* of Samuel Foote and Theodore Hook, etc, 1894. Pl. 223
$3\frac{3}{4} \times 2\frac{1}{4}$ inches
Mr R. A. Harari, London

225 Vignette for p. 102 in *Bon-Mots* of Charles Lamb and Douglas Jerrold, edited by Walter Jerrold and published by J. M. Dent and Company, London, 1893. Pl. 222
$3\frac{7}{16} \times 2\frac{1}{8}$ inches
Mr R. A. Harari, London

226 Vignette for p. 108 in *Bon-Mots* of Charles Lamb and Douglas Jerrold, edited by Walter Jerrold and published by J. M. Dent and Company, London, 1893. Repeated on p. 62 in *Bon-Mots* of Samuel Foote and Theodore Hook, etc, 1894. Pl. 228
$2\frac{13}{16} \times 2\frac{1}{4}$ inches
Mr R. A. Harari, London

227 Full-page grotesque on p. 131 in *Bon-Mots* of Charles Lamb and Douglas Jerrold, edited by Walter Jerrold and published by J. M. Dent and Company, London, 1893. Repeated in a smaller version on p. 65 in *Bon-Mots* of Samuel Foote and Theodore Hook, etc, 1894. Pl. 234
From the line-block

A single example of an attempt by Beardsley to draw like Phil May.

228 Vignette for p. 138 in *Bon-Mots* of Charles Lamb and Douglas Jerrold, edited by Walter Jerrold and published by J. M. Dent and Company, London, 1893. Pl. 227
$3\frac{9}{16} \times 2\frac{11}{16}$ inches
Mr R. A. Harari, London

229 Vignette for p. 156 in *Bon-Mots* of Charles Lamb and Douglas Jerrold, edited by Walter Jerrold and published by J. M. Dent and Company, London, 1893. Repeated on a reduced scale on p. 22 in *Bon-Mots* of Samuel Foote and Theodore Hook, etc, 1894. Pl. 226
$2\frac{13}{16} \times 1\frac{7}{16}$ inches
Mr R. A. Harari, London

This extraordinary grotesque must be unique in the history of art. It might be said to relate to certain types of schizophrenic drawing.

230 Vignette for p. 159 in *Bon-Mots* of Charles Lamb and Douglas Jerrold, edited by Walter Jerrold and published by J. M. Dent and Company, London, 1893. Repeated on p. 71 in *Bon-Mots* of Samuel Foote and Theodore Hook, etc, 1894. Pl. 229
$2 \times 1\frac{3}{4}$ inches
The Drawing Shop, New York

231 Vignette for p. 187 in *Bon-Mots* of Charles Lamb and Douglas Jerrold, edited by Walter Jerrold and published by J. M. Dent and Company, London, 1893. Repeated on p. 153 in *Bon-Mots* of Samuel Foote and Theodore Hook, etc, 1894. Pl. 230
$3 \times 1\frac{13}{16}$ inches
Mr F. M. Gross, London

232 Grotesque accompanying half-title after the Introduction, on p. 15 of *Bon-Mots* of Samuel Foote and Theodore Hook, edited by Walter Jerrold and published by J. M. Dent and Company, London, 1894. Pl. 232
From the line-block

There was another half-title for the section devoted to the *bon-mots* of Hook, with the grotesque ornament at NO. 184. The creature was a caricature of Max Beerbohm (see Herbert Small, 'Aubrey Beardsley', in *The Book-Buyer*, New York, February 1895).

233 Vignette on p. 19 in *Bon-Mots* of Samuel Foote and Theodore Hook, edited by Walter Jerrold and published by J. M. Dent and Company, London, 1894. Pl. 231
From the line-block

234 Drawing for the full-page grotesque facing p. 24 in *Bon-Mots* of Samuel Foote and Theodore Hook, edited by Walter Jerrold and published by J. M. Dent and Company, London, 1894. Pl. 233
$3\frac{7}{8} \times 1\frac{1}{4}$ inches
The Drawing Shop, New York

235 Vignette for p. 31 in *Bon-Mots* of Samuel Foote and Theodore Hook, edited by Walter Jerrold and published by J. M. Dent and Company, London, 1894. Pl. 237
$5\frac{3}{4} \times 2\frac{3}{8}$ inches
Mr R. A. Harari, London

236 Echo of Venice. Second version of a subject drawn for the full-page illustration facing p. 40 in *Bon-Mots* of Samuel Foote and Theodore Hook, edited by Walter Jerrold and published by J. M. Dent and Company, London, 1894. Signed with the artist's names. Pl. 238
$4\frac{9}{16} \times 3$ inches (on page, $9 \times 5\frac{1}{2}$ inches)
Fitzwilliam Museum, Cambridge, England

The drawing was made either in or before the winter of 1894 when Beardsley sent it to the wife of his friend Alfred Lambart. Mrs Enid Lambart was asked to accept it because she disliked the artist's drawings of women. The illustration on which it was based must have been drawn before March 1894, when the *Bon-Mots* of Foote and Hook were published.

237 Vignette for p. 44 in *Bon-Mots* of Samuel Foote and Theodore Hook, edited by Walter Jerrold and published by J. M. Dent and Company, London, 1894. Pl. 235
$3\frac{7}{16} \times 1\frac{13}{16}$ inches
Victoria and Albert Museum, London

The head of the obsessional foetus is linked here to the stylized form of a skeletal old woman.

238 Vignette on p. 56 in *Bon-Mots* of Samuel Foote and Theodore Hook, edited by Walter Jerrold and published by J. M. Dent and Company, London, 1894. Pl. 242
From the line-block

An interesting change-over from the head of Iokanaan. Woman, or at least sterile Woman, may have the urge to possess Man's head, cost him what it may; but Man, and especially a man like Beardsley, has the countervailing tendency to have the head of Woman separated from her body —in a beautiful bonnet. The drawing for this vignette belonged to Pickford Waller, and together with other drawings for the *Bon-Mots* series, it was sold by his daughter Miss Sybil Waller through Christie, London, on 12 November 1965. It is now the property of Mrs Stephanie Maison, London. ($3\frac{1}{2} \times 1\frac{3}{4}$ inches.)

239 Drawing for the full-page grotesque facing p. 58 in *Bon-Mots* of Samuel Foote and Theodore Hook, edited by Walter Jerrold and published by J. M. Dent and Company, London, 1894. Pl. 239
$3\frac{1}{8} \times 1\frac{3}{8}$ inches
The Drawing Shop, New York

No captain of a Rugby football Fifteen could look more ideally gross, arrogant and dangerous.

240 Full-page grotesque on p. 74 in *Bon-Mots* of Samuel Foote and Theodore Hook, edited by Walter Jerrold and published by J. M. Dent and Company, London, 1894. Pl. 241
From the line-block

The irrepressible ambivalence of Beardsley's feelings toward anything that caught his attention is shown in this apparition of a Roman priest, in which many of the physical attributes of a type of man who tends to this vocation are rendered so grotesque as to seem, to the innocent beholder, malignant.

241 Vignette on p. 83 in *Bon-Mots* of Samuel Foote and Theodore Hook, edited by Walter Jerrold and published by J. M. Dent and Company, London, 1894. Pl. 244
From the line-block

The style of the clothes is right for the 1860s, including the wide hat for a young girl; but not including the mahoitered sleeves, which belong to the 1890s. The arms are drawn in such dislocated poses that the whole figure with its shut eyelids and bolt-upright appearance has the semblance of a marionette. Both Beardsley and his sister Mabel had been, from childhood upwards, interested in puppets and marionettes.

242 Vignette on p. 95 in *Bon-Mots* of Samuel Foote and Theodore Hook, edited by Walter Jerrold and published by J. M. Dent and Company, London, 1894. Pl. 243
From the line-block

The elegance and eroticism of this figure appear now quite out of context in late Victorian England.

243 Vignette for p. 110 in *Bon-Mots* of Samuel Foote and Theodore Hook, edited by Walter Jerrold and published by J. M. Dent and Company, London, 1894. Pl. 240
$3\frac{9}{16} \times 1\frac{9}{16}$ inches
Mr Brian Reade, London

A fantasy in the Aesthetic taste, with a parody of Whistler's emblem.

244 Vignette for p. 133 in *Bon-Mots* of Samuel Foote and Theodore Hook, edited by Walter Jerrold and published by J. M. Dent and Company, London, 1894. Pl. 236
$2\frac{5}{8} \times 2$ inches
The Drawing Shop, New York

245 Full-page grotesque on p. 136 in *Bon-Mots* of Samuel Foote and Theodore Hook, edited by Walter Jerrold and published by J. M. Dent and Company, London, 1894. Pl. 245
From the line-block

Reminiscence of some poster by Chéret perhaps lies behind the conception of this figure.

246 Vignette on p. 148 in *Bon-Mots* of Samuel Foote and Theodore Hook, edited by Walter Jerrold and published by J. M. Dent and Company, London, 1894. Pl. 246
From the line-block

A growth of female breasts on odd parts of the body, as on the back of the head of this preposterous grotesque, was one of the strange fantasies often expressed by Beardsley (see also NO. 189). It is foreshadowed in the breast-shapes to be found on the trees in many of the *Morte Darthur* illustrations.

247 Full-page grotesque on p. 150 in *Bon-Mots* of Samuel Foote and Theodore Hook, edited by Walter Jerrold and published by J. M. Dent and Company, London, 1894. Pl. 247
From the line-block

A Japanese man seen in a Japanese print undoubtedly, but the fine angular outlines appear to belong to some drawing from a quarter of a century later.

248 Vignette for p. 168 in *Bon-Mots* of Samuel Foote and Theodore Hook, edited by Walter Jerrold and published by J. M. Dent and Company, London, 1894. Pl. 248
$3 \times 2\frac{3}{8}$ inches
Mr F. J. Martin Dent, London

249 Drawing for the full-page grotesque on p. 171 in *Bon-Mots* of Samuel Foote and Theodore Hook, edited by Walter Jerrold and published by J. M. Dent and Company, London, 1894. Pl. 251
$7\frac{5}{8} \times 3\frac{5}{8}$ inches
Mr Brian Reade, London

The drawing has been called 'Waiting' and 'Woman at Café'. The Foote and Hook volume was the last of the little *bon-mots* books to be illustrated by Beardsley. The silhouetted form of the hat suggests that it may have been done after seeing the similar treatment of a hat and a woman in Toulouse-Lautrec's poster *Le Divan Japonais* (1892), in which however the design is quite different. Beardsley was in Paris during the middle of 1893, so that it looks as if the drawing dates from late in that year, or early in 1894. It must be the earliest, or among the very earliest, of drawings in *The Yellow Book* style.

250 Vignette on p. 186 in *Bon-Mots* of Samuel Foote and Theodore Hook, edited by Walter Jerrold and published by J. M. Dent and Company, London, 1894. Pl. 249
From the line-block

251 Vignette intended for the *Bon-Mots* series (1893–4), but not used. Pl. 250
$3\frac{1}{16} \times 1\frac{5}{8}$ inches
Princeton University Library

252 La Femme Incomprise. Reproduced as NO. 9 in *The Uncollected Work of Aubrey Beardsley*, John Lane, London, 1925. Pl. 257
From the half-tone plate

The proportions of the design and the idea of the elongated thistle suggest the influence, possibly indirect, of Carlos Schwabe, which was then appearing in *proto-art nouveau* trends. Here the artist has plagiarized his own grotesque of the one-eyed spider (? after Redon) which was drawn for p. 41 of the *Bon-Mots* of Smith and Sheridan (see NO. 176), and the Japanese woman and cat on p. 76 of the same book, published in June 1893 (see NO. 185). In spite of its many eccentricities, the drawing is evidence of a rapidly cultivated gift of abstract linear design, which happened to be briefly

descriptive and decorative, with emphasis in this case on meagreness of form, on the contrast of S-shapes against vertical lines, and the rectangle-play so fashionable in the Eighties and Nineties in England, following the Aesthetic craze for Japanese arts and crafts.

The drawing was published in *Today*, Spring 1895, and in *The Idler*, March 1897. In 1974 it was held by Charles Alan, New York.

253 Design for a book-marker, 1893. Signed with the artist's emblem. Reproduced as NO. 9 in *The Later Work of Aubrey Beardsley*, John Lane, 1901. Pl. 258
From the line-block

The original design once belonged to Sir William Geary, Bt. It was a rare example of loose, sketchy drawing in ink, with none of Beardsley's customary insistence on definition. Another interesting point is that it must have been drawn (or memorized) from life. Perhaps the model was Mabel Beardsley getting into bed. The long vertical rectangle enclosing the design, and echoed in the framed picture which is shown on the wall, was one of the modish shapes of the Nineties.

254 A Snare of Vintage, *c.* 1893. Drawing for the illustration facing p. 23 in *Lucian's True History*, translated by Francis Hickes and illustrated by William Strang, J. B. Clark and Aubrey Beardsley, privately printed (251 copies, 4to) by Lawrence and Bullen, London, December 1894. Pl. 252
$7\frac{5}{8} \times 5\frac{1}{2}$ inches
Graphische Sammlung Albertina, Vienna

A fake of this drawing is reproduced for comparison in R. A. Walker's *How to Detect Beardsley Forgeries*, Bedford, 1950, pl. V. On about 15 February 1893, Beardsley wrote in bed to his old school-fellow, G. F. Scotson-Clark, about how he had been thriving. 'Better than the Morte darthur [*sic*]' he observed, 'is the book that Lawrence and Bullen have given me, the "Vera Historia" of Lucian. I am illustrating this entirely in my new manner, or, rather, a development of it. The drawings are most certainly the most extraordinary things that have ever appeared in a book both in respect to technique and conception. They are also the most indecent. I have 30 little drawings to do for it 6 inches by 4. L and B give me £100 for the work. Dent is giving me £250 for the Morte.' As he got deeper into 1893 however Beardsley found himself busy on *Salome* and then at the beginning of 1894 on *The Yellow Book,* and the Lucian commitments were neglected. When the *True History* was published at the end of 1894, there were only two illustrations by him in it, the rest being by the other artists mentioned above.

255 A Snare of Vintage. Proof of a first version of the subject on the plate facing p. 23 in *Lucian's True History*, translated by Frances Hickes, illustrated by William Strang, J. B. Clark and Aubrey Beardsley, with an introduction by Charles Whibley, privately printed (251 copies, 4to) by Lawrence and Bullen, London. December 1894. Not used. Pl. 253
From the line-block, $6\frac{1}{8} \times 4\frac{1}{4}$ inches
Mr W. G. Good, England

Although this version of 'A Snare of Vintage' was not used, a line-block existed, from which the proof was taken. Platinotype copies of the design were made by F. H. Evans however and inserted in 54 copies of the book printed on Japanese vellum. Beardsley wrote to his form-master A. W. King, on 9 December 1892, telling him that Lawrence and Bullen had given him 'Lucian's Comic Voyage' to illustrate.

But the majority of the illustrations were by Strang and Clark; only three by Beardsley seem to have been actually linked with the book, this one resembling in style another one entitled 'Dreams', facing p. 209 (see NO. 256). Two more were rejected altogether (see NOS. 257, 258). This design is remarkable for the curious web-like lines that link up the forms, and for the fantastic ornamental hair that grows on the bodies of the creatures. It illustrates the passage in Hickes's translation where the travellers came among a world of vines 'which towards the earth had firm stocks . . . but the tops of them were women from the hip upwards . . . at their fingers' ends sprung out branches full of grapes . . . They also kissed us with their mouths, but he that was so kissed fell drunk . . . Some of them desired to have carnal mixture with us, and two of our company were so bold as to entertain their offer, and could never afterwards be loosed from them . . . and their fingers began to spring out with branches and crooked wires as if they were ready to bring out fruit.'

256 Dreams. Drawing for illustration, facing p. 209 of *Lucian's True History*, translated by Francis Hickes, illustrated by William Strang, J. B. Clark and Aubrey Beardsley, privately printed (251 copies, 4to) by Lawrence and Bullen, London, December 1894. Pl. 254
$5\frac{15}{16} \times 4\frac{3}{8}$ inches
Scofield Thayer Collection, Fogg Art Museum, Harvard University, Massachusetts

257 Lucian's Strange Creatures. Illustration intended for *Lucian's True History*, published by Lawrence and Bullen, London, December 1894, 4to. Not used, but published in *An Issue of Five Drawings Illustrative of Juvenal and Lucian* (120 sets) published by Leonard Smithers, London, 1906. Pl. 256
From the line-block, 9 × 5 inches
Mr W. G. Good, England

This illustration and the one reproduced at NO. 258 were rejected from the 1894 and 1902 editions of *Lucian's True History*. Among the strange creatures is a caricature of Oscar Wilde.

258 Birth from the Calf of the Leg. Illustration intended for *Lucian's True History*, published by Lawrence and Bullen, London, 1894, 4to. Not used, but published in *An Issue of Five Drawings Illustrative of Juvenal and Lucian* (120 sets) by Leonard Smithers, London, 1906. Pl. 255
From the line-block, 9 × 5 inches
Mr W. G. Good, England

This illustration and the one reproduced at NO. 257 were rejected from the 1894 and 1902 editions of *Lucian's True History*. At the time when it was drawn the artist was obsessed by foetuses and irregular births; creatures derived from the foetus form occur in the *Bon-Mots* series, in *The Kiss of Judas*, in *Salome* and elsewhere. That he chose to illustrate this subject suggests that there may have been a latent strain of homosexuality in Beardsley. Lucian describes in his *True History* the way in which children are born in the kingdom of Endymion on the Moon. 'They are not begotten of women, but of mankind: for they have no other marriage but of males: the name of woman is wholly unknown among them: until they accomplish the age of five and twenty

years, they are given in marriage to others: from that time forwards they take others in marriage to themselves: for as soon as the infant is conceived the leg begins to swell, and afterwards when the time of birth is come, they give it a lance and take it out dead: then they lay it abroad with open mouth towards the wind, and so it takes life: and I think thereof the Grecians call it the belly of the leg, because therein they bear their children instead of a belly'. Lucian also explains that 'their boys admit copulation, not like unto ours, but in their hams, a little above the calf of the leg for there they are open'. (1902 ed. pp. 30–32.)

259 *The Studio*, Vol. I, NO. 1, April 1893. Original wrapper printed in line-block and letterpress on dark green paper, 4to. Pl. 264
Mr W. G. Good, England

The first number of a new art magazine, *The Studio*, was planned towards the end of 1892, with C. Lewis Hind as editor. Hind met Beardsley at Mrs Alice Meynell's during this period, and he was so impressed by some drawings he saw in the young artist's portfolio that he commissioned Joseph Pennell to write for the first number of *The Studio* an article on Beardsley to be illustrated by a selection from Beardsley's own work to date. Beardsley was also asked to design the first wrapper of the magazine. The design for *The Studio* poster was similar but on a larger scale.

260 The Birthday of Madame Cigale. Drawing reproduced in *The Studio*, NO. 1, April 1893, p. 15. Pl. 259
Pen, ink and wash, $9\frac{3}{4} \times 15\frac{1}{8}$ inches
Grenville L. Winthrop Bequest, Fogg Art Museum, Harvard University, Massachusetts

The word 'cigale' means cicada. Could Beardsley have come across the French book *La Cigale*, a symposium of verse and prose and musical compositions by various hands, published in Paris in 1889? He could, but it seems we may never know.
The design is composite, containing one almost identical *Bon-Mots* figure, the boy with the slippers (see NO. 178). The two figures behind him are variations respectively on the right-hand figure in the *Bon-Mots* of Foote and Hook, p. 17 (the man with a hat and cane) and a vignette on p. 174 of the same book (the man with flowers, see NO. 177); while the fantastic birds on the base-line are related to the one in 'King Arthur and the Questing Beast' (NO. 56), which is dated 8 March 1893. A similar Moorish table supports the youth in the rejected 'Toilet' of Salome, which was done later, and in the design for a book-marker (NO. 253) which may have been done at about the same time. Wispy lines, like the ones straying in the foreground and the background without any descriptive function, seem to have been compulsive for Beardsley at this date: his last and most assertive use of them being in his design for the front cover of Dowson's *Verses*, 1896 (NO. 457). Parallel wavy lines occur on the screen-like background in the Japanese manner and bring the whole composition into line with the Aesthetic productions in ceramics and lacquer of the 1870s and 1880s. It will be seen here that Beardsley's contribution to the decline of this decorative style was to render it grotesque. The well-drawn flight of birds in the distance expresses a motif that Beardsley later reduced to a mere arc of V-shapes (NO. 421).

261 J'ai Baisé Ta Bouche Iokanaan. Salome with the head of John the Baptist. Published in *The Studio*, Vol. I, p. 19, April

1893. Signed with the artist's names and with his emblem. Lettered with title. Pl. 272
Indian ink and green water-colour wash, $10\frac{15}{16} \times 5\frac{13}{16}$ inches
Princeton University Library

The green water-colour washes were added after 1893. The drawing in its former black-and-white state featured among others reproduced alongside an article by Joseph Pennell, 'A New Illustrator: Aubrey Beardsley', in the first number of *The Studio*. John Lane's attention having been drawn to this interpretation of a passage in Oscar Wilde's play *Salome*, Beardsley was commissioned by him soon afterwards to illustrate the translation of *Salome* (originally written in French) which Elkin Mathews and Lane published the following year. Later when it came to illustrating the same theme for the book of 1894 (NO. 286), Beardsley improved upon this version and cut out the *Bon-Mots* hair-line flourishes. However, the lilies growing from the pool of blood remained in the later drawing, though they were more tactfully treated. Many of those who opened the first number of *The Studio* must have been sickened by this detail, and it is the outstanding instance of sensationalism in Beardsley's work. At the same time if we dismiss it as purely sensational we should be sharing certain conventions of taste held by the late Victorians, and this would be unreasonable once we see that Beardsley's compulsion to describe such a thought is some rough measure of the strength of the compulsion in him to convert excruciation into a kind of macabre comedy, by way of stylization. There are links between the lilies and the ulcers in NO. 189 and NO. 466, and indeed with everything that is perverse in Beardsley's art. What were the traumatic experiences behind that compulsion? Whatever they were, Beardsley was evidently determined to face the consequences of them, not only in his grotesque drawings, but in his equally grotesque romance *Venus and Tannhäuser*.

262 Of a Neophyte and how the Black Art was revealed unto him by the Fiend Asomuel. Illustration to 'The Black Art', Part II, by James Mew, facing p. 177 of *The Pall Mall Magazine*, Vol. I, June 1893, 8vo. Lettered with title. Pl. 260
From the line-block
Mr W. G. Good, England

The artist invented the name Asomuel, meaning insomnia, for the purpose of this illustration, which was a facetious comment on the article that accompanied it.

263 The Kiss of Judas. Drawing for the plate prefixed to the story 'A Kiss of Judas' by 'X. L.' in *The Pall Mall Magazine*, July 1893, pp. 339–366, 8vo. Signed with the artist's emblem and inscribed with title. Pl. 261
$12\frac{1}{4} \times 8\frac{5}{8}$ inches
Mr R. A. Harari, London

The skilful balance of components in this design can be compared with that of 'A Platonic Lament' (NO. 284) in the illustrations to *Salome*, which however were not published until 1894. There are similar and unusual vertical espaliers in both compositions. They were probably conceived at the same period in 1893, the magazine illustrations being published well ahead of the *Salome* series. About the same time too there must have been drawn the design for the heading of Chapter VI, Book XVII (p. 789 of Vol. II) in *Le Morte Darthur*, which appeared in Part X: in this the forms of the female head and the trees behind

are similar, though less carefully drawn. Indeed the quality of the lines in 'The Kiss of Judas' is as high as Beardsley ever achieved. The curious brevities, as in the simple curve of the woman's arms, and the delicate suggestion of shadows in the thickening of the lines describing her legs are among its many perfections. As to 'The Kiss of Judas', '"It's a Moldavian legend", observed the "great specialist"' in the story by 'X.L.' (p.350). '"They say that children of Judas, lineal descendants of the arch traitor, are prowling about the world seeking to do harm, and that they kill you with a kiss."'

'"Oh how delightful", murmured the Dowager Duchess...'
The author 'X.L.' was Julian Osgood Field, whose 'satanic' stories were published in London and Paris. Later his money-lending activities landed him in gaol (see O. Sitwell, *Great Morning*, London, 1948).

264 Design for the frontispiece (The Landslide) to *Pastor Sang*, the drama of *Over Aevne* by Bjornstjerne Bjornson, translated from the Norwegian by William Wilson, published by Longmans, Green and Company, London and New York, October 1893, 8vo. Signed with monogram. Pl.263
$9\frac{1}{2} \times 6\frac{3}{4}$ inches
Mr F. J. Martin Dent, London

In the monogram and in the Teutonic landscape Beardsley has imitated Dürer. William Wilson was the pseudonym of More Adey, one of Beardsley's early London friends: also a friend of Robert Ross and Oscar Wilde. The cover was designed by Aymer Vallance.

265 Réjane. Profile to left. Signed with the artist's emblem and dated in pencil 1893. Pl. 265
Indian ink, red chalk and pencil, $7\frac{5}{8} \times 6\frac{1}{16}$ inches
Mr Ewan Phillips, London

An excursion into the art of rubbed drawing with red chalk, which Beardsley otherwise did not practise. The result is not technically impressive because he had little experience of how to get the best from this medium. It seems probable that the drawing was meant to be a careful study of Réjane's profile, made from the life, and that it may have been referred to both for the drawing of Réjane reclining on a divan which is now in the Metropolitan Museum in New York (see NO. 327) and for the *Yellow Book* drawing (NO. 359). Formerly in the collection of Beardsley's friend Frederick H. Evans, the present study passed after his death through the saleroom into a French collection, from which it came to the art market in 1967.

266 Réjane. Portrait of Madame Réjane, the actress, holding a fan, half-length. Pl. 266
From the line-block

This portrait was published on p.95 in *A Second Book of Fifty Drawings by Aubrey Beardsley*, Smithers, London, 1899, where it is stated that it was drawn in 1893 and was hitherto unpublished.

267 Design for the frontispiece to large paper copies of *The Wonderful History of Virgilius the Sorcerer of Rome*, published by David Nutt, London, 1893, 8vo. Signed with the artist's emblem. Pl. 262
$9 \times 5\frac{1}{2}$ inches
The Art Institute of Chicago

The placing of the figure of the sorcerer, which is compensated by the movements implied by his gestures, shows the influence of Japanese prints, from which Beardsley learnt also the flat treatment of patterns on garments, as here. The book was issued in January 1894. The drawing was referred to by the artist in a letter of (?) November 1893, to Robert Ross.

68 Design for the title-page to *Pagan Papers* by Kenneth Grahame, published by Elkin Mathews and John Lane, London, December 1893, 8vo. Pl. 267
$9 \times 5\frac{1}{4}$ inches
Mr R. A. Harari, London

The book bears the date 1894 on the title-page and at the foot of the spine.

69 Incipit Vita Nova, *c.* 1893. Pl. 273
Indian ink and chinese white over pencil on brown paper, $7\frac{11}{16} \times 7\frac{13}{16}$ inches
Dr Nicholas Pickard, Kansas City, USA

Chapter-heading II, Book V (p.157 of Vol. I) in *Le Morte Darthur* incorporates in the design the same title of Dante's prose masterpiece (Here Begins a New Life), and was made probably at about the same time as this drawing. The style here has something of the stylized economies of form and tone that signalize the *art nouveau* designs of such artists as Behrens, dating from later in the 1890s.

70 Two drawings on the front cover of Beardsley's copy of the vocal score of *Tristan und Isolde, c.* 1893–4. Pl. 268
Indian ink and chinese white on brown paper, $10\frac{3}{4} \times 6\frac{15}{16}$ inches
Princeton University Library

The copy of the vocal score is in the Gallatin Collection in Princeton University Library. This is an unusual drawing for Beardsley. The home-made lettering is beautifully worked in the free style of many years later, and the broad treatment of the bisected seed is handled with a looser touch than was usual with him. The strange hybrid clematis-passion flowers, which haunt the designs for *Le Morte Darthur*, appear again here very appropriately.

71 Outer sides, front and back, of The Playgoers' Club Menu of their tenth annual dinner, London, 28 January 1894. Pl. 269
Line-block, half-tone and letterpress
Princeton University Library

The carnival costumes are still influenced by Japanese popular art, and a Japanese lantern of the kind that attracted Beardsley, according to Gleeson White in his article 'Aubrey Beardsley: In Memoriam' (*The Studio,* May 1898, p.256) appears on the back of the menu. The inset photographs include one of Carl Hentschel as Honorary Treasurer of the Club. This man was head of the firm of process-engravers which reproduced most of Beardsley's drawings until he worked for *The Savoy.* Hentschel's initials, followed by the letters *sc.* for 'sculpsit', will be found in many of the line-blocks by his firm.

72 Design for the front cover of *Salome* by Oscar Wilde. Not used for the edition of *Salome* of 1894 but reproduced as Plate III in *A Portfolio of Aubrey Beardsley's Drawings Illustrating 'Salome' by Oscar Wilde,* published by John Lane,

London, N.D. [1907]. Signed in the design with the artist's emblem. Pl. 270
From the half-tone plate
Mr Brian Reade, London

Nothing could be more evocative of the late Aesthetic or *fin de siècle* period than these serpentine peacock feathers growing out of a 'Japonesque' ground. An all-over pattern for the cover was rejected for a simpler design (see NO. 273).

273 Front cover of *Salome*. A tragedy in one act, translated [by Lord Alfred Douglas] from the French of Oscar Wilde, pictured by Aubrey Beardsley and published by Elkin Mathews and John Lane, London; Copeland and Day, Boston, March 1894. Edition de luxe limited to 100 copies for England and bound in green silk with covers and spine stamped in gold, 4to. Pl. 271
Stamped design

Mr R.A.Harari, London. Given from Ralph A. Harari's estate by Dr Michael Harari to Brian Reade.

The neat interruption of a tendency to symmetry by the placing of the roses and the inner leaves is characteristic of Beardsley. The diagram roses, with petals something like the scale-shapes he adapted from Whistler's peacock-feathers at 49 Prince's Gate were to become familiar in *art nouveau* decorations in all media.

274– *Salome*. Drawings for illustrations to *Salome,* translated from
83 the French of Oscar Wilde, [by Lord Alfred Douglas], pictured by Aubrey Beardsley, and published by Elkin Mathews and John Lane, London; Copeland and Day, Boston, March 1894, 4to. All signed with the artist's emblem.

274 Title-page. Pl. 274
$8\frac{3}{4} \times 6\frac{1}{2}$ inches
Grenville L. Winthrop Bequest, Fogg Art Museum, Harvard University, Massachusetts

275 The Woman in the Moon (frontispiece). Pl. 275
$8\frac{3}{4} \times 6\frac{1}{8}$ inches
Grenville L.Winthrop Bequest, Fogg Art Museum, Harvard University, Massachusetts

276 Border for the List of Pictures. Pl. 276
$9\frac{1}{4} \times 7\frac{3}{4}$ inches
Grenville L.Winthrop Bequest, Fogg Art Museum, Harvard University, Massachusetts

277 The Peacock Skirt. Drawing for the illustration facing p. 2. Pl. 277
$8\frac{7}{8} \times 6\frac{1}{4}$ inches
Grenville L. Winthrop Bequest, Fogg Art Museum, Harvard University, Massachusetts

278 The Black Cape. Drawing for the illustration facing p. 8. Pl. 278
$8\frac{13}{16} \times 6\frac{1}{4}$ inches
Princeton University Library

279 The Eyes of Herod. Drawing for the illustration facing p. 32. Pl. 279
$8\frac{3}{4} \times 6\frac{7}{8}$ inches
Grenville L.Winthrop Bequest, Fogg Art Museum, Harvard University, Massachusetts

280 The Stomach Dance. Drawing for the illustration facing p. 40. Pl. 280
$8\frac{3}{4} \times 6\frac{7}{8}$ inches
Grenville L. Winthrop Bequest, Fogg Art Museum, Harvard University, Massachusetts

281 The Toilet of Salome. Drawing for the illustration facing p. 48. Pl. 281
$8\frac{13}{16} \times 6\frac{5}{16}$ inches
British Museum

282 The Dancer's Reward. Drawing for the illustration facing p. 56. Pl. 282
$8\frac{3}{4} \times 6\frac{1}{4}$ inches
Grenville L. Winthrop Bequest, Fogg Art Museum, Harvard University, Massachusetts

283 The Burial of Salome (cul-de-lampe). Pl. 283
$6\frac{7}{16} \times 6\frac{3}{4}$ inches
Grenville L. Winthrop Bequest, Fogg Art Museum, Harvard University, Massachusetts

These ten drawings were all reproduced by the line-block craftsman, Carl Hentschel, in the 1894 book. In the published title the male organs were deleted. The 'Toilet' was a second version of the subject, in contemporary clothes, replacing the original composition reproduced at NO. 287. The drawings for 'A Platonic Lament', 'Enter Herodias' and 'The Climax' are not available for reproduction, but the line-blocks after them published in 1907 are at NOS. 284, 285 and 286. 'John and Salome' and 'Salome on Settle' (otherwise called 'La Maîtresse d'Orchestre') were not published in the 1894 book but were included in the 1907 portfolio of reproductions on the same scale as the original drawings.

The *Salome* illustrations have had such a great influence on *art nouveau* design, and have remained so well-known since 1894, that comment on them is almost superfluous. In the minds of many people they represent the whole ethos of Beardsley's art, though in fact they date from before the *Yellow Book* period and are strictly the last of his early works. The dramatic force, the sense of abstraction, and the bold elimination of supporting descriptive details were all Beardsley's own and unmatched in the black-and-white medium before, or since. Such features as the crossing of the lines of the skirt in the frontispiece, and a related self-sufficient form in 'The Toilet' (second version); the plethora of roses and the head of rose-hair in the border for the list of pictures; the brilliant adaptation of Whistler's feather-motifs from The Peacock Room and the trailing and arabesque lines of ragged feathers in 'The Peacock Skirt'; the outswung cloak in 'The Stomach Dance'; the white lines in reserve of the almost early-Greek cloak of Salome in 'The Dancer's Reward', and the sensational executioner's arm; the drawing of the powder-box and puff in the cul-de-lampe; — these are all features that have kept their old power to amaze. The quality of the drawn lines, though much praised by favourable critics in the Nineties, and later, seems, in some cases, as in 'The Stomach Dance', to be rather hesitant, and has not the assurance either of *The Yellow Book* drawings or those for *The Rape of the Lock* and for later works. But the conceptions immortalize in fact those strains in the play which the author shared unconsciously with its illustrator. Wilde disliked them possibly because they did just this, and also because they conveyed what Beardsley could seldom repress, an ironical comment on the text. That Wilde was caricatured mildly in the frontispiece, in 'A Platonic Lament', in 'Enter Herodias' and in 'The Eyes of Herod', doubtless annoyed him, but Beardsley had a habit of caricaturing his friends and acquaintances without real malice. And the notion that he satirized the play and despised Wilde at the date of these drawings cannot be confirmed — especially as his earlier and gratuitous illustration to 'J'ai baisé ta bouche Iokanaan' (which obtained for him the commission from Lane to illustrate the 1894 book) shows that originally he was fascinated by it. Also it should never be forgotten that he offered Wilde a translation of *Salome* which was rejected in favour of another one by Lord Alfred Douglas. For differing reasons, therefore, the illustrations caused a rift in the association between Wilde and Beardsley, an association which developed otherwise than it might have done. The effect of Wilde's trial on Beardsley's life and the jealous influence of Raffalovich later strengthened his alienation from the author whose play contributed in time to Beardsley's wide renown.

284 A Platonic Lament. Reproduction of illustration to face p. 16 in *Salome*, translated from the French of Oscar Wilde [by Lord Alfred Douglas], pictured by Aubrey Beardsley, and published by Elkin Mathews and John Lane, London; Copeland and Day, Boston, 1894. 4to. Signed with the artist's emblem. NO. VII in *A Portfolio of Aubrey Beardsley's Drawings illustrating 'Salome' by Oscar Wilde*, published by John Lane, London [1907]. Second issue. Pl. 284
From the line-block
Mr Brian Reade, London

The observation and skill required to draw this illustration were not stupendous. None the less its imagery is remarkable by virtue of qualities that the technological bias of late nineteenth- and twentieth-century aesthetic criticism has avoided, and they still need to be referred to as qualities of the Imagination. But to invest imagination of this sort takes courage, the courage of deliberation, which itself becomes a foreground to the work of art. The illustration shows the page of Herodias lamenting over the corpse of his friend the Young Syrian Captain, who was so infatuated by Salome that he killed himself when she discovered her passion for John the Baptist. The face of Wilde in the Moon is partly concealed by a narrow cloud in a sky of empty white paper. The clash of near-abstract forms, of topiary tree, of roses on espaliers, of leaning youth, and of the body at full length lying crosswise in front of all the rest, has in it the seeds of the inventions of Kandinsky, Picasso, Mondrian and many others to come, who were to reduce the content of their art to studio arguments. This illustration was also seminal at shorter range in the *art nouveau* of the Glasgow School, and in England, Europe and the United States.

285 Enter Herodias. Proof of the first state of an illustration facing p. 24 in *Salome*, translated from the French of Oscar Wilde [by Lord Alfred Douglas], pictured by Aubrey Beardsley, and published by Elkin Mathews and John Lane, London; Copeland and Day, Boston, 1894. 4to. Signed with the artist's emblem. Inscribed in ink:

> 'Alfred Lambart from Aubrey Beardsley.
> Because one figure was undressed
> This little drawing was suppressed
> It was unkind —
> But never mind
> Perhaps it all was for the best.'

From the line-block, $7 \times 5\frac{1}{16}$ inches. Pl. 285
Princeton University Library

In the second state of this illustration a fig-leaf was shown tied on to the male figure in the background: this was the state printed in the edition of *Salome* published by Mathews and Lane in 1894; and it left part of the meaning of the illustration obscure. For the leaf concealed the point that the youth with the powder-puff, who has removed his mask, is not excited by Herodias and possibly not by women at all; unlike the infantile monster opposite, whose excitement is covered by his clothing and whose hydrocephalous expression is fated to be lustful.

The erotic theme is carried into the pun on the fantastic prickets, or ancient candlesticks, either side of a creature (lifted possibly from a similar one in Rodolphe Bresdin's lithograph 'La Comédie de la Mort', 1854), whose horns outline a female symbol. Meanwhile in the corner, wearing the owl-cap of a mage and holding his prompt copy of the play, together with the caduceus of a physician, Oscar Wilde introduces the scene with the gesture of a showman; although his caduceus is also a crutch, because he leans on a gospel of 'curing the senses by means of the soul, and the soul by means of the senses'.

A proof similar to the one above was stated by A. E. Gallatin to have been inscribed for Frank Harris (*Aubrey Beardsley, Catalogue of Drawings etc.*, 1945, p. 47).

The original drawing was one of a small group belonging to Mrs E. T. Hutchinson, Schloss Weissenstein, Austria. It was sold by auction at Hamburg for £8,000 to David Carritt and partner in 1972. Later it was acquired by Los Angeles County Museum (see Brian Reade, 'Enter Herodias: Or, What Really Happened', *Los Angeles County Museum Art Bulletin*, Vol. XXII, 1976).

286 The Climax. Reproduction of illustration to face p.64 in *Salome*, translated from the French of Oscar Wilde [by Lord Alfred Douglas], pictured by Aubrey Beardsley, and published by Elkin Mathews and John Lane, London; Copeland and Day, Boston, 1894. 4to. Signed with the artist's emblem. NO. XV in *A Portfolio of Aubrey Beardsley's Drawings Illustrating 'Salome' by Oscar Wilde*, published by John Lane, London [1907]. Second issue. Pl.286
From the line-block
Mr Brian Reade, London

This marks a stage in Beardsley's development. The design is based on that of 'J'ai Baisé Ta Bouche Iokanaan', published in the first number of *The Studio* in April 1893. But the hairline flourishes in the former drawing have been decisively abandoned and Beardsley never reverted to this type of fantasy (see NO.261). The lines throughout are firmer, and the curves more rationalized: the cloud-forms at the top left are derived from the short feathers of Whistler's peacocks in the room at 49 Prince's Gate, which Beardsley saw in 1891. The thick, falling blood seems rather to rise upwards, solid and hostile: it helps to link the black ground, which also curves upward oppressively, with the white area in which Salome kneels. Beardsley's evasions of the left foot and left hand of the princess are characteristic. By such means he avoided what to him was unnecessary in the forcible representation of an action or a gesture. The lilies growing in the pool of blood symbolize the chastity of John the Baptist.

287 The Toilet of Salome. First version. Intended for illustration in *Salome*, translated from the French of Oscar Wilde [by Lord Alfred Douglas] and published by Elkin Mathews and

John Lane, London; Copeland and Day, Boston, 1894. 4to. Not used. Signed with the artist's emblem. Pl. 287
Indian ink over pencil, $9 \times 6\frac{3}{8}$ inches
Mr Edward James Matthews, New York

This drawing was supplied by Beardsley as one of the illustrations to the text of the English translation of *Salome* published by Elkin Matthews and John Lane in 1894. It was rejected however on account of the seated youth, and Beardsley produced another version of the subject with Salome in contemporary clothes, which was published in the book (see NO. 281).

The drawing was given to the present owner by Mr Jim Barney, before the 1939 War.

288 The Toilet of Salome. Working proof of a line-block made for illustration to *Salome* by Oscar Wilde, published by Elkin Mathews and John Lane, London, 1894. 4to. Signed with the artist's emblem. This version of the subject was replaced by that at NO. 281. Pl. 288
From the line-block
Mr W. G. Good, England

The drawings illustrating *Salome* contained several erotic details, some of which were more than Mathews and Lane could let pass for publication. The bent spine of the youth sitting on the Moorish stool is intended to convey that in accordance with Victorian beliefs he has been indulging in auto-erotism, and he is shown practising this art as he gazes at the boy with the coffee tray. This was too much for the publishers, and it is quite likely that the proof was one of those taken in 1894 and which enabled them to judge and to discard this block and to require that Beardsley should make another version of 'The Toilet', in fact the one which was published in the 1894 volume. The extra black masses show where the background had not been removed from the block. Remarkable features of the design are the frail, black dressing-table in the Aesthetic style of furniture designed by the architect E. W. Godwin, and the form of Salome in which all the details that would have gone to complete its definition in the literal sense, legs, chair, bottom edge of the cloak, are dispensed with, and there is only a linear evocation of essentials. In *The Early Work of Aubrey Beardsley*, first published by Lane in 1899, this block was used, but the pubic hair and turgescent penis of the sitting youth were removed. In Lane's *Portfolio of Aubrey Beardsley's Drawings Illustrating 'Salome'*, where all the line-blocks are approximately the same size as the original drawings, a larger version of this illustration, unexpurgated, was published.

289 Salome on Settle, or Maîtresse d'Orchestre. Signed, in the pleat lines of the upholstery, with the artist's emblem. NO. XVI in *A Portfolio of Aubrey Beardsley's Drawings Illustrating 'Salome' by Oscar Wilde*, published by John Lane, London [1907]. Second issue. Pl. 289
From the line-block
Mr Brian Reade, London

This drawing has no reference to any passage in the play, *Salome*, and was a larger version of a grotesque on p. 53 of *Bon-Mots* of Foote and Hook, London, 1894. The debt to Japanese print-makers in general should be clear enough, even to the back-view of a figure, which has a slight element of novelty. The drawing was not published in the 1894 volume, possibly because the baton could be interpreted as a dildo; and it first appeared in line-block facsimile as plate XVI in the *Salome* portfolio of 1907 published by Lane.

290 John and Salome. Signed with the artist's emblem. NO. VIII
in *A Portfolio of Aubrey Beardsley's Drawings Illustrating
'Salome' by Oscar Wilde*, published by John Lane, London,
[1907]. Second issue. Pl. 290
From the line-block
Mr Brian Reade, London

Although this is one of the most powerful of the *Salome*
illustrations it was excluded from the 1894 volume and was
first published as Plate VIII in the *Salome* portfolio of 1907.

It is difficult to analyse a drawing in which every detail
contributes so forcibly to the subject of tension between the
yearning Salome on the right and the resistant John the
Baptist on the left—in whom something nevertheless responds to the princess. Here and there the lines in the background run through the figure of John as if his thinness was
near to transparency. A bentwood rose-bush with geometrical roses is the prototype of much *art nouveau* decoration.
And rising up from the bottom edge of the paper, like
apparitions, the figures of John and Salome are distracted by
sharp masses of black abstracted from the rational forms of
their garments.

291 Music. Headpiece in the periodical *St Paul's*, Vol. I, NO. I,
March 1894. Reproduced as NO. 95 in *The Early Work of
Aubrey Beardsley*, John Lane, London, 1899. Pl. 292
From the line-block

292 Design for a headpiece in the periodical *St Paul's*, Vol. I, NO.
I, March 1894. Signed with the artist's emblem. Pl. 294
$4\frac{3}{4} \times 4\frac{1}{4}$ inches
Graphische Sammlung Albertina, Vienna

The foetus was deleted from the reproduction of this drawing in *St Paul's* and in Plate 96 of *The Early Work of Aubrey
Beardsley*, John Lane, 1899.

293 The Man that holds the Watering Pot. Design for a tailpiece
in the periodical *St Paul's*, Vol. I, NO. I, March 1894. Signed
with the artist's emblem. Pl. 293
$3\frac{5}{8} \times 5$ inches
Graphische Sammlung Albertina, Vienna

This drawing was reproduced at an eccentric angle in Plate
94 of *The Early Work of Aubrey Beardsley*, John Lane, 1899.

294 Pierrot and cat. Headpiece in the periodical *St Paul's*, 20 July
1895. Pl. 291
From the line-block
Mr W. G. Good, England

With Beardsley the dramatic value of the silhouette had
priority over descriptive logic: thus the cat has only two legs
visible. Like all the four drawings Beardsley made for *St
Paul's*, this one was done late in 1893, but not used until
eighteen months later than the rest.

295 Design for the front cover and title-page of *Keynotes* by
George Egerton (Mrs Chavelita Dunne Bright), published
by Elkin Mathews and John Lane, London, and by Roberts
Brothers, Boston, December 1893 (Vol. I in the *Keynotes*
series). Signed with the artist's emblem. Pl. 295
$9\frac{9}{16} \times 6\frac{1}{4}$ inches
Princeton University Library

The blank panel contained the letterpress of the title etc. In
the title-page the panel is smaller and in the line-block the
right-hand kite flies outside it.

296 Title-page of *The Dancing Faun,* by Florence Farr, Vol. II in
the *Keynotes* series, published by Elkin Mathews and John
Lane, London, and Roberts Brothers, Boston, June 1894.
Pl. 298
Crown 8vo.
From line-block and letterpress, with title in red
Mr W. G. Good, England

The standard lamp, in a form typical of the Nineties, is
attenuated to the consistency of wire. The high picture-rail
of the late Victorians comes in as a black bar. The faun sits
on a daintified Regency sofa wearing the hair and the monocle
of Whistler, and Whistler's patent shoes, with black bows.
The novel is a light-hearted affair and has nothing to do with
Whistler; Florence Farr was more interested in Bernard
Shaw. The layout of the title-page is an expression of
Beardsley's taste for one-sidedness in design and in this
respect follows the posters by him. The second and third
volumes in the *Keynotes* series had title-pages and front covers
following the same layouts, with panels on the left. The
remainder of the series had panels of ornament below the
titles (see NOS. 298–312 and 315, 316).

297 Title-page of *Poor Folk* translated from the Russian of F.
Dostoievsky by Lena Milman, etc, Vol. III in the *Keynotes*
series published by Elkin Mathews and John Lane, London,
and Robert Brothers, Boston, June, 1894. Crown 8vo.
Pl. 299
From the line-block and letterpress
Mr Brian Reade, London

The girl's white silhouette was probably a new version in
contemporary clothes of the mediaeval-looking maiden in
the heading of Chapter VI, Book XV (p. 749 of Vol. II) in
Le Morte Darthur. Possibly behind both was a remembrance
of the picture 'Vespertina Quies' by Burne-Jones (1893).
This panel, with the stately drainpipe and beautifully planned
lines and masses, is one of the best of Beardsley's smaller
designs.

298 Title-page of *A Child of the Age* by Francis Adams, Vol. IV
in the *Keynotes* series published by John Lane, London, and
Roberts Brothers, Boston, November 1894. Crown 8vo.
Pl. 300
From the line-block and letterpress
Mr Brian Reade, London

Francis Adams (1862–1893) spent a number of years in
Australia working on the staff of *The Sydney Bulletin*. He
suffered from tuberculosis and became so depressed that
he committed suicide at Margate just over one year before
this mysterious novel was published. Beardsley's design in
the bottom panel, like so many of his *Keynotes* designs, has
near-symmetry, or rather symmetry contradicted by a few
small details.

299 Design for the front cover and title-page of *The Great God
Pan and The Inmost Light* by Arthur Machen, Vol. V in the
Keynotes series published by John Lane, London, and by

Roberts Brothers, Boston, December 1894. Crown 8vo.
Pl. 301
$8\frac{13}{16} \times 4\frac{11}{16}$ inches
Princeton University Library

00 Unfinished and unused design for the title-page and front
cover of *The Great God Pan and the Inmost Light* by Arthur
Machen, Vol. V in the *Keynotes* series published by John Lane,
London, and Roberts Brothers, Boston, December 1894.
Crown 8vo. On the back is the completed design which was
used (see NO. 299). Inscribed variously in pen and pencil.
Pl. 302
Indian ink over pencil, 8×4 inches
Princeton University Library

This provides evidence that Beardsley completed his borders
in ink before coming to grips with the design within them.
Failure in the drawing of the horned head of Pan in this case
may have been one reason for abandoning the design.

01 Design for the front cover and title-page of *Discords* by
George Egerton (Mrs Chavelita Dunne Bright), Vol. VI in
the *Keynotes* series published by John Lane, London, and
by Robert Brothers, Boston, December 1894. Crown 8vo.
Pl. 303
$8\frac{3}{4} \times 4\frac{3}{4}$ inches
Princeton University Library

02 Design for the front cover and title-page of *Grey Roses* by
Henry Harland, Vol. X in the *Keynotes* series published by
John Lane, London, and Roberts Brothers, Boston, May
1895. Crown 8vo. Pl. 304
$7\frac{11}{16} \times 4\frac{1}{2}$ inches
Princeton University Library

Volume X of the *Keynotes* series, a group of stories by Harland,
had been advertised as *The Bohemian Girl and Other Stories*.
It is possible that the change of title to the visual imagery of
Grey Roses, and the better typographical design resulting,
may have been suggested by Beardsley.

03 Title-page of *At the First Corner and Other Stories* by H. B.
Marriott Watson, Vol. XI in the *Keynotes* series published by
John Lane, London, and Roberts Brothers, Boston, May
1895. Crown 8vo. Pl. 305
From the line-block and letterpress
Mr W. G. Good, England

The motif of the bottom panel is a large double poppy, with
three seed-pods at three of the corners. There may have been
an unconscious memory of Morris's 'Horn Poppy' wallpaper. The plant is treated as if it were a tree or springing
from a very short, thick stem. It looks as though Beardsley
got into a habit of drawing the supports of his flowers in this
manner ever since he discovered the formula in his *Morte
Darthur* borders.

04 Title-page of *Monochromes* by Ella D'Arcy, Vol. XII in the
Keynotes series published by John Lane, London, and Roberts
Brothers, Boston, June 1895. Crown 8vo. Pl. 306
From the line-block and letterpress
Mr Brian Reade, London

The very lack of geometrical purity in the curves of this long
plant from the corner of Beardsley's imagination is what gives
it a strange effect of vitality.

305 Title-page of *At the Relton Arms* by Evelyn Sharp, Vol.
XIII in the *Keynotes* series published by John Lane, London,
and Roberts Brothers, Boston, June 1895. Crown 8vo.
Pl. 309
From the line-block and letterpress
Mr Brian Reade, London

An ingenious motif of an inn sign bearing the imprint of
John Lane's firm and supported by a symmetrical *art nouveau*
tree.

306 Title-page of *The Girl from the Farm* by Gertrude Dix, Vol.
XIV in the *Keynotes* series, published by John Lane, London,
and Roberts Brothers, Boston, June 1895. Crown 8vo.
Pl. 310
From the line-block and letterpress
Mr W. G. Good, England

The same design was used for the front cover. Occasionally
Beardsley deviated into symmetry, as he did in the title-page
of *The Relton Arms* in the *Keynotes* series (NO. 305). At first
glance he has done so again here: but no; such a principle
seems to have made him uneasy and it will be noticed that of
the two white hemispherical forms near the base-line the
right-hand one has the outline of a nipple, while its counter-
part is without this detail. Meanwhile all but one of the inter-
lacing branches grow across the central feature into their
opposite numbers—a quite irrational concept. The central
feature itself, like the rising cloud of an exploded hydrogen
bomb, is a mystery suggesting all kinds of possible readings.
Beardsley's one fatal weakness, from a strictly intellectual
viewpoint, is disclosed by the addition of his favourite dots,
blown-up like the spots on a bandana handkerchief, and
sprinkled over areas which they detach from the surrounding
space without any purpose except to introduce another
decorative dimension.

307 Design for the front cover and title-page, and key monogram
on the spine and the back cover (and within) of *The Mirror of
Music* by Stanley Mackower, Vol. XV in the *Keynotes* series
published by John Lane, London, and by Roberts Brothers,
Boston, August 1895. Pl. 308
$7\frac{11}{16} \times 4\frac{7}{16}$ inches
Princeton University Library

The angel with the bass viol is related to a similar figure
designed for the heading of Chapter XXV, Book VIII, p. 334
in *Le Morte Darthur* (1893–4) (NO. 80).

308 Design for the front cover and title-page of *Yellow and White*
by W. Carlton Dawe, Vol. XVI in the *Keynotes* series published
by John Lane, London, and Roberts Brothers, Boston,
August 1895. Crown 8vo. Enclosed in the panel for letterpress is a design for the key monogram for the spine and
back cover of *The Three Impostors* by Arthur Machen, published by Lane and Roberts in November 1895 (Vol. XIX
of the *Keynotes* series). Pl. 314
$7\frac{11}{16} \times 4\frac{7}{16}$ inches
Princeton University Library

309   Design for the front cover, title-page and key monogram on spine and back cover of *The Mountain Lovers* by Fiona Mac-Leod (pseudonym of William Sharp), Vol. XVII in the *Keynotes* series published by John Lane, London, and Roberts Brothers, Boston, July 1895. Crown 8vo. Pl. 307
$7\frac{5}{8} \times 4\frac{7}{16}$ inches
Princeton University Library

310   Title-page of *Nobody's Fault* by Netta Syrett, Vol. XX in the *Keynotes* series, published by John Lane, London, and Roberts Brothers, Boston, February 1896. Crown 8vo. Pl. 313
From the line-block and letterpress
Mr W. G. Good, England

In the lower panel two of Beardsley's principles of design are reduced to their simplest terms. First, a larger version of the prevailing motif, in this case a flower of dubious botany, stands out in one corner: secondly, all the stems sway on a diagonal twist.

311   Design for the front cover and title-page of *The British Barbarians* by Grant Allen, Vol. XXI in the *Keynotes* series published by John Lane, London, and G. P. Putnam's Sons, New York, November 1895. Crown 8vo. Pl. 315
$8\frac{3}{16} \times 5$ inches
Princeton University Library

312   Design for the front cover and title-page of *Platonic Affections* by John Smith, Vol. XXIII in the *Keynotes* series, published by John Lane, London, and Roberts Brothers, Boston, April 1896. Crown 8vo. Pl. 316
$7\frac{1}{2} \times 4\frac{1}{2}$ inches
Princeton University Library

313   Eight designs for key monograms for volumes in the *Keynotes* series, published by Elkin Mathews and John Lane, London, and Roberts Brothers, Boston, 1893–6. Reproduced in *Early Work*, 1899. Pl. 311
From line-blocks

From left across the monograms are those of Fiona Mac-Leod, Henry Harland, F. Dostoievsky and Lena Milman (together), Evelyn Sharp, George Egerton (Mrs Chavelita Dunne Bright), Gertrude Dix, Grant Allen and Arthur Machen. See also NO. 314.

314   Six designs for key monograms for volumes in the *Keynotes* series, 1894–5; and one design for a key monogram for *The Barbarous Britishers* by Henry Duff Traill, January 1896. Pl. 312
From line-blocks

From left to right on the top row the monograms are those of Ella D'Arcy, Florence Farr, W. Carlton Dawe, Stanley Makower. Below are the monograms of Netta Syrett and Victoria Crosse (pseudonym of Vivian Cory); and one of H. D. Traill, for whose book *The Barbarous Britishers* Beardsley designed a title-page, cover and key monogram (the drawings are reproduced at NO. 316) burlesquing his designs for *The British Barbarians* by Grant Allen (Vol. XXI in the *Keynotes* series). These odd, original, monograms could

scarcely have been conceived except in the age of *art nouveau*: needless to add they flout most academic pieties of good design.

315   Title-page of *Young Ofeg's Ditties* by Ola Hansson, translated from the Swedish by George Egerton (Mrs Chavelita Dunne Bright), published by John Lane, London, and Roberts Brothers, Boston, 1895. Crown 8vo. Pl. 317
From the line-block and letterpress
Dr Ian Fletcher, Reading

The same design was used blind-stamped on the dark rose-coloured front cover. The format is in the style of the *Keynotes* series, but the book was not published in that series. Curiosity about life and literature in Scandinavia at this date found its champion in the feminist George Egerton, who wrote many stories with Scandinavian settings.

In the bottom panel organic logic is sacrificed to Beardsley's primary inclination towards pattern and arabesque, so that the twig in one corner coils into the twig opposite by means of a loop like the back of a bentwood chair—that form which seems to have haunted the late nineteenth century (see also Brian Reade, *Art Nouveau and Alphonse Mucha*, HMSO, London, 1967). The eight loose leaves in the middle serve to break the symmetry but, like the surrounding dots, they are equally arbitrary.

316   Design for the front cover and title-page and for the key monogram of *The Barbarous Britishers*, a novel by Henry Duff Traill, published by John Lane, London, 1896. Crown 8vo. Signed with a grotesque version of the artist's emblem. Pl. 318
$5\frac{3}{4} \times 3\frac{1}{2}$ inches
Princeton University Library

The maidservant's features caricature Ada Lundberg, the actress. The design for cover and title is a burlesque of Beardsley's design for *The British Barbarians* by Grant Allen published in November, 1895, as Vol. XXI in the *Keynotes* series (NO. 311).

317   Design for the frontispiece to *Plays* by John Davidson, published by Elkin Mathews and John Lane, London, 1894. 8vo. Signed with the artist's emblem. Pl. 321
Indian ink over pencil, $11\frac{1}{4} \times 7\frac{2}{3}$ inches
Tate Gallery, London

The people represented here are said (see Tate Gallery Catalogue, 4172) to be (from left) Mabel Beardsley, Henry Harland (literary editor of *The Yellow Book*), Oscar Wilde, Sir Augustus Harris (manager of Covent Garden, Drury Lane and Her Majesty's Theatre), Richard Le Gallienne (man-of-letters) and the dancer Adeline Genée (later and still [1967] Dame Genée-Isitt). The figure with the faun's legs and ears does not resemble Harland, and it will be seen that he partly conceals the figure of Mabel Beardsley, beside whom is Oscar Wilde with his legs apparently thonged together. The innuendo may be that Mabel is interested in Wilde, or the reverse, but safe from him because his legs are tied together (in other words he has become heterosexually impotent); in which case it is possible that Beardsley intended the faun to represent himself. The drawing is mentioned in a letter to Robert Ross of (?) November 1893, as being an illustration to the fifth and last of the plays in the volume, entitled

'Scaramouch in Naxos: A Pantomime', which had been written by Davidson in 1888.

The landscape details are remarkable for their date, being almost abstractions.

318 Masked pierrot in black. Drawing for the vignette on the title-page, and in gold on the front cover, of *Plays* by John Davidson, published by Elkin Mathews and John Lane, London, 1894. 8vo. Pl. 319
6¾ × 2¾ inches
Grenville L. Winthrop Bequest, Fogg Art Museum, Harvard University, Massachusetts

A few copies of this book had white cloth covers, the rest covers of plum-coloured cloth.

319 Poster advertising the play *A Comedy of Signs* by John Todhunter, preceded by the one-act play *The Land of Heart's Desire* by W. B. Yeats, at the Avenue Theatre, London, 29 March 1894. Pl. 297
From the colour lithograph, 30 × 20 inches
Victoria and Albert Museum, London

The subtlety of this design lies in its simplicity. The placing of the spots on the abstract curtains, the white line, in reserve, forming the hair, the languid hand—all combine to produce a harmony in four tones, of which two are colours in modified contrast.

On this poster Owen Seaman wrote a 48-line poem, *Ars Postera*, which began:

'Mr. Aubrey Beer de Beers,
　You're getting quite a high renown;
Your Comedy of Leers, you know,
　Is posted all about the town;
This sort of stuff I cannot puff,
　As Boston says, it makes me "tired";
Your Japanee-Rossetti girl
　Is not a thing to be desired.'

(*Battle of the Bays*, London, 1896)

320 Chopin Ballade III. Op. 47. Pl. 325
Indian ink and ink and water-colour washes, 10⅛ × 9½ inches
Colonel Mahlon C. Sands, England

The drawing, made early in 1894, appears to be identical with a portrait of the Comtesse d'Armailhacq exhibited at the Royal Society of Portrait Painters in October, 1895. The relations to an (?) imaginary countess on the the one hand, and to a ballade of Chopin on the other, seem tenuous. It has the static quality of a bas-relief, and the riding-school pose of the horse is in the manner of equestrian portraits of the seventeenth and eighteenth centuries. The drawing is unusual in that Beardsley has used washes to render intermediate tones, a technique he was to develop in less monumental drawings of 1897. This was first reproduced in *The Studio*, May 1898.

321 Poster advertising Singer sewing machines. Reproduction on p. [132] of *The Poster*, Vol. I, October number, 1898. Signed in capitals with the artist's names. Pl. 342
From the half-tone plate
Victoria and Albert Museum, London

The label at the bottom left records that the Polychrome Printing Company, London, printed this poster in colour lithography, from Beardsley's design mentioned in a letter to John Lane, March 1894. It does not seem to have been used, or used at all widely. The pun on the name Singer makes the subject of the design, a woman singing to her own piano accompaniment in the middle of a field, an extension of the subject of the title-page of *The Yellow Book*, Vol. I, April 1894, where a woman is shown playing a piano likewise in a field (NO. 345). In this design, however, Beardsley has introduced double outlines everywhere, partly to cope with the scale, and he has used water-colour washes in the background and for the pattern on the dress. The lettering is characteristic. But the general effect is not characteristic, and has the dreamy bifocal quality of average English *art nouveau*, and little of the purpose and vitality of Beardsley's drawings at their best.

322 La Dame aux Camélias. 1894. Published as 'Girl at her Toilet' in the journal *St Paul's*, 2 April 1894. Later published with the present title on p. [57] as NO. IV of 'Four Drawings by Aubrey Beardsley' (Art Index Plate VI) in *The Yellow Book*, Vol. III, October 1894. On the back is written in pencil 'Yellow Book Immediate/today'. Pl. 323
Indian ink and water-colour, 11 × 7⅛ inches
Tate Gallery, London

NOS. 147 and 1060 in Gallatin's catalogue refer to other representations by Beardsley of the heroine of the play by Dumas fils. Since this drawing was first reproduced with another title, there seems no need to regard it seriously as Beardsley's conception of La Dame aux Camélias. Both the early reproductions were line-blocks, but between 1894 and 1897 (see Tate Gallery Catalogue, 4608) Beardsley added water-colour washes of pinkish-purple. Apart from the saturation of floor and wall up to the dado with black shadow, the design is, for Beardsley, stable and simple, which may be why it has always been popular.

323 A Caprice. On the right a woman clothed in black with green trimmings turns toward a beckoning negro dwarf clothed in red. Behind the dwarf is a view of a town through an archway. c. 1894. On the back of the canvas is the painting described at NO. 324. Pl. 329
Oil on canvas, 30 × 25 inches
Tate Gallery, London

Of the two paintings on one canvas this was presumably the first, since the 'Masked Woman' was painted within the area enclosed by the stretchers. No other paintings in oil by Beardsley are known to have survived, and these two should be regarded as experimental. Both are unfinished. The subject of 'A Caprice' is similar to that of NO. I of 'The Comedy Ballet of Marionettes', published in *The Yellow Book*, Vol. II, July 1894 (see NO. 353). William Rothenstein's early paintings may have given Beardsley the idea of these bold, gloomy saturated forms; otherwise the general atmosphere is similar to that of the Venetian artist Longhi. Beardsley's favourite colours—like black and white—were the complementary shades of red and green. It is interesting to reflect that here again, in a field he never exploited, he sought the drama primarily of direct contrast. For the provenance of this painting, see NO. 324.

324 A masked woman, half-length, in black, with a white mouse on a table before her. *c.* 1894. Pl. 330
Oil on canvas, $25\frac{3}{4} \times 20\frac{1}{4}$ inches
Tate Gallery, London

This painting is on the back of the canvas supporting the painting 'A Caprice', the only other painting in oil by Beardsley. The canvas was found by Mrs Pugh when she took over the lease of 114 Cambridge Street, Pimlico, London SW1, after the Beardsleys left the house, and it was bought from her by R. A. Walker in 1920. He sold it to the Tate Gallery three years later.

Sickert offered to teach Beardsley oil-painting, but nothing came of it. Neither the 'Masked Woman' nor 'A Caprice' have any particular reference to Sickert's method; rather to the paintings of Longhi. Although Beardsley had only a dormant colour sense, the handling of the flesh shows promise and the possibilities of development. The symbolism of the picture is Freudian, and Beardsley's choice of it is miraculous, considering that Freud's mythology was unknown in England in 1894.

325 The Fat Woman. Inscribed on the back 'A mon ami Will Rothenstein Aubrey Beardsley fec. et don.' Further inscribed over a phallic caricature of a Queen Victoria penny stamp, 'Received by Will Rothenstein'. Pl. 322
Indian ink and wash, $7 \times 6\frac{3}{8}$ inches
Tate Gallery, London

This was intended as a caricature of Whistler's wife and was published in the journal *To-Day*, 12 May 1894. Whistler was offended. William Rothenstein, who at this period shared a work-room in Pimlico with Beardsley, was given the drawing and later returned it, urging Beardsley to destroy it. It was not destroyed. It is related to the earlier drawing 'Waiting' (see NO. 249) but is less sinister and the composition is more stable. It also has half-tones rendered in indian ink wash.

326 Front wrapper of *The Cambridge A.B.C.*, NO. I, 8 June 1894. Published by Elijah Johnson, Cambridge. 8vo. Signed with the artist's names. Pl. 328
From the line-block and letterpress
Mr W. G. Good, England

While he was an undergraduate at Cambridge Maurice Baring helped to bring out this magazine, and he wrote to Beardsley for a wrapper design. The artist dissuaded him from having a dark red cover and charged him ten guineas for the drawing. The cover was white with the design in black. In it there is a characteristic atmosphere of mystery, and the carnival suit worn by the boy, with its short voluminous legs, heralds the pierrot costumes of later designs. The garden with its fountains has been evolved from the *Morte Darthur* backgrounds, but the balustrade comes perhaps from the memory of Adelaide Crescent in Hove.

327 Rejane [*sic*]. Portrait of Madame Réjane (Gabrielle Charlotte Réju) full-length on a chaise-longue, left profile. Signed with the artist's emblem and inscribed with title. Pl. 332
Indian ink and wash, $13\frac{1}{4} \times 8\frac{3}{4}$ inches
Metropolitan Museum of Art, New York

In this drawing, one of Beardsley's most graceful achievements, he used indian ink wash for intermediate tones, as well as the undiluted medium. He made numerous drawings of Madame Réjane of which this is the most elaborate. She acted the role of Catherine in *Madam Sans Gêne* at the Gaiety Theatre, on 23 June 1894, her first appearance in London.

328 Design for the frontispiece to *Baron Verdigris. A Romance of the Reversed Direction*, by Jocelyn Quilp, published by Henry and Company, London, July 1894. Signed in brown ink with the artist's names. Pl. 327
$7\frac{3}{4} \times 4\frac{3}{4}$ inches
British Museum

The author's name may have been a pseudonym. The story, which is pseudo-mediaeval and facetious, is dedicated to 'Fin-de-Siècle-ism, the Sensational Novel, and the Conventional Drawing-Room Ballad'.

329 Design for the invitation card to the opening of the Prince's Ladies Golf Club at Mitcham, Surrey, on 16 July 1894. Signed with the artist's names. Pl. 326
$9 \times 5\frac{1}{2}$ inches
Mrs R. Hippisley-Coxe, England

This is the most remarkable of Beardsley's silhouette treatments of women in contemporary clothes, which he exaggerated. The drawing has been well forged (see R. A. Walker, *How to Detect Beardsley Forgeries*, Bedford, 1950, p. 11).

330 Page 192 of *The Idler*, September 1894, published by Chatto and Windus, London. 8vo. Headpiece in the shape of an inverted L. Signed with the artist's names, and lettered The Idler's Club. Pl. 335
From the line-block and letterpress
Mr W. G. Good, England

A similar design of the same shape on a smaller scale was printed in black on the salmon-coloured front wrapper of the periodical. The article by H. E. Abbott was the first of a series on 'How to Court the "Advanced Woman"'.

331 The Idler's Club. Design for a full-page border intended for *The Idler*, 1894, but not used for that periodical. Signed with the artist's names and inscribed with title. Pl. 334
$8\frac{3}{8} \times 6\frac{1}{2}$ inches
Princeton University Library

332 Les Passades. Published in the magazine *To-Day*, Winter Number, 17 November 1894. Pl. 336
From the half-tone plate, 10×5 inches
Mr W. G. Good, England

The drawing compares with 'A Night Piece' (NO. 348), which is related in subject and composition. The introduction of grey indian ink wash in the sky and elsewhere made the use of a half-tone plate necessary, instead of the customary line-block facsimile. Beardsley has carried the positive approach of Whistler in the 'Nocturnes' to extremes by simply lifting the shapes of the prostitutes out of a background saturated with the blackness of night.

333 The Pseudonym and Autonym Libraries. Poster published by T.Fisher Unwin, London, 1894. Signed with the artist's names. Pl.296
From the colour lithograph, 30 × 20¼ inches
Victoria and Albert Museum, London
The design here differs in various details from Beardsley's original drawing for the poster (see NO.334). According to Vallance the colour scheme was suggested to Beardsley by a French poster (Vallance, 77) and according to A.E.Gallatin the poster was coloured by the artist (Gallatin, 789). It was in use for some years after 1894 with varied letterpress; and the design was adapted for a small advertisement slip issued by Unwin, for the cover of *Unwin's Chap Book* (1899 – 1900), and for the front cover of *The Dream and the Business* by John Oliver Hobbes, published by Unwin in 1906.

A water-coloured ink drawing, slightly larger in scale but point-by-point similar, had formerly belonged to Fisher Unwin. This came on to the market during recent years and was acquired by A. d'Offay. A companion drawing for the *Children's Books* poster (see NO.335) from the same source influenced the present author to accept both drawings as by Beardsley, and as used for photographic reproduction in the colour lithographed posters.

334 Girl and a Bookshop, 1893. Later used as a design for a poster advertising The Pseudonym and Autonym Libraries published by T.Fisher Unwin, London, 1894. Pl.320
Indian ink over pencil, 14⅛ × 5⅝ inches
Philip H. and A.S.W. Rosenbach Foundation, Philadelphia

The positive parts of the drawing are all on one side and towards the top: an excellent example of the disbalance learnt from Japanese prints. The result is to dramatize the figure and to suggest motion towards the empty space, as in the figure of 'Virgilius the Sorcerer' (see NO.267). In the poster certain details were changed and the proportion of the design altered by the inclusion of more white background, on which the titles of books appeared (see Pl.296). The drawing was exhibited in the 1893 winter exhibition of the New English Art Club.

335 Poster advertising *Children's Books* published by T.Fisher Unwin, London, 1894. Signed with the artist's names and emblem. Pl.324
From the colour lithograph, 30 × 20 inches
Mr Anthony d'Offay, London

Such winged chairs were known as grandfathers' chairs, and Beardsley may have intended to represent a grandmother sitting in an appropriate chair and reading to her grandchildren from one of the books advertised in the letterpress panel. The gown with its leg-of-mutton sleeves is of the Nineties, but the feather is in the mode of the late eighteenth or early nineteenth century. Instead of age and maturity therefore Beardsley has formulated a disturbing sensuality in the features of the woman. This was the kind of negligent irony which repelled so many of his own generation. See NO.333 above.

336 Caricature of Whistler on a garden seat, pointing to a butterfly, c.1893–4. Pl.333
8 1/16 × 4 7/16 inches
Rosenwald Collection, National Gallery of Art, Washington
A distorted-looking butterfly was Whistler's emblem, and as such it appeared on numerous etchings and drawing by him. Here the butterfly has been partly erased. The drawing was never published in Beardsley's lifetime and was not widely known until it was reproduced in R.A.Walker's *Some*

Unknown Drawings by Aubrey Beardsley, London, 1923. It is among the boldest of Beardsley's early drawings. The balance, or rather disbalance, of what is actually drawn, all in the upper right corner, against the empty foreground, produces a sense of perspective learnt from Japanese art, but here carried to extremes. The seat on which Whistler sits is either meant to be Japanese (like the ones in Japanese prints), or is meant to look like an example of the frail 'Aesthetic' furniture made after the designs of E.W.Godwin which were much influenced by Japanese furniture. Beardsley mentioned this drawing in a letter to Raffalovich in December 1896, saying it was a 'very malicious caricature of Whistler' that had been hung on the Christmas tree put up by Mabel and himself in 1894.

337 The Murders in the Rue Morgue. The first of four illustrations to *The Works of Edgar Allan Poe,* published by Herbert S. Stone and Company, Chicago, 1894–5. Signed with the artist's emblem. Pl.337
9⅞ × 6¼ inches
Mr Albert Reese, New York

Four drawings were commissioned from Beardsley for this edition of Poe's works in ten volumes. The line-block plates however accompanied only the Japanese paper issue of ten sets. Stone republished the plates in 1901 (250 copies).

338 The Black Cat. The second of four illustrations to *The Works of Edgar Allan Poe,* published by Herbert S. Stone and Company, Chicago, 1894–5. Pl.338
9⅞ × 6¼ inches
Mr Albert Reese, New York

See NO.337. As with the powder-puff in the cul-de-lampe of *Salome,* the white chest of the cat, which is white paper left in reserve, reminds us that Beardsley was not only a master of line and of meaningful black and white shapes, but of the possibilities of indian ink and its limitations.

339 The Fall of the House of Usher. The third of four illustrations to *The Works of Edgar Allan Poe,* published by Herbert S. Stone and Company, Chicago, 1894–5. Pl.339
9⅞ × 6¼ inches
Mr Albert Reese, New York

See NO.337. The figure is based upon that of Chopin in an earlier drawing of 1892 in the Japonesque style, subtitled 'Frederic [*sic*] Chopin' (see *The Uncollected Work of Aubrey Beardsley,* John Lane, London, 1925, NO.13).

340 The Mask of the Red Death. The fourth of four illustrations to *The Works of Edgar Allan Poe,* published by Herbert S. Stone and Company, Chicago, 1894–5. Signed with the artist's emblem. Pl.340
9⅞ × 6¼ inches
Mr Albert Reese, New York

See NO.337. This illustration was first reproduced in *The Chap Book,* Chicago, 15 August 1894; and again in the same periodical on 1 April 1898.

341 Design for a poster to advertise *The Yellow Book,* 1894. Signed with the artist's names. Pl.341
15 1/16 × 10⅞ inches
Princeton University Library
The Yellow Book was conceived on New Year's Day 1894 by

Beardsley and Henry Harland, the novelist, at Harland's house in the Cromwell Road. The first volume came out in April 1894, published by Elkin Mathews and John Lane in London at the Bodley Head, and by Copeland and Day in Boston. The design on the small poster was reduced to a height of $13\frac{5}{8}$ inches and was printed in dark blue from the line-block on yellow paper. In the panel on the right were printed 'Sold Here. The Yellow Book. Contents of Vol. I, April, 1894, etc.'

342 Design for the front cover of the prospectus of *The Yellow Book*, Vol. I, April 1894, published by Elkin Mathews and John Lane, London, and Copeland and Day, Boston. 4to. Signed with the artist's emblem. Pl. 343
$9\frac{1}{2} \times 6\frac{1}{8}$ inches
Victoria and Albert Museum, London

The suggestion contained in the design is that the enterprising young woman who is free to decide what she reads will be interested in just this sort of periodical. *The Yellow Book* was a hard-back quarto with yellow covers and with designs and title etc. in black. The elderly pierrot looking on from the doorway was said to represent Elkin Mathews, the partner of John Lane at the Bodley Head (where *The Yellow Book* was published), who by comparison with Lane was somewhat apprehensive and prudish.

343 Design for the front cover of *The Yellow Book*, Vol. I, April 1894. Published by Elkin Mathews and John Lane, London; Copeland and Day, Boston. 4to. Signed with the artist's emblem. Pl. 344
Indian ink over pencil, $10 \times 8\frac{1}{2}$ inches
Tate Gallery, London

All the cover designs of *The Yellow Book* were printed in black on yellow cloth boards. There lingers in this conception something of the gaiety of Chéret's iconography, particularly when associated with the Quatz' Arts ball of 1893 in Paris. The mephistophelian man gives a sinister note however. What is remarkable is the exaggerated form of the woman's hat cut from the darkness behind—of which it is literally a part—by two bold white curved lines. The balancing of hat, hair and shoulders in this figure inside a rectangle of such a shape, the exceptionally hard, flat, jagged treatment of the gown, differentiated by heavy dots: the dots themselves—vestigial of pointilliste spots or of the spatter on Toulouse-Lautrec's posters—all contribute to a startling design which appears to have in it the seeds of Cubism and of many kinds of abstract art.

344 Decoration on the back covers of Vols. I–V of *The Yellow Book*, published by John Lane, London; Copeland and Day, Boston, 1894–5. 4to. Signed twice with the artist's emblem. Pl. 346
From the line-block

Although Beardsley's contributions to the fifth volume of *The Yellow Book* were withdrawn at the last minute, including the front cover design (see *Catalogue of Aubrey Beardsley Exhibition at the Victoria and Albert Museum*, 1966, NOS. 484,

485), the spine and the back cover were overlooked: the back cover design had remained the same ever since the first volume of a year before.

345 Title-page of *The Yellow Book*, Vol. I, April 1894, published by Elkin Mathews and John Lane, London; Copeland and Day, Boston. 4to. Pl. 345
From the line-block

On learning that there was widespread criticism of this design, Beardsley sent a letter to *The Pall Mall Budget* in which he recalled that Bomvet described Glück, the composer, as accustomed to placing himself in the middle of a field with his piano [*sic*] before him and a bottle of champagne on each side, and that he wrote in the open air his two 'Iphigenias', 'Orpheus' and some other works. 'I tremble to think', Beardsley wrote, 'what critics would say had I introduced those bottles of champagne. And yet we do not call Glück a decadent'. None the less, the composition would have suited the requirements of the Surrealists of the 1930s.

346 L'Éducation Sentimentale. Illustration to the novel of 1869 by Gustave Flaubert reproduced on p. 55 in *The Yellow Book*, Vol. I, April 1894, published by John Lane, London; Copeland and Day, Boston. 4to. Pl. 349
From the half tone plate

The original drawing of the left-hand figure, later covered by Beardsley with pink and green water-colour, survives in the Fogg Art Museum, Harvard University (see NO. 347). The differing qualities of cynicism in age and youth are contrasted here and subconsciously emphasized by the black and white contrast in the clothes of the two women. Beardsley's analysis of the edges of the features of the older woman comes near to forestalling a principle in the art of Wyndham Lewis.

347 Part of the drawing 'L'Éducation Sentimentale' reproduced in *The Yellow Book*, Vol. I, April 1894 (see NO. 346). Pl. 348
Pen and ink and water-colour, $10\frac{3}{4} \times 3\frac{1}{2}$ inches
Grenville L. Winthrop Bequest, Fogg Art Museum, Harvard University, Massachusetts

For some reason, apparently not recorded, Beardsley divided his original drawing into two parts, this part containing the older woman holding the letter. He then added pink and green water-colour, which entirely changed the character of the drawing.

348 A Night Piece. Reproduced in half-tone in *The Yellow Book*, Vol. I, April 1894 (pl. VII in Index), published by Elkin Mathews and John Lane, London; Copeland and Day, Boston. 4to. Pl. 351
Indian ink and wash, $12\frac{5}{8} \times 6\frac{1}{8}$ inches
Fitzwilliam Museum, Cambridge, England

Sold at Christie, London, 20 December 1901, Lot 71, as 'Aubrey Beardsley—in Leicester Square—Black and White'. In fact the wash in the drawing introduced half tones, and the reproduction could not be carried out in line-block. Apart from the disbalance typical of compositions by Beardsley during the *Yellow Book* period, there is the unusual feature of a form being raised by a few white lines out of a black background. These lines were made partly by erasure with a knife, apparently. The well-poised spaces of white for the lamps, head and shoulders, sleeve and instep show Beardsley's memorization of paintings by Whistler; such as, for example, 'Battersea Bridge'. The half-tone buildings in the background are also in the manner of the 'Nocturnes'.

349 Mrs Patrick Campbell. Reproduced in half-tone on p. [157] of *The Yellow Book*, Vol. I, April 1894 (Pl. X in Index), published by Elkin Mathews and John Lane, London; Copeland and Day, Boston. 4to. Pl. 347
Indian ink and wash, $13\frac{1}{16} \times 8\frac{3}{8}$ inches
National Gallery of Berlin

A letter from Beardsley to the actress Mrs Patrick Campbell survives, written in February or March 1894. In this he thanks her for giving him a sitting (see *Catalogue of Aubrey Beardsley Exhibition at the Victoria and Albert Museum*, 1966, NO. 481). At the time, Mrs Patrick Campbell was playing the part of Paula Tanqueray in A.W. Pinero's play *The Second Mrs Tanqueray* at the St James's Theatre, London. In February 1894 Oscar Wilde wrote to her asking to present Beardsley to her (see Rupert Hart-Davis, (ed.) *Letters of Oscar Wilde*, p. 353). The present drawing was evidently the fruit of this encounter: it is of course an elegant caricature rather than a literal likeness and it caused indignation when it was published in *The Yellow Book*. The drawing became the property of Oscar Wilde.

350 Design for the bookplate of John Lumsden Propert. Reproduced in *The Yellow Book*, Vol. I, April 1894 (Pl. XIV in Index), published by Elkin Mathews and John Lane, London; Copeland and Day, Boston. 4to. Pl. 350
$7\frac{3}{4} \times 4\frac{7}{8}$ inches
Mr R. A. Harari, London

Another instance of Beardsley's gift of achieving poise in a composition by calculated disbalance. Stabilizing elements are in the curves of the *art nouveau* style branch, the candle, and in the more important figure of the beseeching pierrot, who implores attention from the contemptuous and malicious-looking female.

351 Design for the front cover of *The Yellow Book*, Vol. II, July 1894: published by Elkin Mathews and John Lane, London; Copeland and Day, Boston. 4to. Signed with the artist's emblem. Pl. 353
$8\frac{1}{8} \times 6\frac{3}{16}$ inches
Princeton University Library

The disbalance of the woman's form here is more in line with European conventions than was customary with Beardsley. Her thick lips, the soft outlines of her nose and her abundant hair are all features of erotic and 'emancipated' suggestion, of the anti-genteel, anti-Du Maurier style of late Victorian woman. The background is half plain white, and half covered by a wallpaper decorated with large cup-shaped flowers anticipating the large floral motifs in *art-nouveau* designs of some five years later. The exaggerated perspective of the bookcase intruding at an angle, and the drawing of the bowl of flowers which is not in perspective, are together characteristic of Beardsley's type of visual wit.

352 Design for the title-page of *The Yellow Book*, Vol. II, July 1894. Published by Elkin Mathews and John Lane, London;

Copeland and Day, Boston. 4to. Signed with the artist's emblem. Pl. 352
$3\frac{11}{16} \times 3\frac{5}{8}$ inches
Princeton University Library

There are strange premonitions here of the severer kinds of abstract art to come: the bands of black which represent the lawns; the self-sufficient form arrived at by running the girl's black sash into the patch of lawn behind her, and the odd way in which the dotted T-form of the junction of paths in the foreground is crossed by the black-gloved hand and walking-stick combined. The near-parallel relation between the line of the stick and the line of the edge of the lawn beyond it to the right is a typical instance of Beardsley's wit, and once more reveals his pleasure in kinds of visual experience that were unexplored by artists at this time.

353 Design for NO. I of 'The Comedy Ballet of Marionettes, as performed by the troupe of the Theatre-Impossible, posed in three drawings'. Reproduced on p. 87, Pl. III (in Index) of *The Yellow Book*, Vol. II, July 1894. Published by Elkin Mathews and John Lane, London; Copeland and Day, Boston. 4to. On the back a slight pencil sketch of a woman. Pl. 356
$13\frac{3}{8} \times 10\frac{1}{16}$ inches
Princeton University Library

Here the dwarf is shown holding a small box: in *The Yellow Book* plate he holds a mask in his right hand with which he points to the archway in the background. The drawing was altered in this detail when the design was used as a small poster for Geraudel's pastilles. Beardsley made use of a similar composition for his oil painting 'A Caprice' now in the Tate Gallery (see NO. 323).

The strong disbalance of the black mass of the woman's garment is countered by the suggestion of her movement to the left and by the posture of the dwarf who turns inwards and backwards, and finally by the stabilizing effect of the distant archway and street at the top left. But as usual with Beardsley, the off-side black mass is the first, because it is the most arresting, act in the visual drama. There is a reminiscence of the Venetian painter Longhi, more evident still in the picture 'A Caprice'. But the dramatic elements are Beardsley's own. The dwarf invites the woman with her eighteenth-century clothes to pass with him through the archway to a world beyond. Being a dwarf he cannot share the life of a normal woman, but his features are congested with a lust for vicarious pleasure.

354 The Comedy Ballet of Marionettes, II. Plate IV (in Index) of *The Yellow Book*, Vol. II, July 1894. Published by Elkin Mathews and John Lane, London: Copeland and Day, Boston. 4to. Pl. 358
From the line-block

The woman in the first design of this group of three (see NO. 353) is now in clothes of the Nineties and has been joined by a female in jacket and bloomers who is making advances to her. The receding chin of the lesbian denotes, in the phrenological terms of the nineteenth century, absence of moral fibre equivalent to anti-morality. The dwarf in the first design is here again, pointing with sarcastic glee at the situation he has helped to bring about. The quality of the outlines, apparently, yet not quite, of even width, speaks for itself.

355 The Comedy Ballet of Marionettes, III. Plate V (in Index) of *The Yellow Book,* Vol. II, July 1894. Published by Elkin Mathews and John Lane, London; Copeland and Day, Boston. 4to. Pl. 357
From the line-block

The heroine of the first two designs in this group of three (see NOS. 353, 354) is here seen wearing the short skirts of a ballet dancer and pointing with a mask held behind her back to her lesbian friend. The lesbian in reply points with an outstretched finger behind her back to the woman. Slightly behind them, on the left, the elderly husband or 'protector' of the young woman, wears the horns of a cuckold and dances clumsily. The dwarf is now the conductor of an orchestra of midgets who are pleased to be the voyeurs of a situation which, like their own condition in the first degree, is abnormal.

356 The Dancer. The central figure cut from the original drawing of 'The Comedy Ballet of Marionettes, III' made for *The Yellow Book,* Vol. II, July 1894 (Pl. V in Index): published by Elkin Mathews and John Lane, London; Copeland and Day, Boston. 4to. Signed with the artist's emblem (added). Pl. 359
$8\frac{1}{8} \times 5\frac{1}{8}$ inches
The Cooper Union Museum, New York

Beardsley's emblem was not used in the design for *The Yellow Book,* and may have been added by another hand when this figure was cut away from the rest of the drawing. It was re-named 'The Black Domino', and later 'The Dancer'. The poise of the figure and the subtle outline of her silhouetted garment are totally stylized; yet they suggest what the dashing lines of the realist draughtsman seldom achieve, the swaying movements of the clothes on the body of the dancer (see also the complete composition at NO. 355).

357 Garcons de Café. Plate IV of 'Six Drawings by Aubrey Beardsley', on p. 93 in *The Yellow Book,* Vol. II, July 1894, published by John Lane, London; Copeland and Day, Boston. 4to. Pl. 354
From the line-block

The drawing for this plate seems to have been lost or destroyed. Originally Beardsley called it 'Les Garcons du Café Royal'. From the heel of the waiter on the left to the end of the sleeve of the waiter on the right there is a continuous black continent absorbing all details within it in the same tone. This saturation effect, combined with the attempt at realism, is a tribute to the woodcut style of Félix Valloton (1865 – 1925) who was one of the group known in France as the Nabis. Presumably Beardsley became aware of Valloton's graphic art when he went to Paris in 1892 and 1893, though the impact could have been made through reproductions in *The Studio* (see Vol. I, May 1893) and elsewhere.

358 The Slippers of Cinderella. Plate V of 'Six Drawings by Aubrey Beardsley' on p. 95 in *The Yellow Book,* Vol. II, July 1894, published by Elkin Mathews and John Lane, London; Copeland and Day, Boston. 4to. Pl. 355
From the line-block

The drawing was in ink and first reproduced as shown here. Later the artist coloured it in green and scarlet water-colour.

359 Madame Réjane. Plate VI of 'Six Drawings by Aubrey Beardsley' on p. 97 of *The Yellow Book,* Vol. II, July 1894, published by Elkin Mathews and John Lane, London; Copeland and Day, Boston. 4to. Pl. 360
From the line-block

The profile of Réjane here is similar to those at NOS. 265 and 327, but the drawing was probably made in the previous month when this actress appeared for the first time in London at the Gaiety Theatre.

360 Design for the front cover of *The Yellow Book,* Vol. III, October 1894. Published by John Lane, London; Copeland and Day, Boston. 4to. Pl. 361
$8\frac{1}{16} \times 6\frac{1}{8}$ inches
Princeton University Library

By the date of the publication of this volume, Elkin Mathews had ceased, in September 1894, to be a partner with Lane at The Bodley Head. The black masses on the right are compensated by the movement of the figure to the left. The fleecy lining of the gown is heavily outlined to contain a self-sufficient white mass, which has an echoing form in the black mass of hair. The weak, pert and narcissistic features of the woman are opposed by the looking-glass on her dressing-table, which she scrutinizes and which tells her nothing because there is no reflection to be seen in it. But the bracketed lights on the glass are like London street lamps and the flames within are like gas-jets. The insinuation is that the woman, although too rich to be a street-walker, is so charged with desire to see the love of herself reflected in the eyes of others that she is vulnerable to any bold encounter in the streets of London's night life.

361 Title-page of *The Yellow Book,* Vol. III, October 1894, published by John Lane, London, and Copeland and Day, Boston. 4to. Pl. 362
From the line-block and letterpress

Another example of Beardsley's obsession with bulging pantaloons in harlequin and pierrot costumes. The result is a very small leg with the action of a four-footed beast.

362 Portrait of Himself [by Beardsley]. Par Les Dieux Jumeaux Tous Les Monstres Ne Sont Pas En Afrique. The artist is shown in a bed with enormous curtains. Reproduced on p. [51] as NO. I of 'Four Drawings by Aubrey Beardsley' (Art Index Plate III) in *The Yellow Book,* Vol. III, October 1894, published by John Lane, London, and Copeland and Day, Boston. 4to. Pl. 363
From the line-block

Beardsley has visualized himself in a night-cap more like a mob-cap, lying alone in a late seventeenth-century bed. The designation of himself by implication as a monster was a rationalization of his early feeling at school, and later, that he was markedly different from the other people around him, and therefore grotesque. By this date, however, he took a humourous pride in this difference.

363 Lady Gold's Escort. Reproduced on p. [53] as NO. II of 'Four Drawings by Aubrey Beardsley' (Art Index, Plate IV) in *The Yellow Book,* Vol. III, published by John Lane, London,

and Copeland and Day, Boston, October 1894. 4to. Pl. 364
From the line-block

During 1894 Beardsley seems to have become attracted to the problem of showing figures in darkness, whether the darkness of night, as in this case, and in 'Les Passades' and 'A Night Piece', or the darkness of the auditorium as in 'The Wagnerites' (NO. 364). Thus a positive technique was of little avail and he was obliged to leave white lines in reserve, as here, or actually paint them or scratch them out as in 'A Night Piece' (NO. 348). The original stimulus to this phase of his work was undoubtedly his appreciation of the poetic qualities of Whistler's 'Nocturnes'; only for Beardsley darkness was sinister.

364 The Wagnerites. Drawing reproduced on p. [55] as NO. III of 'Four Drawings by Aubrey Beardsley' (Art Index Plate V) in The Yellow Book, Vol. III, October 1894. Published by John Lane, London; Copeland and Day, Boston. 4to. Inscribed on the back in pencil with a note by Joseph Pennell (see Catalogue of the Aubrey Beardsley Exhibition at the Victoria and Albert Museum, 1966, NO. 405). Pl. 366
Indian ink touched with white, $8\frac{1}{8} \times 7$ inches
Victoria and Albert Museum, London

The plate in The Yellow Book was reproduced in Le Courrier Français on 23 December 1894. This is one of the best-known Beardsley's works, because of the bold break-up of the crowded scene into a comparatively few areas of black and white to represent the darkness of the auditorium Some of the white lines running into this lower half have been put in with chinese white, not left in reserve. Paint occurs elsewhere on the whites of the drawing.

The figures of men are indicated in the boxes, but only one man appears in the stalls, presumably a Jew. There is a legend that the woman drawn with a three-quarter profile represents Elizabeth Browning. The programme on the floor in the right bottom corner tells us that the audience is listening to Tristan and Isolde, an opera which had an especial attraction for Beardsley. He delights here in the irony of this opera with its theme of idealized love affecting an audience of worldly and vicious-looking women.

365 Front cover and spine of The Yellow Book, Vol. IV, January 1895, published by John Lane, London; Copeland and Day, Boston, 4to. Pl. 365
Design in black on yellow cloth boards
Mr W. G. Good, England

366 The Mysterious Rose Garden. Drawing for Plate NO. XIV (Index) in The Yellow Book, Vol. IV, January 1895, published by John Lane, London; Copeland and Day, Boston. 4to. Pl. 367
Indian ink over pencil, $8\frac{3}{4} \times 4\frac{3}{4}$ inches
Grenville L. Winthrop Bequest, Fogg Art Museum, Harvard University, U.S.A.

Beardsley was busy on this drawing in late 1894, and it appears there was a former version destroyed at the pencil sketch stage (see NO. 367). Originally he had intended it to be 'the first of a series of Biblical illustrations representing nothing more nor less than the Annunciation'. However, he changed his mind and entitled the drawing for publication 'The Mysterious Rose Garden'. As such it acquired a different

significance. The messenger with the winged slippers of Mercury is whispering a message at dusk to a young girl, evidently pregnant, wandering in a garden with a background of symbolic roses on trellises. The import of his message is left to the imagination. The form of the girl is sufficiently like that of Beardsley's sister, Mabel, for us to suspect that the underlying association was with her (compare the left-hand figure in the frontispiece to Plays by John Davidson, 1894. See NO. 317). The future of the pregnant young woman in late Victorian society was not easy, and whatever joy the girl in the 'Mysterious Rose Garden' may have derived from the news of her condition, would have been offset by the messenger's warning of her future tribulations as an unmarried mother.

367 Discarded drawing, for 'The Mysterious Rose Garden' as published in The Yellow Book, Vol. IV, January 1895. On nineteen fragments of paper reassembled. On the back, a faint scribble and sketch of a nude girl. Pl. 368
Pencil and indian ink, $10\frac{5}{16} \times 5\frac{13}{16}$ inches
Mr A. J. Ballantine, London

The drawing was re-discovered in 1963, torn into nineteen fragments held together at the back by lengths of gummed margins from British postage-stamp issues of c. 1881–1902 (See Catalogue of Aubrey Beardsley Exhibition at the Victoria and Albert Museum, 1966, NO. 422). Formerly it had belonged to John Lane and was sold with others from his collection in 1922.

Pencil sketches by Beardsley are uncommon, as his practice was to use them as foundations for his finished designs in ink. Ink border lines, as here, were frequently drawn by him before proceeding with the inking-in of the design. This version of 'The Mysterious Rose Garden' (originally conceived as an 'Annunciation') is in reverse of the final version in the Fogg Museum of Art at Harvard (See NO. 366), and there are other differences. It would seem this sketch was torn up (?because of the badly drawn border) and the fragments rescued perhaps without his knowledge.

368 The Repentance of Mrs . . . , Plate XV (Index) in The Yellow Book, Vol. IV, January 1895, published by John Lane, London; Copeland and Day, Boston. 4to. Pl. 369
From the line-block

The upper part of the kneeling figure of the repentant adulteress is related to the equivalent part of the figure of St John in Mantegna's engraving The Entombment (Armand-Durand, NO. 3). Beardsley had memorized the same agonized profile of St John for the kneeling figure of Mary Magdalen in 'The Litany of Mary Magdalen' 1891 (see NO. 20). Indeed the periwigged figure and the dwarf and the cut-away figure on the right all have their counterparts in the earlier composition.

369 Portrait of Winifred Emery. Plate XVI (Index) in The Yellow Book, Vol. IV, January 1895, published by John Lane, London; Copeland and Day, Boston. 4to. Pl. 370
From the line-block

One of the most delicate of Beardsley's drawings, here photo-engraved in line-block by Carl Hentschel. What is unusual is that for once the linear description of the clothes is precise and without exaggeration.

370 Frontispiece for Juvenal. Two monkeys in livery bearing an elderly person in a sedan chair along a London street. Double-page supplement at the end of *The Yellow Book*, Vol. IV, 1895, published by John Lane, London; Copeland and Day, Boston. 4to. Pl. 371
From the line-block

The last plate by Beardsley to be published in a *Yellow Book*. From Vol. V the plates after his designs were withdrawn before publication. The rest of his illustrations to Juvenal were published by Leonard Smithers (see NOS. 468–70, 483). Here the architecture of the street may have been intended to be Roman, but the buildings are indisputably of eighteenth century and Regency London as they survived in the Nineties.

371 Design for the prospectus and the front cover of *The Yellow Book*, Vol. V, to be published by John Lane, London, in April 1895, but withdrawn. On the back is a slight pencil sketch of a woman's profile and a two-line border in ink. Pl. 373
$8\frac{1}{8} \times 6\frac{1}{8}$ inches
Brighton Art Gallery, England

This design is similar in some respects to one used for the front covers of the earlier rare-book catalogue issued by Leonard Smithers in 1895 and 1896. It survives in black on yellow cloth on one cover of Vol. V of *The Yellow Book* as originally planned, which forms part of a dummy copy obtained by Sir Edmund Gosse. The published front cover was re-designed by Patten Wilson; the back cover and spine were overlooked, but five plates after Beardsley inside the volume were withdrawn while it was actually in production. This crisis in the history of *The Yellow Book* arose because of Beardsley's dismissal from his post as art editor of the journal at the time of the Wilde scandal (See *Catalogue of Aubrey Beardsley Exhibition at the Victoria and Albert Museum*, 1966, NOS. 425, 426).

372 Atalanta in Calydon. An illustration to the poem by Algernon Charles Swinburne, 1895. Pl. 372
Indian ink and wash, $12 \times 4\frac{3}{8}$ inches
British Museum

The disbalance aids the suggestion of movement to the right, into a black background. Some of the flowers were brushed over with ink wash, thus making the full reproduction of this drawing impossible by line-block. It was to have been published in Volume V of *The Yellow Book* in April 1895, but was withdrawn from the volume as issued, along with three other plates and a title-page after Beardsley, when John Lane dispensed with his services as art editor of the magazine.

373 Portrait of Miss Letty Lind. Reproduced as NO. 84 in *The Early Work of Aubrey Beardsley*, John Lane, London, 1899. Pl. 374
From the half-tone plate

This fine drawing is described in *Early Work* as hitherto unpublished. It represents Letty Lind in the play called 'The Artist's Model' and was among five plates after Beardsley's drawings that were to have been published in Vol. V of *The Yellow Book*, April 1895, but were withdrawn at the last minute when Beardsley's connection with the periodical was terminated at the time of Oscar Wilde's arrest. It was then

that certain pious authors, published by the Bodley Head, conspired to force Lane to abandon the young artist.

374 A Nocturne of Chopin. Pl. 375
Pen, ink and wash, $7\frac{3}{4} \times 7\frac{1}{8}$ inches
Grenville L. Winthrop Bequest, Fogg Art Museum, Harvard University, Massachusetts

First reproduced in *Early Work*, 1899, this drawing is an essay in the technique adopted for some of the *Madomoiselle de Maupin* series, involving varied tones rendered by ink washes. It was one of the drawings intended for reproduction in the original Volume V of *The Yellow Book*, but withdrawn (see NOS. 372, 373, 394).

375 Design for a poster to advertise *The Yellow Book*, but not used. Signed with the artist's emblem. Pl. 376
$13\frac{5}{8} \times 10\frac{1}{8}$ inches
Princeton University Library

A typical Beardsley poster with a panel for lettering on one side. The alarmingly rising shoulders of the jacket and the jewelled-moth hair ornament (shades of Whistler's butterfly emblem) symbolize the aggressive nature of the New Woman, who holds the mannikin pointing to what could have been an announcement of *The Yellow Book*.

376 Design for a front cover of *The Yellow Book*, but not used. Signed with the artist's names. Pl. 378
$7\frac{5}{8} \times 6\frac{1}{8}$ inches
Princeton University Library

The bars in the background representing shelves are noteworthy. Considered as visual formulae they are derived from similar features in Japanese prints. The books which the lady is about to place on her shelves include *The Yellow Book*, of course, *Discords* by George Egerton (one of the *Keynotes* series by a New Woman), and Beardsley's own *Story of Venus and Tannhäuser*, first advertised in the Bodley Head list at the back of Volume III of *The Yellow Book* in October 1894, but never in fact to be completed by Beardsley or published by Lane.

377 A title-page ornament. First published in plate NO. 81 of *The Early Work of Aubrey Beardsley*, John Lane, 1899. 4to. Pl. 379
From the line-block

It is not known for what purpose this drawing was made. At the time of its reproduction in *Early Work* it was described as 'hitherto unpublished'. It dates probably from 1895. A nude male figure playing a double-bass was in the same category as a woman playing a piano in a field (NO. 345); except that the actions of this figure in bowing and fingering the strings of the female-shaped instrument are not only eccentric, they are charged with erotic symbolism, by the very fact of his nudity. The original drawing ($6\frac{1}{8} \times 2\frac{1}{8}$ inches) was bought at Sotheby's, London, by Brian Reade, 19 July 1967.

378 Madame Réjane. Drawing in pen, ink and wash first reproduced on p. 65 in *A Second Book of Fifty Drawings by Aubrey Beardsley*, Leonard Smithers, 1899. Pl. 377
From the half-tone plate

The subject, the conception of the foot and the pen and brush work suggest that Beardsley was thinking of Constantin Guys when he made this drawing. As art editor of *The Yellow Book* he may have arranged for the reproduction of a drawing of three men by Guys in Plate XII of Vol. V of *The Yellow Book*, April 1895. His own contributions to Vol. V were removed before publication, at the time when John Lane was influenced by a group of Bodley Head authors to drop Beardsley.

379 Caricature of Beardsley painted apparently by himself over a photograph of him (mounted on card) by Frederick Hollyer. Inscribed in pen 'Max Beerbohm from Aubrey Beardsley'. Inscribed on back in red ink 'Fred^r Hollyer/9 Pembroke Sq^{re} Kensington W'. Pl. 331
Water-colour and chinese white over photograph, $4\frac{3}{16} \times 6\frac{7}{16}$ inches
Mr Alan Thomas, London

The style of the painting imitates the style of Beerbohm's caricatures, up to a point. It does not seem as lightly executed as it might have been by Beerbohm himself however, and although he had a habit of imitating inscriptions from well-known persons for his own amusement, the photograph is from the same negative by Hollyer from which another print was made and similarly inscribed, again presumably by Beardsley himself, to William Rothenstein.

380 Design for a small poster advertising *The Spinster's Scrip* as compiled by Cecil Raynor and published by William Heinemann, 1895. Signed with the artist's names. Pl. 380
$14\frac{1}{4} \times 9\frac{5}{16}$ inches
Princeton University Library

A. E. Gallatin, in his catalogue of 1945, maintained that this design was never used; but an example of the small poster or show-card for *The Spinster's Scrip*, with lettering in the panel on the left and 'Sold Here' in capitals at the top left corner exists in the Print Room of the Victoria and Albert Museum. The book by Rayner was issued in December 1895. A reproduction of the design in *Early Work* (1899) includes the semblance of a dog at the end of the leash, which is not in the original drawing. The design is remarkable for the arresting and angular silhouette of the standing woman's garment, and for the half-clothed, sphinx-like female leaning on the panel. The space above the second female has been heightened with chinese white to obliterate a discarded feature. In execution the drawing is rougher than was usual in Beardsley's work at this date.

381 Autumn. Design for a calender first published as NO. 91 in *The Early Work of Aubrey Beardsley*, John Lane, London, 1899. Pl. 396
From the line-block
The original drawing ($10\frac{1}{2} \times 5\frac{1}{2}$ inches) was reproduced in the above-mentioned book by permission of William Heinemann in 1899, and was described as hitherto unpublished. It does not seem to have been used for any calendar. On 12 July 1961 it was sold by Messrs Sotheby for £200 to Mrs H. V. Brunner.

382 Invitation card for John Lane's 'Sette of Odd Volumes Smoke', on 22 February 1895. Pl. 383
From the line-block and letterpress, $4\frac{3}{8} \times 3\frac{1}{4}$ inches
Mr W. G. Good, England

It was characteristic of Beardsley that he should see any social occasion as an opportunity for the wearing of carnival costume. The design is unusual amongst his work of this period in that it is vignetted like some of the earlier *Bon-Mots* drawings; which is to say, that the forms are not closed up, the lines being left to end in an undefined space. It is also unusual in that the figure has a 'lost' profile and is viewed three-quarters from the back. Later reproductions of the design (see *Early Work*, pl. 127) have the letterpress capitals O and V omitted, together with the initials of Carl Hentschel, the line-block engraver, while a dotted line is added to the right-hand end of the sofa.

The design was first reproduced in *The Studio*, September 1895.

383 Drawing for the frontispiece to *A Full and True Account of the Wonderful Mission of Earl Lavender, which lasted one Night and one Day* by John Davidson, published by Ward and Downing, London, 1895. 8vo. Pl. 381
$10\frac{1}{8} \times 6\frac{3}{16}$ inches
Grenville L. Winthrop Bequest, Fogg Art Museum, Harvard University, Massachusetts

John Davidson's peculiar humour, of which *Earl Lavender* is a good example, is scarcely reflected in Beardsley's delicate outlines, or in the stilted posture of the woman who holds up a whip in one hand and her dress in the other, and places her feet as if in some sort of dance. This is, for all that, one of the most splendid drawings of the nineteenth, or of any other century. The delineation of the early Victorian fireplace and fender is a wonderful transformation of the commonplace into the grand; and, on second glance, the stilted figure of the *flagellateuse* does suggest, without broken or impressionist lines, the various movements she would make, with a languid, *fin-de-siècle* gentility.

384 The Scarlet Pastorale. Illustration on p. 16 in *The London Year Book*, 1898, and accompanying an article entitled *Aubrey Beardsley* by W. L., pp. 46–50. Published by the Grosvenor Press, London. 8vo. Titled 'The Scarlet Pastorale'. Pl. 384
$10\frac{9}{16} \times 7\frac{5}{16}$ inches
Scofield Thayer Collection, Fogg Art Museum, Harvard University, Massachusetts

This composition was first published in *The Sketch*, 10 April, 1895; then again in *A Book of Fifty Drawings by Aubrey Beardsley*, Smithers, London, 1897, p. 35. The first use of scarlet for the block was in *The London Year Book* of 1898.

The arrested movement of the dancer on the stage is cleverly aided by a suggestion of the motions that brought him to the posture he is in. This is done by the gradual elongation of the lozenges on his harlequin costume to the left, and by the serpentine alignment of the lozenges along the front leg to the shoulder on the left. The masqueraders behind him are not in the same dimension, for they are on the backcloth and are literally images on the backcloth haunting the dancer on the stage. The two candlesticks are in another dimension again, because they are not visibly supported by anything and are in a different scale from the figures. For some reason hard to explain the transitions in this design make it one of the most memorable of Beardsley's works. If the editor of *The London Year Book* had not been at Brighton Grammar School with Beardsley it is doubtful whether the article in memory of the artist, who had just died, would have appeared in such a publication.

385   Front cover of *Sappho*, a memoir with text, selected renderings and a literal translation by Henry Thornton Wharton, published by John Lane, London, and A. C. M'Clurg and Company, Chicago, July 1895. Third edition, and the first with this format. 8vo. Pl. 382
Blue cloth stamped with a design in gold
Mr W. G. Good, England

Beardsley's cover designs are all remarkable for their restraint, for meagre or minimal elegance, in its way another expression of an aesthetic ideal held by such poets as Lionel Johnson and Ernest Dowson, and in the graphic arts by Charles Ricketts.

386   The Mirror of Love. Design for the frontispiece to a book of poems by Mark André Raffalovich, entitled *The Thread and the Path*, published by David Nutt, London, 1895; but not used. Pl. 385
$10\frac{13}{16} \times 6$ inches
Victoria and Albert Museum, London

This drawing was intended to illustrate the line 'Set in a heart as in a frame Love liveth', which was the first line of the first poem in the book. Nutt refused to publish it as a frontispiece, observing that 'whatever you may say the figure is hermaphrodite'. (See *Catalogue of Aubrey Beardsley Exhibition at the Victoria and Albert Museum*, 1966, NO. 555). The candelabrum is a curious conception springing from a form derived from that of a German goblet of the sixteenth century.

387   Venus between Terminal Gods. Design for the frontispiece to Beardsley's romantic novel, *The Story of Venus and Tannhäuser*, advertised to be accompanied by twenty-four illustrations in John Lane's list of 1894, but never completed. Lettered 'Venus'. Pl. 386
Indian ink touched with white, $8\frac{7}{8} \times 7$ inches
Cecil Higgins Art Gallery, Bedford, England

An expurgated version of the incomplete novel was published as *Under the Hill* in *The Savoy*, NOS. 1 and 2, 1896. When this drawing was made in 1895 it was much admired by Lord Leighton, among others (see Haldane Macfall, *Aubrey Beardsley*, London, 1928, p. 69). It is static and frontal: the ideal figure of Venus is flanked by two sinister Terms, a typical Beardsley contrast. The background reverts in style to decorative passages in *Le Morte Darthur*. According to Vallance it reflects the influence of Charles Ricketts or Laurence Housman (R. Ross, *Aubrey Beardsley*, London, 1909; List of Drawings compiled by A. Vallance, p. 95, NO. 101). If Vallance was referring to the background of the title-page in *The End of Elfintown*, which was designed by Housman and published in 1894, then it was more likely that Housman was influenced by Beardsley's early work for *Le Morte Darthur*. Vallance also says the design was intended for 'a version of the Tannhäuser legend to be published by Messrs H. Henry & Co., Ltd.', by which he implies that Henry & Co. as well as the Bodley Head were interested in publishing the novel.

388   Venus. Design for a title-page intended for Beardsley's

romantic novel, *The Story of Venus and Tannhäuser*, but not used. Lettered with title. Pl. 388
$4\frac{3}{8} \times 3\frac{1}{8}$ inches
Grenville L. Winthrop Bequest, Fogg Art Museum, Harvard University, Massachusetts

This design was first published in *The Studio*, 1898, Vol. 13.

389   Frontispiece to *The Story of Venus and Tannhäuser* etc., Beardsley's unfinished novel, intended to be published by John Lane at The Bodley Head, London, in 1895. Signed with the artist's initials and dated 1895 in a roundel. Reproduced in plate 92 in *The Early Work of Aubrey Beardsley*, John Lane, London, 1899. Pl. 387
$11\frac{11}{16} \times 7$ inches
Grenville L. Winthrop Bequest, Fogg Art Museum, Harvard University, Massachusetts

The exclusion of erotic overtones from this design and its astonishing poise bring it close to the work of Anning Bell, and they also suggest that Beardsley's story of Venus and Tannhäuser was something with serious meanings for him beyond, or beside, its lascivious innuendos. Here the candlestick has an exaggerated delicacy of form: the sixteenth-century German goblet, which struck Beardsley's fancy at this date and occurs again in 'The Mirror of Love' (NO. 386) appears just as a student might have drawn it in a museum. The fountain and the park seen through the windows take us back once more to *Le Morte Darthur*. The title-page designed alongside this frontispiece is reproduced at Pl. 389.

390   The Story of Venus and Tannhäuser, etc. Designs intended for the frontispiece and title-page of Beardsley's unfinished novel, advertised in *The Yellow Book*, Vol. III, October 1894, as on this title-page. Signed with the artist's initials and the date 1895 in a roundel in the frontispiece. Reproduced in plate 92 of *The Early Work of Aubrey Beardsley*, John Lane, London, 1899. Pl. 389
From the line-block

After the 1895 crisis, when Lane authorized the dismissal of Beardsley from *The Yellow Book* staff, there could be no question of *Venus and Tannhäuser* being published by The Bodley Head. When the story, in a bowdlerized version, was published by Smithers in *The Savoy*, NOS. 1 and 2, these designs were not used.

The architectural frames and the composite capitals are linked perhaps with memories of woodcuts in the *Hypnerotomachia Poliphili* of 1499; and the title-page on the right, crammed with Roman lettering, doubtless follows the precedent found in the epitaph NO. 108 in Appell's facsimile of the *Hypnerotomachia* published in 1889.

391   The Return of Tannhäuser to the Venusberg. Drawing intended to illustrate Beardsley's romantic novel *The Story of Venus and Tannhäuser*, announced with twenty-four full-page illustrations in John Lane's 1894 list, but not completed. Signed with monogram. Inscribed on the back with title and 'To J. M. Dent my kind friend, & first publisher; from Aubrey Beardsley. Sept. 1896'. Pl. 390
Indian ink and wash, $5\frac{1}{4} \times 5\frac{3}{16}$ inches
Mr F. J. Martin Dent, London

The first reproductions of this drawing were in reverse, as in

The Idler, May 1898, and *Later Work,* pl. 74. An earlier wash drawing of the same subject dates from 1891 (see NO. 19). The theme of Tannhäuser's return, in pilgrim's clothes, to the realm of Venus, fascinated Beardsley over the years, and the present design is one of the most moving ever to be conceived by him.

2 Isolde. Drawing reproduced in colour lithography (red, green, grey and black) as a supplement to *The Studio,* October 1895. Titled as above. Pl. 391
Pen and ink and water-colour, $11\frac{1}{16} \times 7$ inches
Grenville L. Winthrop Bequest, Fogg Art Museum, Harvard University, Massachusetts

The colours used by Beardsley were purple-grey wash in the background and grey wash and indian ink for the figure. In the lithograph published in *The Studio* the backcloth is toned flat, the drawing is hardened, while the colours are bright. There exists a proof of a colour-lithograph after this drawing, inscribed by A. J. A. Symons as taken before publication in plate 24 of *The Early Work of Aubrey Beardsley,* 1899; in this state the backcloth is orange, and no green appears. The plate in *Early Work* ended by being the same in colouring as *The Studio* supplement.

Beardsley's interpretation of one of his favourite Wagnerian heroines as a woman of his own period may be compared with the right-hand woman in 'Café Noir' (NO. 394), who wears a similar hat, turned up to give the impression of the outlines of an exotic butterfly's wing.

3 Messalina returning home. 1895. Illustration to the Sixth Satire of Juvenal. On the back a drawing in ink, possibly for an ornamental initial; also a guarantee by Leonard Smithers dated 27 April 1898. Pl. 392
Pencil, indian ink and water-colour, 11×7 inches
Tate Gallery, London

The pinkish-purple water-colour was added apparently by Beardsley before 1898 and was not part of the original drawing.

4 First frontispiece to *An Evil Motherhood* by Walt[er] Ruding, published by Elkin Mathews, London, 1896. 8vo. Pl. 393
Pen, ink and wash, $6\frac{1}{8} \times 6\frac{1}{4}$ inches
Scofield Thayer Collection, Fogg Art Museum, Harvard University, Massachusetts

Beardsley introduced a grey wash into the drawing which meant it could only be reproduced by half-tone. This frontispiece appeared in six copies only (or twelve, according to Mathews himself) of the first issue of the book in November 1895. It had formerly been entitled 'Black Coffee' (Café Noir) and was intended for publication in *The Yellow Book,* Vol. V, April 1895, but was withdrawn at the last minute from that volume along with four other plates and the front cover after Beardsley's designs when Lane authorized his dismissal from *The Yellow Book* staff. The drawing was then supplied by the artist to Mathews for Ruding's story, with which it has no connection. Lane objected; and Mathews made Beardsley design a fresh frontispiece (see NO. 395) which replaced 'Black Coffee' in the rest of the issue. Later issues of the book had 'Black Coffee' tipped in alongside. It has many familiar characteristics of Beardsley's style and is related to 'Waiting'

(see NO. 249) and, in the shape of the right-hand woman's hat, to 'Isolde' (see NO. 392).

395 Second frontispiece to *An Evil Motherhood* by Walt[er] Ruding, published by Elkin Mathews, London, 1896. 8vo. Pl. 394
From the line-block
Mr Brian Reade, London

For the first frontispiece see NO. 394. When Mathews saw the advance copies of the book with the first frontispiece ('Black Coffee') substituted for the portrait of Ruding that had been stipulated, he was, not unreasonably, annoyed: so was Lane, who had commissioned the drawing for Vol. V of *The Yellow Book,* from which it had been withdrawn, along with the front cover design and four other designs within, when Beardsley was dismissed from the art-editorship. But Mathews went to Beardsley's rooms and would not leave until he had seen the present frontispiece (which was more or less a portrait of Ruding) well advanced. Ruding gave Beardsley two or three sittings.

Of all Beardsley's compositions this is perhaps the most evocative of the *fin-de-siècle* drama: the props are the oil-lamp, the antimacassar, the loose-covered armchair, the rug and the fender; the actors are the youth with long hair and pierrot-style slippers and trousers (Beardsley's specific contributions) and the ruthless mother, looking down on her son.

396 Illustration to 'At a Distance', a poem by Justin Huntly M'Carthy (p. 189) on p. 191 of *A London Garland,* an anthology of verse selected by W. E. Henley with pictures by members of the Society of Illustrators, published by Macmillan and Company, London and New York, December 1895. 4to. Pl. 395
From the line-block
Mr W. G. Good, England

On p. 190 was another illustration by W. D. Almond. In *A Second Book of Fifty Drawings by Aubrey Beardsley,* Smithers, London, 1899, Beardsley's illustration in *A London Garland* is reproduced on p. 115 with the title 'A Suggested Reform in Ballet Costume (unfinished drawing)', and is described as 'hitherto unpublished'. The scale there is enlarged and the three-line border on the right re-drawn from the end of the artist's signature. The original drawing included another figure on the left which appears to have been deleted before the block-making stage. Had Beardsley survived into the period of the Ballet Russes he would undoubtedly have been taken up by Diaghilev, who met him once before his death and had a profound admiration for his work.

397 Designs for the front covers and spines of the volumes in the 'Pierrot's Library', a series of novels published by John Lane, London; Henry Altemus, Philadelphia (Vols. I and II) and Rand McNally and Company, Chicago (Vols. III and IV), 1896. Pl. 397
$6\frac{1}{4} \times 4\frac{11}{16}$; $5\frac{9}{16} \times \frac{5}{16}$ inches
Princeton University Library

These designs were used for all the volumes but were stamped in different colours (red, blue, green and brown) on buff cloth for each title.

398 Decoration on back covers of volumes in the 'Pierrot's Library', published by John Lane, London; Henry Altemus, Philadelphia (Vols. I and II); and Rand McNally and Company, Chicago (Vols. III and IV), 1896. 8vo. Design stamped in red, blue, green and brown on buff cloth for each different volume. Reproduced as NO.138 in *The Early Work of Aubrey Beardsley*, John Lane, London, 1899. Pl.399
From the line-block

Beardsley had been anticipated in the idea of this motif by Tom Meteyard, who designed the front cover of *Songs from Vagabondia* by Bliss Carman and Richard Hovey, published by Elkin Mathews and John Lane, London, 1894. In Meteyard's design, which is stamped in black on grey board, there are three faces in the dark portion of the Moon, and a light crescent.

399 Design for the title-pages in the 'Pierrot's Library', a series of novels published by John Lane, London; Henry Altemus, Philadelphia (Vols. I and II) and Rand McNally, Chicago (Vols. III and IV), 1896. Pl. 398
$6\frac{1}{16} \times 4\frac{3}{16}$ inches
Princeton University Library

400 Design for the front end-papers of the volumes in the 'Pierrot's Library', published by John Lane, London; Henry Altemus, Philadelphia (Vols. I and II) and Rand McNally, Chicago (Vols. III and IV), 1896. Signed with the artist's name. Inscribed in pencil near top of tree '1st end paper'. Pl. 400
$6\frac{1}{2} \times 9\frac{3}{16}$ inches
Princeton University Library

The design was printed in olive green.

401 Design for the back end-papers of the volumes in the 'Pierrot's Library', published by John Lane, London; Henry Altemus, Philadelphia (Vols. I and II) and Rand McNally, Chicago (Vols. III and IV), 1896. Signed with the artist's names. Inscribed in pencil behind ruff of right-hand figure '2nd end paper'. Pl. 401
$6\frac{1}{2} \times 9\frac{3}{16}$ inches
Princeton University Library

The design was printed in olive green.

402 Front wrapper of the *Catalogue of Rare Books* offered for sale by Leonard Smithers, Effingham House, Arundel Street, London, NO. 6, 1896. 8vo. Pl. 402
From the line-block and letterpress
Mr W. G. Good, England

The wrappers of the catalogues NOS. 1–4 issued by Smithers bore a design similar to the one for Vol. V of *The Yellow Book*, though different in proportion and details. The wrappers of NOS. 5–7 were printed in black on pink (5), light blue (6) and violet grey (7).

403 Design for the front cover of *The Rape of the Lock,* an heroi-comical poem in five cantos written by Alexander Pope, embroidered with nine drawings by Aubrey Beardsley. Published by Leonard Smithers, London, May 1896. Crown 4to. Signed with intials left and right. Pl. 404
$9\frac{7}{8} \times 6\frac{15}{16}$ inches
Mr R. A. Harari, London

It was at the suggestion of Edmund Gosse that Beardsley undertook to illustrate this poem. But he seldom illustrated anything literally: rather he made graphic comments on the text, as he did on *Salome,* which explains the use of the word 'embroidered' on the title-page of *The Rape of the Lock.* The cover design is one of the finest ever conceived. The strength and beauty of the drawing in indian ink were somewhat modified in gold on the covers of the ordinary edition, which were turquoise-blue, and even more so on those of the edition-de-luxe, which were of vellum.

404 The Dream. Drawing for the frontispiece of *The Rape of the Lock,* an heroi-comical poem in five cantos written by Alexander Pope embroidered with nine drawings by Aubrey Beardsley. Published by Leonard Smithers, London, May 1896. Crown 4to. Pl. 405
$10 \times 6\frac{3}{4}$ inches
Mr John Hay Whitney, New York

The eclectic confusions of this design gave birth to some of the most typical pre-1914 styles of ornament. The decorations on the bed curtains drawn in Beardsley's stippled manner must have remained in the unconscious of many an artist; for here are the posies in baskets, the garlands and swags of flat roses, the tassels and the peacocks with spreading tails which appeared in the medium of dots, just as they do here, over many a wallpaper, textile, Christmas card and end-paper of the 1900s. These are motifs taken from the Louis Seize and Aesthetic periods. As for the clothes of the courtier, they are modelled on those of a ballet dancer of the first half of the eighteenth century, when the wide-spreading *tonnelet* was in vogue. But the *tonnelet* here is enriched with roseate garlands of the 1770s, as popularized by Louis Boquet, the costume designer of the Opéra under Louis XVI. The sense of space achieved by lines of slightly different values is remarkable.

405 The Billet-Doux. The second illustration reproduced as a headpiece on p. [1] in *The Rape of the Lock* an heroi-comical poem in five cantos written by Alexander Pope embroidered with nine drawings by Aubrey Beardsley. Published by Leonard Smithers, London, May 1896. Crown 4to. Pl. 403
From the line-block

This illustration has been much admired because it is pretty. It has the absurd prettiness of a work by some *petit maître* of the *ancien régime.* In the title-pages of some of the *Keynotes* series Beardsley explored decorative symmetry disturbed by unruly details. And the style of this illustration runs counter to the disintegrative compositions of his former drawings inspired by Japanese art: here the figure is off-centre with counterbalancing details, and with a near-symmetrical bedhead and wallpaper above. *The Rape of the Lock* was a turning point in Beardsley's development: thenceforward centralized compositions like this became more frequent. The simplification of the hand follows a trend in much decorative drawing of this date, whereby details were taken for granted. But Beardsley's outline treatment of it nearly deprives it of meaning.

406 The Toilet. Drawing for the third illustration facing p.6 in *The Rape of the Lock* an heroi-comical poem in five cantos written by Alexander Pope embroidered with nine drawings

by Aubrey Beardsley. Published by Leonard Smithers, London, May 1896. Crown 4to. Pl. 406
10 × 6¾ inches
Cleveland Museum of Art, U.S.A.

Graded dots are used in a stippled effect to suggest varied tones in the landscape decorations on the screen, on the flounces of the women, and for the vertical pattern on the wallpaper.

407 The Baron's Prayer. Drawing for the fourth illustration facing p. 8 in *The Rape of the Lock* an heroi-comical poem in five cantos written by Alexander Pope embroidered with nine drawings by Aubrey Beardsley. Published by Leonard Smithers, London, May 1896. Crown 4to. Pl. 407
10 × 6¹³⁄₁₆ inches
Scofield Thayer Collection, Fogg Art Museum, Harvard University, Massachusetts

The design illustrates Pope's lines about the Baron, who

'. . . to *Love* an Altar built,
Of twelve vast *French* Romances, neatly gilt.
There lay three Garters, half a Pair of Gloves,
And all the Trophies of his former Loves.
With tender *Billet-doux* he lights the Pyre,
And breathes three am'rous Sighs to raise the Fire.
Then prostrate falls, and begs with ardent Eyes
Soon to obtain, and long possess the Prize.'

The prize being a lock of Belinda's hair.

408 The Barge. Fifth illustration facing p. 10 in *The Rape of the Lock* an heroi-comical poem in five cantos written by Alexander Pope embroidered with nine drawings by Aubrey Beardsley. Published by Leonard Smithers, London, May 1896. Crown 4to. Pl. 408
From the line-block

409 The Rape of the Lock. Sixth illustration facing p. 20 in *The Rape of the Lock* an heroi-comical poem in five cantos written by Alexander Pope embroidered with nine drawings by Aubrey Beardsley. Published by Leonard Smithers, London, May 1896. Crown 4to. Pl. 409
From the line-block

A moment of suspense is evoked, the moment just before the Baron cuts off the lock of hair. The sagacious dwarf conniving at the reader and taking a cup of chocolate is the nearest, and almost the central, feature of the composition, an irony characteristic of Beardsley's art. Everything else is successfully balanced behind him—the clothes (first noticeable because of their elaborate decorations), the figures, the curtains (all stipple), the window and the view of the park outside it. The furniture is scarcely of the eighteenth century: indeed the chair Belinda sits on is like a Thonet chair with unlikely carvings attached; and, as in other illustrations in the book, the clothes are more or less appropriate for the man, but for the women they are taken from fashions of the 1780s. In spite of anachronisms however the illustration is a record of Beardsley's skill and taste. In his day this particular mastery had never been achieved in any medium: nor has it been achieved since, for the reason that it springs as much from limitations as from gifts that can hardly be found in combination again.

410 The Cave of Spleen. Drawing for the seventh illustration facing p. 24 in *The Rape of the Lock* an heroi-comical poem in five cantos written by Alexander Pope embroidered with nine drawings by Aubrey Beardsley. Published by Leonard Smithers, London, May 1896. Crown 4to. Pl. 411
9⅞ × 6⅞ inches
The Boston Museum of Fine Arts, U.S.A.

This strange design, in which some of the creatures appear to be ornamental motifs coming to life, seems to have had a considerable influence on Beardsley pasticheurs in the early twentieth century: for example, Alan Odle, in his earlier works.

411 The Battle of the Beaux and the Belles. Drawing for the eighth illustration facing p. 34 in *The Rape of the Lock* an heroi-comical poem in five cantos written by Alexander Pope embroidered with nine drawings by Aubrey Beardsley. Published by Leonard Smithers, London, May 1896. Crown 4to. Pl. 410
9¹⁵⁄₁₆ × 6¾ inches
The Barber Institute of Fine Arts, Birmingham

Beardsley's illustrations to *The Rape of the Lock* were the most admired of all his works during the years following his death. The variety of tone and texture suggested by the dots and the close-laid lines is a marvel of craftsmanship. While the clothes of the men are more or less appropriate to the date of the poem, the clothes of the women are based on styles of the 1780s. The chair is based on rococo designs of the mid-eighteenth century.

412 The New Star. Drawing for the cul-de-lampe on p. 38 in *The Rape of the Lock* an heroi-comical poem in five cantos by Alexander Pope embroidered with nine drawings by Aubrey Beardsley. Published by Leonard Smithers, London, May 1896. Crown 4to. Signed with the artist's intials. Pl. 412
12⅛ × 7⅛ inches
Grenville L. Winthrop Bequest, Fogg Art Museum, Harvard University, Massachusetts

The periwig and tiny cap with vast plumes suggest the style of the costumes of the famous Carrousel of 1662 held by Louis XIV in Paris—though there is no written evidence that Beardsley knew of the engravings that record this event. The rest of the costume differs little from other gala or carnival costumes conceived by Beardsley.

413 Front cover of the bijou edition of *The Rape of the Lock* an heroi-comical poem by Alexander Pope etc., published by Leonard Smithers, London, 1897. Demy 16mo. Pl. 413
Red cloth stamped with title, and design in gold

The plates of the bijou edition of 1897 were similar to those of the big edition of 1896, but reduced in scale. Plate 1 repeated in line-block the design of the front cover, without the lettering. Plate 2 reproduced in line-block a reduced version of the design for the front cover of the 1896 edition (NO. 403). Beardsley's original drawing for the present design was intended for the actual cover of the little red edition. Writing to Smithers from Paris on 27 April 1897, he enclosed a slip for the lettering of the title which was arranged as shown here; and he warned Smithers that there was some chinese white on the drawing, 'so let it not be touched with india Rubber'.

414 Design for the front cover of the prospectus of *The Savoy*, NO. 1, January 1896; edited by Arthur Symons and published by Leonard Smithers, London. 4to. Signed with the artist's names in capitals below the design. Reproduced on pink paper. Pl. 414
$9\frac{3}{8} \times 6\frac{9}{16}$ inches
Scofield Thayer Collection, Fogg Art Museum, Harvard University, Massachusetts

According to Bernard Shaw (see Grant Richards, *Author Hunting*, 2nd ed. 1948, note on pp. 33, 34) Beardsley's other design for the prospectus, showing a pierrot on the right in a reversed posture to John Bull (reproduced in *Later* Work, NO. 107), was objected to by Smithers as too flippant. The pierrot design was printed, but Beardsley having provided the Bull design, this too was printed (without his signature) and distributed in December 1895. When it was too late, George Moore and other *Savoy* contributors, including Shaw, told Smithers he must withdraw a prospectus which showed John Bull with a diminutive erection under his breeches. Not having any of the prospectuses left, Smithers agreed.

415 Siegfried. Drawing used for the publisher's emblem of Leonard Smithers, on the back cover of the prospectus of *The Savoy*, NO. 1, issued in December 1895; and on the back cover of *The Savoy*, NOS. 1 and 2. Pl. 417
$3\frac{11}{16} \times 2\frac{13}{16}$ inches
Princeton University Library

The top panel contained the word 'Leonard' and the bottom panel 'Smithers'. Owen Seaman greeted the appearance of *The Savoy* with a 36-line poem entitled 'A New Blue Book', of which the first stanza ran:

> ' "The world's great age begins anew,"
>   Cold virtue's weeds are cast;
> Our heads are light, our tales are blue,
>   And things are moving fast;
> And no one any longer quarrels
> With anybody else's morals.'

And the fifth:

> 'O cease to know your Bodley pap
>   Whence all the spice is spent!
> The splendour of its primal tap
>   Was gone when Aubrey went;
> Behold that subtle Sphinx prepare
> Fresh liquors fit to lift your hair.'

(*The Battle of the Bays*, London 1896)

416 The Savoy. Design for the front cover of *The Savoy*, NO. 1, January 1896. Reproduced on pink boards for that number, edited by Arthur Symons and published by Leonard Smithers, London, January 1896. 4to. Signed in ink with the artist's names and dated 1896; titled in ink 'The Savoy', and in pencil 'NO. 1 January 1896'. Pl. 415
Indian ink and pencil, $14\frac{5}{8} \times 11$ inches
Grenville L. Winthrop Bequest, Fogg Art Museum, Harvard University, Massachusetts

The design was used also in NO. 2 of *The Savoy*, April 1896. Proofs were made from a line-block reproducing the design completed, with the pencilled lettering and numerals inked in. The putto is shown as if about to urinate on a copy of *The Yellow Book* on the ground, Beardsley revealing here some bitterness over his ejection from the staff of that

magazine eight months before. George Moore having criticised this detail, *The Yellow Book* and the genitals of the putto were deleted for publication.

417 Drawing for the title-page of *The Savoy*, NO. 1, January 1896, edited by Arthur Symons and published by Leonard Smithers, London. 4to. Signed with the artist's names and dated 1896. Pl. 416
$14\frac{5}{8} \times 11$ inches
Grenville L. Winthrop Bequest, Fogg Art Museum, Harvard University, Massachusetts

This title-page was first used in the first number of *The Savoy* and again for the second number; also for the gold-stamped design on the front covers of the publisher's cases of violet cloth as provided for binding the eight numbers of the periodical in three volumes; and also for the gold-stamped designs on the de luxe front covers of vellum.

418 John Bull in a cloak, holding with his right hand a quill and a draughtsman's pencil and pointing with his left hand toward the word Contents in Gothic lettering which was added on the printed page. Design for p. 7 preceding the page with the contents list in *The Savoy*, NO. 1, January 1896, edited by Arthur Symons and published by Leonard Smithers, London. 4to. Pl. 418
$9\frac{1}{16} \times 7$ inches
Scofield Thayer Collection, Fogg Art Museum, Harvard University, Massachusetts

The figure here was a non-provocative re-statement of the figure of Bull as formerly drawn for the second prospectus of *The Savoy*.

419 The Three Musicians. Intended illustration to the poem by Beardsley thus entitled on p. 65 of *The Savoy*, NO. 1, January 1896, edited by Arthur Symons and published by Leonard Smithers, London. 4to. Not used. Pl. 419
From the line-block

This design was considered provocative and was replaced by the one reproduced at Pl. 420. It was first published in *A Book of Fifty Drawings by Aubrey Beardsley*, Smithers, London, 1897, p. 167.

420 The Three Musicians. Illustration to the poem (p. 65) by Beardsley thus entitled on p. 64 of *The Savoy*, NO. 1, January 1896, edited by Arthur Symons and published by Leonard Smithers, London. 4to. Pl. 420
From the line-block

This design replaced the one at NO. 419. The actress, Sophie Menter, was, according to Beardsley in a letter to his sister, the heroine of the poem.

421 The Bathers. Illustration to the article 'Dieppe: 1895' by Arthur Symons on p. 87 of *The Savoy*, NO. 1, January 1896, edited by Arthur Symons and published by Leonard Smithers, London. 4to. Pl. 422
From the line-block

In the summer of 1895 Beardsley and Symons had been staying in Dieppe, and the illustrated article was one of the results of their encounters. While Symons enjoyed seeing women bathing on the beach, Beardsley seldom went out of doors and paid very little attention to the sea. The result is a moonscape with the familiar arc of flying birds in the sky to suggest the open air. Even more strange is the central figure with her high shoulders, flat breasts, long sixteenth-century waist and exaggerated pelvis. This is intended to be the actress Cléo de Mérode, who is referred to in the article as wearing a gold chain over her bathing dress—though in other respects the drawing scarcely corresponds with the description by Symons. Cléo de Mérode died in 1966.

2 Moska. Illustration to 'Dieppe: 1895' by Arthur Symons on p. 91 of *The Savoy*, NO. 1, January 1896, edited by Arthur Symons and published by Leonard Smithers, London. 4to. Pl. 421
From the line-block

'The dance has begun: it is the Moska, with its funny rhythm, its double stamp of the heels'. This passage in the article 'Dieppe: 1895' by Arthur Symons refers to a dance in the *Bals des Enfants* in the Casino at Dieppe, which occurred on certain afternoons and fascinated Beardsley. It is possible that such a fan would have been suspended on a ribbon, but Beardsley has not indicated this and the position of the hand is the only weakness in an otherwise remarkable drawing.

3 The Abbé. Drawing for illustration to *Under the Hill* by Aubrey Beardsley, reproduced on p. 157 in *The Savoy*, NO. 1, January 1896; edited by Arthur Symons and published by Leonard Smithers, London. 4to. Pl. 423
$9\frac{13}{16} \times 6\frac{7}{8}$ inches
Mr R. A. Harari, London

Under the Hill was the original title of Beardsley's unfinished novel which was to have been published by John Lane as *The Story of Venus and Tannhäuser*. The spavin-legged dandy originally represented the 'Abbé Aubrey' as the hero of the story: the Abbé Aubrey however was changed to the 'Abbé Fanfreluche', in *Under the Hill* as published in *The Savoy*, and to the 'Chevalier Tannhäuser' in the version of *The Story of Venus and Tannhäuser* published by Leonard Smithers in 1907. The drawing illustrates a passage at the beginning of *Under the Hill* on p. 156 of *The Savoy*, NO. 1. 'The place where he stood waved drowsily with strange flowers, heavy with perfume, dripping with odours. Gloomy and nameless weeds not to be found in Mentzelius. Huge moths, so richly winged they must have banqueted upon tapestries and royal stuffs, slept on the pillars that flanked either side of the gateway, and the eyes of all the moths remained open and were burning and bursting with a mesh of veins'.

4 The Toilet. Illustration to *Under the Hill* by Aubrey Beardsley, Chapter II, reproduced on p. 161 of *The Savoy*, NO. 1, January 1896, edited by Arthur Symons and published by Leonard Smithers, London. 4to. Pl. 424
From the line-block

This illustration was later called 'The Toilet of Helen', under which name the Venus of the original story appears in *Under the Hill*. The seated figure on the right represents 'Mrs Marsuple', the fat manicure and fardeuse.

Pl. 424 has been made from one of the prints of 1896 in which parts of the reproduction were defective, giving broken lines, patches of white etc. in the floor and the figures of the two dwarfs. Later reproductions were made from the same line-block print of 1896, and exaggerated these defects.

425 The Fruit Bearers. Drawing for illustration to *Under the Hill* by Aubrey Beardsley, Chapter III, reproduced on p. 167 of *The Savoy*, NO. 1, January 1896; edited by Arthur Symons and published by Leonard Smithers, London. 4to. Pl. 425
$9\frac{3}{4} \times 6\frac{7}{8}$ inches
Scofield Thayer Collection, Fogg Art Museum, Harvard University, Massachusetts

426 A Large Christmas Card. The Virgin and Child on a card loosely inserted at the end of *The Savoy*, NO. 1, January 1896; edited by Arthur Symons and published by Leonard Smithers, London. 4to. Signed with the artist's names. Pl. 429
From the line-block

Beardsley himself had a low opinion of this design for a Christmas card.

427 Choosing the New Hat. Front cover of *The Savoy*, NO. 2, April 1896, edited by Arthur Symons and published by Leonard Smithers, London, 4to. Pl. 427
From the line-block

The cover was of pink boards with the design in black. The same design was printed on white paper as a plate at the end of the volume, p. 201. Beardsley's very personal ideas of tall Roman capitals, with the unbalanced S, the high-barred A and the small Y, which appeared first on the front cover of NO. 1 of *The Savoy*, were retained for NOS. 2–7. The background of the composition has been evolved from looking at French prints of the 1780s, whether by Moreau, Eisen or St Aubin scarcely matters. The clothes of the women are strictly of the late nineteenth century, but survive well in a Louis Seize atmosphere. The page, or hatter's apprentice, is a creature of the 1780s, but also the last-but-one manifestation of the foetal obsession of 1893 to occur in Beardsley's work; *not* an infant, he wrote to Smithers, 'but an unstrangled abortion'. The name of the hat-shop 'Elise', in slanted facsimile handwriting, and the date 19 . . ., are memories of the dying nineteenth century carried over to a dream of the living present, which for Beardsley at that date was in the last years of the *ancien régime* of the previous century.

428 A Footnote. Illustration on p. 185 preceding the instalment of *Under the Hill* in *The Savoy*, NO. 2, April 1896; edited by Arthur Symons and published by Leonard Smithers, London. 4to. Pl. 428
From the line-block

This self-portrait by Beardsley was reproduced in gold on the scarlet front cover of *The Second Book of Fifty Drawings by Aubrey Beardsley*, Smithers, London, 1899, but with Pan's torso and the cord deleted. It is a vital point to comprehend that the artist saw himself as tethered to the pagan god Pan, and he emphasizes this affinity by exaggerating the faun-like ears. Also it must be noted that this is the only representation of Beardsley's legs that we have: if they were really like this, then the spavin-shaped Abbé (who was originally the 'Abbé Aubrey', NO. 423), the knock-kneed Siegfried (NO. 164) and similar figures in his work as a whole can be understood as partly self-identified.

429 The Ascension of Saint Rose of Lima. Illustration to a passage in *Under the Hill* by Aubrey Beardsley (Chapter IV) on p. 189 in *The Savoy*, NO. 2, April 1896; edited by Arthur Symons and published by Leonard Smithers, London. 4to. Pl. 426
From the line-block

The aesthetic and baroque elements in later Roman Catholic legends began to appeal to Beardsley, especially in 1896 when his friendship with André Raffalovich and John Gray, both homosexuals converted to Catholicism, became more necessary to him. This illustration and its treatment are leading in a direction later explored in literary terms by Ronald Firbank, in such novels as *The Flower Beneath the Foot* (1923).

430 The Third Tableau of Das Rheingold. Drawing reproduced on p. 193 in *The Savoy*, NO. 2, April 1896; edited by Arthur Symons and published by Leonard Smithers, London. 4to. Pl. 430
$10 \times 6\frac{7}{8}$ inches
Museum of Art, Rhode Island School of Design, U.S.A.

The figures represent Wotan, Loge and Fafner in Wagner's operatic cycle The Ring, and the drawing is one of a group by Beardsley illustrating subjects in *Das Rheingold* (see NOS. 438, 446, 447, 448, 449).

431 The Driving of Cupid from the Garden. Design for the panel below the title on the front wrapper of *The Savoy*, NO. 3, July 1896; edited by Arthur Symons and published by Leonard Smithers, London. 4to. Signed in capitals 'Aubrey Beardsley Etc.' Pl. 431
$9\frac{3}{4} \times 7\frac{3}{8}$ inches
National Gallery of South Australia, Adelaide

The design was printed in black, with title in red, on light blue paper for the wrapper, and in black on white paper for the first page of the volume.
The old man in the odd cap is making advances to the young woman. Cupid, muffled in a cloak, is hastening away from them.

432 Puck on Pegasus. Drawing for decoration on the title-pages of *The Savoy*, NOS. 3–8; edited by Arthur Symons and published by Leonard Smithers, London, 1896. 4to. Signed with the artist's initials. Pl. 432
$9 \times 6\frac{7}{8}$ inches
Scofield Thayer Collection, Fogg Art Museum, Harvard University, Massachusetts

A small version of the Puck emblem was used for the imprint on many of the books published by Smithers.

433 The Coiffing. Reproduction in *The Savoy*, NO. 3, July 1896, p. [90]; edited by Arthur Symons and published by Leonard Smithers, London. 4to. Illustration to Beardsley's own poem

'The Ballad of a Barber' on p. [91]. Signed with the artist's names. Pl. 434
From the line-block

To understand this composition in the sense that Beardsley intended, it should be necessary to read the poem it illustrates. It is sufficient to say that the capable, brilliant barber, with his ornate hair framing a sly, domed, constipated, feminine face set on the form of a female, and wearing a symbolic apron tied with a sash at the back, is so ravished by the pretty little princess of thirteen whose hair he has been tending that he destroys her, and then tiptoes out of the room on pointed feet. Soon afterwards he is hanged.

The drawing is in the same line of development as the second frontispiece to *An Evil Motherhood* (NO. 395) which itself links up iconographically with the outline engravings of Henry Moses and other Neo-Classic artists of the Regency. The varying strengths of line help to give depth, or an illusion of space, to the composition. The orderly flight of birds outside the window is contrasted with the dangerously placed *art nouveau* vase on the edge of the Victorian table with its attenuated and abruptly-curved cabriole leg. For all the richness of the background, the whole effect is suggestive not of a palace but of a late Victorian house in the suburbs, which makes the illustration all the more alarming, because the barber's act becomes furtive and commonplace. From a technical standpoint this must count as one of Beardsley's finest drawings: and yet, looking back upon it now, it seems to betray and not to illustrate his poem.

434 Cul-de-lampe illustrating Beardsley's poem 'The Ballad of a Barber' on p. [93] in *The Savoy*, NO. 3, July 1896; edited by Arthur Symons and published by Leonard Smithers, London. 4to. Signed with the artist's initials. Pl. 436
From the line-block

A reminder that Beardsley's craft was linked to the silhouette tradition of the eighteenth and nineteenth centuries. How far he had studied pictorial silhouettes, if at all, is not known. A silhouette caricature of himself was published in *A Book of Fifty Drawings by Aubrey Beardsley*, Leonard Smithers, London, 1897. His maternal grandmother, Susan Lambe, had been a skilled silhouettist; but there is no evidence that Beardsley was inspired by, or even saw, her portraits in this medium.

435 Design for the panel below the title on the front wrapper of *The Savoy*, NO. 4, August 1896, edited by Arthur Symons and published by Leonard Smithers, London. 4to. Signed with the artist's names. Pl. 433
$9\frac{3}{8} \times 7$ inches
Mr John Hay Whitney, New York

The design was printed in black with title in red on light blue paper for the wrapper, and on white paper for the first page of the volume. The heaped grapes, symbolizing August, are comparable with the heaped fruit on a much more ornate stand, approached by a woman in similar fashion, in Beardsley's drawing called 'Autumn' made for a calendar (see NO. 381). The figure and stand on *The Savoy* wrapper are the other way round, however. And the figure's relation to the curtain is comparable with the relation of figure and curtain in the poster for the Avenue Theatre (NO. 319). But the design of the poster is more successful. Here the curtain simply takes up half the panel and is perfunctorily drawn. The sequence of the three forms is ineffective: the heavy stand, the white but transparent figure and the transparent but seemingly opaque curtain do not succeed as a witty composition, but they leave the impression that Beardsley's former mastery of disbalance was beginning to desert him. This in fact was the case, as many of his latest works indicate.

436 Front wrapper of *The Savoy*, NO. 5, September 1896; edited by Arthur Symons and published by Leonard Smithers, London. 4to. Signed in capitals at left bottom 'Giulio Floriani'. Pl. 438
From the line-block and letterpress

The signature was a joke. The original drawing for this cover was done at Boscombe, Bournemouth, when Beardsley was seriously ill. The backgrounds of certain pictures by Watteau, and even by Claude, are distantly echoed in the atmosphere of the lake, with its dark banks and overgrown Terms. There are affinities here with 'The Mysterious Rose Garden' (NO. 366), though the drawing is by comparison perfunctory. As on all the wrappers from NO. 3 to NO. 7, the title was printed in red, the rest being printed in black; the paper was light blue.

437 The Woman in White. Plate reproducing a sketch in white on toned paper on p. 53 of *The Savoy*, NO. 5, September 1896; edited by Arthur Symons and published by Leonard Smithers, London. 4to. Signed with the artist's names. Pl. 437
From the half-tone plate

The drawing evokes the title of Wilkie Collins's famous novel, but was not necessarily an illustration connected with it. In fact it was based, though it is not known exactly when, on a drawing reproduced as a vignette in *Bon-Mots* of Lamb and Jerrold, 1893, p. 48; and again in *Bon-Mots* of Foote and Hook, 1894, p. 17, as the left half of a composite headpiece.

438 The Fourth Tableau of Das Rheingold. Drawing for the front wrapper of *The Savoy*, NO. 6, October 1896; edited by Arthur Symons and published by Leonard Smithers, London. 4to. Signed with initials. Inscribed in pencil in top panel 'pierce' within an oval flourish. Pl. 440
12 × 8⅝ inches
Mr R. A. Harari, London

For the 'Third Tableau' see NO. 430. Together with a design for a frontispiece, and drawings of 'Flosshilde', 'Alberich', and 'Erda', this formed part of a series illustrating 'Das Rheingold' which Beardsley never completed. The figures here represent Wotan and Loge in Wagner's operatic cycle. The composition is one of the most boldly disbalanced of all Beardsley's inventions; and the flame-shaped hair on the head, chest and navel of Loge, harmonizing with his draperies, has no precedent in European art, except in the hair of the elderly Lacedemonian ambassador in plate 8 of *The Lysistrata* (1896), which however grows in clusters downwards.

439 The Death of Pierrot. Illustration on p. 33 in *The Savoy*, NO. 6, October 1896; edited by Arthur Symons and published by Leonard Smithers, London. 4to. Signed with the artist's names. Pl. 435

From line-block proof on Japanese vellum, 8 × 5⅜ inches
Mr W. G. Good, England

A text printed (on p. 32) opposite this illustration reads: 'As the dawn broke, Pierrot fell into his last sleep. Then upon tip-toe, silently up the stair, noiselessly into the room, came the comedians Arlecchino, Pantaleone, il Dottore, and Columbina, who with much love carried away upon their shoulders, the white frocked clown of Bergamo; whither we know not.' The brilliance of the composition and the rendering of different textures and patterns are among Beardsley's triumphs. Identifying himself in some degree, like so many men of the Nineties, with the character of Pierrot in the old Commedia dell'Arte, Beardsley was haunted by the irony of his own acceptance of rapidly approaching death.

440 First page of *The Savoy*, NO. 7, November 1896; edited by Arthur Symons and published by Leonard Smithers, London. 4to. Same design on front wrapper of light blue paper with title in red. Pl. 439
From the line-block

The headdress of the Pedant, like a bandage, and even his profile, take us back to the man with a foetus in the *Bon-Mots* of Smith and Sheridan, p. 26 (NO. 172). He wears a smock and cravat like an artist of the old guard. The youth who suffers from his pedantry has the bald forehead and the cap of Watteau's pierrots: characteristically the pattern on his jacket has a life apart from the form of the garment, even though a few lines representing folds break the continuity; and the effect beside the grass, stylized in a Japanese manner, is almost that of a painting by Braque, in terms of black and white only.

441 Ave Atque Vale. Illustration to the translation by Aubrey Beardsley of Carmen CI by Catullus. Reproduced on p. 53 in *The Savoy*, NO. 7, November 1896; edited by Arthur Symons and published by Leonard Smithers, London, 4to. Signed with the artist's names and initials. Inscribed in pencil on the back 'Keep the white dots as small as possible AB'. And inscribed also in pencil in another hand 'No reduction, Satur morn Smithers'. Pl. 441
6¾ × 4⅛ inches
Mr John Hay Whitney, New York

It was because Beardsley was such a master of design, in the sense that he knew how to make the most of black against white, that this drawing is so riveting. For example, nobody questions the solidity of the youth's torso, which is defined by the very minimum of detail, a navel and a nipple (placed slightly too far to the right so as to give a broad-chested effect, and also the effect of an arrested movement of the youth to his right); yet the body of the torso is as white as the white background. The absence of the trees behind the head would have impoverished the design. As usual the heavy disbalance is redeemed, in this case by the upflung arm breaking the white ground on the left. There is a single weakness, and that a typical one: the thumb is too small.

Only the initials AB appeared in the line-block in *The Savoy*, NO. 7. It must be admitted that the poem and the drawing which illustrates it had a fatal relevance to Beardsley's own short life, then nearing its end: 'Hail and Farewell'.

442 First page of *The Savoy*, NO. 8, December 1896, edited by

Arthur Symons and published by Leonard Smithers, London, 4to. Signed with the artist's initials and lettered with title. Same design, all in black, on front wrapper of light blue paper. See also NO. 453. Pl. 442
From the line-block

The figure was probably intended for one of the Ali Baba series (see NOS. 458, 459).

443 Mrs Pinchwife: From Wycherley's *Country Wife*. Reproduction on p. 31 in *The Savoy*, NO. 8, December 1896, edited by Arthur Symons and published by Leonard Smithers, London. 4to. Signed with the artist's initials and lettered with title. Pl. 443
From the line-block

Floating on the tide of sexual ambivalence released by Gautier in *Mademoiselle de Maupin*, Beardsley, who illustrated that book (see NOS. 487–492), was attracted to any manifestation of transvestism, whether by males in female clothes, or by females in male clothes, as here. Male impersonation had been a recognized feature of theatrical entertainment, especially pantomime, since the eighteenth century in England and was not considered burlesque. Female impersonation by males, although going back to *Twelfth Night*, had become by the nineteenth century largely an excuse for the soothing of unconscious ambivalence by laughter.

444 A Repetition of 'Tristan und Isolde'. Drawing reproduced on p. [11] in *The Savoy*, NO. 8, December 1896; edited by Arthur Symons and published by Leonard Smithers, London. 4to. Signed with initials. Pl. 444
$7\frac{1}{4} \times 6\frac{3}{8}$ inches
Mr R. A. Harari, London

445 Don Juan, Sganarelle, and the Beggar. From Molière's *Don Juan*. Illustration reproduced on p. 29 of *The Savoy*, NO. 8, December 1896; edited by Arthur Symons and published by Leonard Smithers, London. 4to. Pl. 445
$8 \times 4\frac{3}{4}$ inches
Scofield Thayer Collection, Fogg Art Museum, Harvard University, Massachusetts

The postures of Sganarelle leaning on his cane, and of Don Juan with his extended arm were undoubtedly suggested by the two chief figures on the left of Watteau's painting 'The Italian Comedians', after which an engraving was made in the eighteenth century. Beardsley has given his own type of Pierrot head, itself inspired by Watteau's pierrots, to the figure of Don Juan.

446 Frontispiece to The Comedy of the Rheingold. Reproduction on p. 43 in *The Savoy*, NO. 8, December 1896; edited by Arthur Symons and published by Leonard Smithers, London. 4to. Signed 'By Aubrey Beardsley' in capitals after the bottom line of the title as above, and dated 1897 in Roman numerals. Pl. 450
From the line-block.

'The Comedy of the Rhinegold' was a publication never achieved. It was to have included Beardsley's 'Third Tableau' (*Savoy*, NO. 2) and 'Fourth Tableau' (*Savoy*, NO. 6), and 'Flosshilde', 'Erda' and 'Alberich', these last three and the frontispiece being published in *The Savoy*, NO. 8. The use of

waves and strands of female hair as symbolic and decorative formulae was by now well established by *art nouveau* artists, among others by Mucha in Paris. Beardsley's treatment of it is in terms of the close-laid lines he used so frequently; but when he illustrated *Le Morte Darthur* his rendering of hair, however fetichist, was much more abstract, and in that sense more prophetic (see NO. 105).

447 Flosshilde. The second in a series of four illustrations intended for 'The Comedy of the Rhinegold' (never completed), reproduced on p. 45 in *The Savoy*, NO. 8, December 1896; edited by Arthur Symons and published by Leonard Smithers, London. 4to. Inscribed in pencil on the back 'Flosshilde Same size Smithers'. Stamped with collector's mark. Pl. 446
$2\frac{1}{2} \times 3\frac{1}{2}$ inches
Mr John Hay Whitney, New York

In the same last volume of *The Savoy* also appeared the 'Frontispiece to The Comedy of the Rhinegold' (NO. 446), 'Erda' (NO. 449), and 'Alberich' (NO. 448). The survival of the Japanese-Burne-Jones formula for land in the middle distance is notable in the waves of the hair of Flosshilde. The drawing has all of Beardsley's wing-movement compositional style, but the dots of the scarf are, for him, rough and uneven. Contemporary German interest in Beardsley is proved by the reproduction on a small scale of this illustration, from the *Savoy* plate, on the penultimate page on *Jugend*, NO. 5, 29 January 1898. Flosshilde was one of the daughters of the Rhine who guarded its gold in 'Das Rheingold', the first of the four music dramas in *Der Ring des Nibelungen* (1869).

448 Alberich. The third in a series of four illustrations intended for 'The Comedy of the Rheingold' (never completed) reproduced on p. 47 in *The Savoy*, NO. 8, December 1896; edited by Arthur Symons and published by Leonard Smithers. 4to. Pl. 451
Scofield Thayer Collection, Fogg Art Museum, Harvard University, Massachusetts

The drawing for this illustration belonged at one time to Herbert J. Pollitt, a friend of Beardsley, and of Wilde, and who later took up the study of Black Magic with Aleister Crowley. The Nibelung, Alberich, is depicted here as a sort of Caliban, a *Bon-Mots* monster more realistically conceived. In 'Das Rheingold', the first of the four music dramas forming Wagner's *Der Ring des Nibelungen*, Alberich is the malevolent character who renounces Love to acquire the Rhine gold by theft.

449 Erda. The fourth in a series of four illustrations intended for 'The Comedy of the Rheingold' (never completed) reproduced on p. 49 in *The Savoy*, NO. 8, December 1896; edited by Arthur Symons and published by Leonard Smithers, London, 4to. Inscribed with title. Pl. 447
$5\frac{7}{16} \times 3\frac{1}{2}$ inches
The British Museum

The pouches under the eyes, the tired mouth, the voluminous breasts and the hair which envelops her, all contribute to Beardsley's idea of the goddess of wisdom and mother of the Valkyrs in Wagner's music drama *Der Ring des Nibelungen*. But the artist is working in the vein of Baudelaire and Rops, in which Woman was the instrument of Evil, presumably without conscious effort. The breasts are diagrammatic and suggest once again that there was a limit to Beardsley's feeling for the secondary sexual characteristics. Erda's rolling hair is in the movement, since hair fetishism was recurrent from the days of Rossetti, both in English and continental art; but it is somewhat confused with the landscape, perhaps because it illustrates the passage in 'Das Rheingold' in which she emerges from a rocky cleft.

450 Felix Mendelssohn-Bartholdy. The composer with his head and bow-tied cravat on a larger scale than the rest, sitting in a chair to right, holding a large quill. Drawing reproduced on p. 63 of *The Savoy* NO. 8, December 1896; edited by Arthur Symons and published by Leonard Smithers, London. 4to. Signed with the artist's initials and titled as above. Pl. 448
$6\frac{3}{8} \times 4\frac{1}{16}$ inches
Grenville L. Winthrop Bequest, Fogg Art Museum, Harvard University, Massachusetts

451 Count Valmont. Illustration to *Les Liaisons Dangereuses* by Choderlos de Laclos, on p. 71 of *The Savoy*, NO. 8, December 1896; edited by Arthur Symons and published by Leonard Smithers, London. 4to. Pl. 452
From the line-block

Only Beardsley would have thought of representing the pivotal character of this novel, naked apparently, under a cloak. The aggressive-looking hand expresses a similar impatience to the snapping toes on the feet of 'The Impatient Adulterer' (not reproduced). The peculiar thick-featured face will be found again in 'The Impatient Adulterer' and 'Juvenal Scourging Woman' (NO. 468) and seems to have represented for Beardsley a symbol of masculine violence and virility.

452 Et in Arcadia Ego. Drawing reproduced on p. 89 in *The Savoy*, NO. 8, December 1896; edited by Arthur Symons and published by Leonard Smithers, London. 4to. Signed with initials. Pl. 449
$8\frac{1}{2} \times 5\frac{7}{8}$ inches
Princeton University Library

The middle-aged dandy with button-boots and waxed moustache approaches on tip-toe the mysterious monument to one who, like himself, had once lived in Arcady. There is a burlesque reference to the inscription on the tomb in Poussin's picture 'Les Bergers d'Arcadie' in the Louvre; and moreover to Leonard Smithers's shop which at this date had been moved to the Royal Arcade, London. Perhaps Beardsley had noticed the phrase in Kenneth Grahame's 'The Olympians' in *Pagan Papers*, 1894, for which he designed a title.

453 *The Savoy* complete in three volumes, price one guinea nett. Leonard Smithers, Royal Arcade, W. A small poster or show-card with the design of Beardsley's front wrapper of *The Savoy*, NO. 8, December 1896. Signed with intials in left bottom corner. Pl. 453
Colour lithograph, $9\frac{5}{16} \times 6\frac{7}{8}$ inches
Mr Anthony d'Offay, London

This show-card advertises the set of three volumes bound in violet cloth containing all eight numbers of *The Savoy*.

Beardsley's growing desire to embellish his black-and-white designs with colours is shown in the way this litho-graph was produced. On 23 October 1896 he wrote to Smithers asking for two or three pulls from the line-block used for the wrapper of *The Savoy*, NO. 8. These were to be 'on water-colourable paper, it will be better not to paint on the original [drawing]'. Then on 1 November he wrote: 'Here is the posterette. Do not be troubled about the unevenness of colour (not intentional). Lithographer must not of course attempt to reproduce brush marks which are inevitable. The green is *emerald green* & a little black the red, *pure vermilion* the yellow chrome orange the grey simple black and white mixture.'

The chief additions to the *Savoy* cover design (which was all black) were the thick vertical and horizontal bars of black. The backgrounds to those in the top and bottom panels were green and the outlines of the tops of the letters of the word 'Savoy' were of the same colour. The backgrounds of the central panel and the border and the shoes, were red; and the ankles and pink jacket were achieved by grained 'tints' of this colour. The grey hat was obtained by a grained 'tint' of black.

454 Pencil sketch in pencil and ink of a young girl. On the back of the drawing 'A Footnote', Beardsley's self-portrait reproduced in *The Savoy*, NO. 2, April 1896 (see NO. 428). Reproduced as Pl. 7 in *Early Work*, 1899.
From the half-tone plate
It was Beardsley's habit to begin his work with a baroque scribble of pencil lines which suggested a great deal, later to be fused into the beautifully poised pattern of outlines he placed over them. Such a technique demands concentration and firmness of touch in quite unusual degrees.

455 Apollo pursuing Daphne. Unfinished drawing. Pl. 455
Indian ink and pencil, size unknown
Present owner unknown

The incomplete left leg ends in a pencil sketch of the left ankle and foot. The rest of the drawing is in ink, apparently. Once it belonged to Herbert J. Pollitt, who bought several drawings from Beardsley, including the bookplate design at NO. 471 and 'The Impatient Adulterer'. It was exhibited at the Galeries Shirleys, Paris, in February 1907, and was NO. 13 in a catalogue of this exhibition, which contained a brief foreword by Pollitt. 'Ali Baba', 'Erda' and the bookplate design, all in Pollitt's collection, were shown at this exhibition and were marked as not for sale; the Apollo drawing however was afterwards the property of Count Robert de Montesquiou-Fezansac, the poet and social paladin who died in 1921 (information from Mr W. G. Good, based on entries in an unpublished catalogue by R. A. Walker in his possession). Together with the 'Children Decorating a Terminal God', which Beardsley presented in 1892 to Puvis de Chavannes, the drawing is among the few works by Beardsley known to have been in French hands. Incomplete as it is, this design is one of his most successful achievements in pure outline, and dates probably from 1896. The figure of Daphne is missing, but a nipple of one of her breasts and part of a laurel tree remain beside Apollo's outstretched hand.

The drawing was first reproduced in R. A. Walker's *Some Unknown Drawings of Aubrey Beardsley*, London, 1923, NO. 29.

456 Design for the front cover of *The Life and Times of Madame Du Barry* by R. B. Douglas, published by Leonard Smithers,

London, 1896. Signed with initials, right and left. Pl. 456
$9\frac{9}{16} \times 6\frac{1}{16}$ inches
Princeton University Library

The design was stamped in gold, without the surrounding lines, on the violet book cover. The form of the canopy is to be found in French stage designs of the eighteenth century.

457 Design for the front cover of *Verses* by Ernest Dowson, published by Leonard Smithers, London, 1896. Signed with initials. Pl. 457
$7\frac{3}{8} \times 5\frac{3}{8}$ inches
Mrs Hippisley-Coxe, England

The curves of this exceptionally economic design, which is near to nothing, may be said to reflect, in Beardsley's idiosyncratic style, a current *art nouveau* form. The design was stamped in gold on parchment board.

458 Ali Baba. Drawing for the front cover design of *The Forty Thieves,* a projected publication never undertaken. Signed with initials and titled as above. Pl. 458
$9\frac{7}{16} \times 7\frac{13}{16}$ inches
Grenville L. Winthrop Bequest, Fogg Art Museum, Harvard University, Massachusetts

The drawing was reproduced in *A Second Book of Fifty Drawings,* Smithers, London, 1899, pl. 41.

It combines something of the old *Yellow Book* dramatic contrast between black and white forms and, in the seemingly coruscating jewels, something of the tense detail of *The Rape of the Lock* series. The lettering of the title is remarkable in being as near as Beardsley ever got to true Roman lettering: compare the title of the cover of *The Savoy,* NO. 1, which has a more period look.

459 Ali Baba in the Wood. Illustration intended for a projected version of *The Forty Thieves.* First published in *A Book of Fifty Drawings by Aubrey Beardsley,* Smithers, London, 1897, p. 147. Pl. 459
$9\frac{5}{16} \times 6\frac{15}{16}$ inches
Scofield Thayer Collection, Fogg Art Museum, Harvard University, Massachusetts

The crowded leaves of the thicket are suggested, or rather symbolized, by white dots of varying sizes and at calculated distances from each other on a black background, in which close-laid lines represent the trunks of the trees. All the whites in this drawing are left in reserve, not applied on the black background—an amazing technical feat.

460–66 Drawings for *The Lysistrata of Aristophanes* Now First Wholly Translated into English and illustrated with eight full-page drawings by Aubrey Beardsley, and published by Leonard Smithers for private distribution, London, 1896. All signed with the artist's names, except for the fifth which is unsigned. The first titled 'Lysistrata'.
Indian ink with traces of pencil, each $10\frac{1}{4} \times 7$ inches
In private possession, London

The eight drawings by Beardsley for *The Lysistrata* (translated by Samuel Smith and published in a limited edition by Smithers) were made at the Spread Eagle Hotel, Epsom, in the summer of 1896. Seven of the eight drawings are reproduced here: the other one, which belonged at one time to

Herbert Horne and was destroyed in a fire, is represented by a reproduction from the collotype facsimile made of it for a portfolio of reproductions after the whole series in the 1920s.

460 Lysistrata shielding her Coynte. Drawing for the frontispiece. Pl. 460

461 The Toilet of Lampito. Drawing for the illustration facing p. 4. Pl. 461

462 Lysistrata Haranguing the Athenian Women. Drawing for the illustration facing p. 12. Pl. 462

463 Lysistrata Defending the Acropolis. Drawing for the illustration facing p. 30. Pl. 463

464 Cinesias Entreating Myrrhina to Coition. Drawing for the illustration facing p. 44. Pl. 464

465 The Examination of the Herald. Drawing for the illustration facing p. 46. Pl. 465

466 The Lacedaemonian Ambassadors. Drawing for the illustration facing p. 50. Pl. 466

Beardsley had studied Greek vase painting in 1894 at the British Museum, and the Lysistrata drawings reflect something of the Greek vase spirit, including the bawdiness, without perhaps much of the spontaneity of Greek draughtsmanship. The absence of backgrounds, as in the *Salome* illustrations, makes the designs of closed outlines and bold dots and rare decorated blacks, all the more dramatic. The most elegant of the series are 'The Toilet of Lampito' and 'Cinesias Entreating Myrrhina to Coition': the boldest are the first, which was reproduced as a frontispiece; 'Lysistrata Haranguing the Athenian Women', where the heroine of the play is seen urging a band of Athenian women to give up sexual relations with their husbands – and the frustration of these women is inspiring, in one case, a lesbian gesture; and 'The Lacedaemonian Ambassadors' which has startling and absurd qualities. The tallest and youngest of the ambassadors has a heaped-up head of hair like the 'hermaphrodite' figure in 'The Mirror of Love' (see NO. 386), and like so many of the young males in the *Morte Darthur* illustrations. The phalluses are abnormally large to symbolize frustration and anticipation. But the morbid defect of this drawing lies not in the sizes of the phalluses, which are referred to in the text of the play at this point, but in the comic cartoon rays which may symbolize an inflamed ulcer on the dwarf – the inference being that this undersized person reaches oversize in one respect, not to be outdone by manipulations in the manner of accomplished Japanese courtesans. This was perhaps Beardsley's reference to the representations of that subject in the erotic prints by Utamaro which William Rothenstein had given him. Oddly enough the footgear of the elderly man is designed in the mediaeval vein of *Le Morte Darthur*; that of the tall youth in a style of late seventeenth-century pastiche, which seems to have followed the eighteenth-century pastiche of *The Rape of the Lock*.

It is difficult to believe that the decorated black stockings in 'The Toilet of Lampito' and 'Lysistrata Defending the

Acropolis' were not, in fact, stylized and dramatized memorizations of those similar stockings in prints by Félicien Rops —'Pornokrates' and 'Les Cousines de la Colonelle', for example—although Robert Ross denied that Beardsley knew anything about this Belgian interpreter of Woman as the instrument of Evil (R. Ross, *Aubrey Beardsley*, London, 1909, p. 40). Yet Beardsley mentioned Rops in a letter of December 1896 to Smithers.

467 Two Athenian Women in Distress. Reproduction of the drawing for the illustration facing p. 34 in *The Lysistrata of Aristophanes* Now First Wholly Translated into English and illustrated with eight full-page drawings by Aubrey Beardsley. Printed privately by Leonard Smithers, London 1896. 4to. Signed with the artist's names. Pl. 467
From a collotype
Victoria and Albert Museum, London

See NOS. 460–466. Beardsley's fifth drawing for *The Lysistrata* was never in the possession of Herbert Pollitt but belonged to Herbert Horne. The rest of Horne's series of *Lysistrata* drawings were copies, but all were subsequently destroyed in a fire. Before the fire a set of collotypes, reproducing the seven Pollitt drawings and the one Horne original, was issued by Philip Sainsbury, on paper water-marked AB. This set was not dated but appeared about 1925. The original drawing for 'Two Athenian Women in Distress' was of course reproduced by line-block in the book issued by Smithers in 1896. The later collotype plate however was a closer reproduction of the drawing and has been used here instead of the contemporary line-block for that reason.

The subjects of this illustration are in fact less erotic than might, at first glance, have been supposed. They refer to Lysistrata's complaints that she cannot keep the women away from their husbands. 'I found . . . another one slipping down by the pulley ; . . . and another one I dragged off a sparrow by the hair yesterday just as she was ready to fly down to the house of Orsilochus (A well-known pander. *Translator's note*).' The passage occurs on p. 36 of the book printed by Smithers in 1896.

468 Juvenal Scourging Woman. Illustration to the Sixth Satire of Juvenal, 1896. Signed with the artist's names and dated. Pl. 468
$9\frac{3}{8} \times 6\frac{3}{4}$ inches
Princeton University Library

This was one of the drawings published by Leonard Smithers in *An Issue of Five Drawings Illustrative of Juvenal and Lucian*, London, 1906.

Stylistically it belongs to the same group as 'The Lysistrata' illustrations: strong outlines, no massed blacks, no backgrounds. Beardsley's ambivalent approach to women is revealed in the treatment, let alone choice, of the subject. For his conception of the reversal of roles in flagellation see the frontispiece to *Earl Lavender* (NO. 383).

469 Bathyllus in the Swan Dance. Illustration to the Sixth Satire of Juvenal. Entitled 'Bathyllus'. Pl. 469
$6\frac{1}{8} \times 5\frac{3}{8}$ inches
Mr R. A. Harari, London

A companion drawing to this was called 'Bathyllus Posturing' (NO. 470). Both were published by Leonard Smithers in *An Issue of Five Drawings Illustrative of Juvenal and Lucian*, London, 1906. There is a brief reference early in the Sixth Satire to an effeminate young man, Bathyllus, acting the part of Leda in a ballet.

470 Bathyllus Posturing. Illustration to the Sixth Satire of Juvenal. From *An Issue of Five Drawings Illustrative of Juvenal and Lucian*, published by Leonard Smithers, London, 1906. Pl. 470
From the line-block
Victoria and Albert Museum, London

Smithers published smaller versions of the three Juvenal designs in Pompeian-red line-blocks, in 1903, at 'The Jesus Press'.

471 Design intended for the bookplate of the artist; not used by Beardsley but by Herbert J. Pollitt. Signed with the artist's initials. Pl. 471
$6\frac{7}{8} \times 4\frac{5}{8}$ inches
Scofield Thayer Collection, Fogg Art Museum, Harvard University, Massachusetts

In the Gallatin Collection at the Princeton University Library is a proof of the bookplate embodying this design, and Roman lettering in the space at the top spelling the name of Pollitt. This man, Herbert Charles Pollitt (1871–1942), who took the name of Jerome, came to know Beardsley late in the artist's life, and formed a collection of his drawings including 'The Impatient Adulterer', intended as a Juvenal illustration, but too amusingly nasty for publication, and not one of Beardsley's best works. The proof of the bookplate is inscribed in pencil, 'This could be better A.B.'. Whether by that Beardsley meant the design, or the quality of the line-block, it is difficult to see how the result could in fact have been better. The fully-fashioned nude woman gratified a singular impulse of Beardsley's own, and the misshapen punchinello, bald and neurotic in appearance, with a peascod stomach falling over his sash and both covering and revealing an erection, looks prudishly away from the woman's delta which promises a pleasure not for the likes of him. The position of the knot on his sash is very strange, and has a similar effect to that of the rose on the figure of the saint in the 'Ascension of Saint Rose of Lima' (NO. 429). That such an arresting vision should happen to be drawn with obvious conviction is a sadly ironical comment when considered in the light of Beardsley's personal history.

472 Self-portrait by Beardsley. Half-length, profile to the left, in outline. Pl. 472
From the line-block

First published in Percival Pollard's *Posters in Miniature*, New York, 1896. The coat is Regency in cut, the frilled shirt an imaginary garment.

473 Design for the front cover of *A Book of Fifty Drawings by Aubrey Beardsley*, with an iconography by Aymer Vallance, published by Leonard Smithers, London, 1897. 4to. Signed with the artist's names and initials. Pl. 473
$8\frac{1}{8} \times 6\frac{3}{4}$ inches
Scofield Thayer Collection, Fogg Art Museum, Harvard University, Massachusetts

On the front cover was added in capitals at bottom left of the right-hand panel, 'London Leonard Smithers Royal Arcade. W 1897'. In September 1896 Smithers had moved his bookselling premises from Effingham House, Arundel Street, Strand, London, to 4 and 5 Royal Arcade, Bond Street, which address appeared on the title-page of the book. The design for the cover appears to have been made by Beardsley about this time, in September 1896. 'The Death of Pierrot', which was published in NO. 6 of *The Savoy*, and the present drawing were the last to bear Beardsley's full names as his signature.

The empty panel on the left, linked by a flying bird to the pictorial panel on the right, is a witty feature typical of Beardsley, who could always transform a fashionable lay-out by introducing some unexpected element of design.

474 Title-page of *The Parade*, an Illustrated Gift Book for Boys and Girls, 1897, published by H. Henry and Company Ltd., 93 St Martin's Lane, London, 1897. 4to. Pl. 474
From the line-block and letterpress

The lettering is in golden brown. Beardsley designed the black decorative branch only. This has its antecedents in *Le Morte Darthur*, but the hairpin bends and whiplash curves are no longer related to natural forms, and the floral lamp with tasselled cords, which grows out of the bottom twig, is even more capricious.

475 Frontispiece to *A Book of Bargains* by Vincent O'Sullivan, published by Leonard Smithers, London, 1896. 8vo. Signed with initials. Pl. 475
From the line-block
Dr Ian Fletcher Reading, England

The frontispiece illustrates 'The Business of Madame Jahn', one of a collection of macabre short stories by O'Sullivan. The figure represents an apparition, cleverly suggested from the shoulders downwards by dotted outlines and contrasted with the hard actuality of the boldly outlined desk.

476 Design for the front cover of Ernest Dowson's *The Pierrot of the Minute*, a dramatic phantasy in one act, published by Leonard Smithers, London, March 1897. Pl. 476
8 × 3¾ inches
Rosenwald Collection, Library of Congress, Washington

The covers of the edition of 300 copies were bound in green cloth: those of the edition de luxe printed on Japanese vellum were bound in vellum. The design by Beardsley was stamped in gold on the front covers of both editions.

477 Drawing for the frontispiece to Ernest Dowson's *The Pierrot of the Minute*, a dramatic phantasy in one act, published by Leonard Smithers, London, March 1897. Signed with initials. Pl. 477
8½ × 4⅝ inches
Rosenwald Collection, Library of Congress, Washington

The scene, with the trellis, lilies, stylized roses, tall trees and Eros on a pedestal, is supposed to be in the garden of the Palace of Versailles, and is a translation into Beardsley's medium of a type of scene painted by Watteau. The figure of Pierrot, which has a noticeably helpless posture and a dazed expression, was clearly linked reminiscently with one of Watteau's pierrots, probably 'Gilles' in the Louvre.

478 Drawings for a headpiece and the initial letter P (on one sheet) in Ernest Dowson's *The Pierrot of the Minute*, a dramatic phantasy in one act, published by Leonard Smithers, London, March 1897. Pl. 478
5¼ × 3¾ inches
Rosenwald Collection, Library of Congress, Washington

479 Design for the cul-de-lampe in Ernest Dowson's *The Pierrot of the Minute*, a dramatic phantasy in one act, published by Leonard Smithers, London, March 1897. Pl. 479
5⅛ × 3⅝ inches
Rosenwald Collection, Library of Congress, Washington

The garden background with the urn is in the manner of Watteau. Beardsley's gift of design is revealed once more in the white disbalanced figure of Pierrot moving out of the picture. His head, divided by a bald line from his hat, might be said to derive in that feature alone from one of Watteau's pierrots; but the embittered expression is Beardsley's comment on the character of the Pierrot in what he called a 'foolish playlet'. The shells, stylized roses, garlands and ribbons surrounding the vignette in dots (simulating an eighteenth-century pin-prick picture—though the artist may not have known of such things) inspired illustrators in Russia, Germany and England, whose eighteenth-century pastiches in this manner came into vogue following the decline of *art nouveau* decorative styles in the 1900s.

480 Head of Balzac. Design for the decoration stamped in black on the front covers of *Scenes of Parisian Life* from *La Comédie Humaine* by Honoré de Balzac in eleven volumes, and published by Leonard Smithers in scarlet cloth, London, 8vo. Pl. 480
3⅞ × 2¾ inches
The British Museum

A design remarkable for its near-symmetry. The spines of the two series were decorated with the mask reproduced at NO. 481 which however was stamped in gold.

481 Design for a mask to be stamped in gold on the spines of *Scenes of Parisian Life* from *La Comédie Humaine* by Honoré de Balzac in eleven volumes published by Leonard Smithers, London, 1897, 8vo. Pl. 481
2⅝ × 1⅞ inches
Mr R. A. Harari, London

In a letter to Smithers dated 9 February 1897, Beardsley wrote, alluding to this drawing, '. . . Let me know if the white lines should be *firmer*. I didn't like to make them too hard'.

482 Atalanta in Calydon (with the hound). The figure of Atalanta is represented on the right and prancing in front of her is her hound clothed in a decorated overcoat with a coronet at the bottom of the flap near his left hind-quarters. Pl. 482
From the line-block

This drawing was reproduced in *A Book of Fifty Drawings by Aubrey Beardsley*, Smithers, 1897, p. 151, and in *The Idler*, March 1897. It has also been known as 'Diane'. Beardsley's former mastery of disbalance was exercised again at a period when he was less inclined to it. Atalanta's hair is unique in being represented entirely by the graded dots usually used for other purposes. For an earlier version of the subject, see NO. 372.

483 Messalina returning from the bath. Illustration to the *Sixth Satire of Juvenal*. Titled 'Messalina'. Pl.483
6⅞ × 5⅛ inches
Mr R.A.Harari, London

The gross power of Messalina is conveyed by stouter and heavier lines than were used by Beardsley in any drawing since the design for the cover of *The Yellow Book*, Vol. I, 1894. This illustration was published on p.191 of *A Second Book of Fifty Drawings by Aubrey Beardsley*, Smithers, London, 1899, where it is stated that it was drawn in 1897 and hitherto unpublished. 'Bath' here should be understood as bagnio.

484 La Dame aux Camélias. Water-colour and pencil sketch made in 1897 on the fly-leaf of a copy of the book presented to Beardsley by the author, Alexandre Dumas *fils*, in 1895. Signed with the artist's initials. Pl.484
From the half-tone plate

The sketch was first reproduced in *A Second Book of Fifty Drawings by Aubrey Beardsley*, Smithers, London, 1897. While staying at Dieppe in the late summer of 1895, Beardsley and Arthur Symons went on a pilgrimage to Puy, where Dumas *fils* was living in the house of his father, the author of *The Three Musketeers*. By 1897, when Beardsley made the drawing on the front fly-leaf of the book Dumas had given him, he had assimilated for the purpose something of the loose, watery touch of the painter Charles Conder.

485 Front cover of *The Houses of Sin* by Vincent O'Sullivan, published by Leonard Smithers, London (400 copies), 1897. 8vo. Signed with the artist's initials. Pl.485
Parchment board stamped with the design in gold
Mr R.A.Harari, London

The same design was repeated on the back cover. Of all his book covers this must be considered one of Beardsley's most daring and most successful. De-centred according to the advanced principles of the period, the amazing growth on the column surpasses most of his abstractions born out of an interest in the Rococo. It is tempting to believe that the winged pig-face, which is also the face of a woman, was a reminiscence, much transformed, and on a different psychological plane, of the pig leading a blindfold woman in the etching 'Le Femme au Cochon' ('Pornokrates') by Félicien Rops, especially as flying cherubs in the manner of Watteau's cherubs in 'The Embarcation for Cythera' precede the woman. This famous etching was published first in 1887 and then, in reverse, in 1896. The journal *La Plume* published a symposium of essays on Rops in 1896: Beardsley must surely have been aware of the works of this artist (see NOS. 460–66).

486 Front cover of Vol.I of *The Souvenirs of Léonard, Hairdresser to Queen Marie-Antoinette*, now first rendered into English with a preface and annotations by A.Teixeira de Mattos, privately printed by Leonard Smithers, London, August 1897. Two volumes, 8vo. Pl.486
Design stamped in gold on violet cloth boards
Mr W.G.Good, England

Another instance of severity and purity of design in book covers. Compare NOS.385, 457.

487 Mademoiselle de Maupin. Drawing for the frontispiece to the series *Six Drawings Illustrating Théophile Gautier's Romance Mademoiselle de Maupin by Aubrey Beardsley*, reproduced by Houssod, Valadon and Company in photogravure in 50 sets and published by Leonard Smithers and Co [*sic*], London, 1898. Signed with the artist's initials beneath the design. Pl.487
Pen, ink and green and pink watercolour, 6 × 3⅞ inches
Grenville L. Winthrop Bequest, Fogg Art Museum, Harvard University, Massachusetts

One of the least satisfactory of Beardsley's drawings, this was separately published in colour on white satin (10 copies) and on Japanese vellum (15 copies) by Smithers. Gautier's famous book was first published in 1835.

488 D'Albert. The second in the series of *Six Drawings Illustrating Théophile Gautier's Romance Mademoiselle de Maupin by Aubrey Beardsley*, published by Leonard Smithers and Co. [*sic*], London, 1898. Signed with the artist's initials. Pl.488
From the photogravure
Mrs Pierre Matisse, New York

Beardsley's drawing of the faces of his 'ideal' characters at the end of his life is quite unlike anything else in the history of art; nor could his imitators ever succeed in copying it.

489 D'Albert in Search of His Ideals. Drawing reproduced as the third in the series *Six Drawings Illustrating Théophile Gautier's Romance Mademoiselle de Maupin by Aubrey Beardsley*, published by Leonard Smithers and Co. [*sic*], London, 1898. Signed with the artist's initials. Pl.489
Pen, ink and wash, 7⅞ × 6⅝ inches
Grenville L. Winthrop Bequest, Fogg Art Museum, Harvard University, Massachusetts

Beardsley's leaning toward caricature, which was his means of expression as a boy, developed into a subtle sense of irony. But here everything is exaggerated, and there seems to be an insistent reversion to facile curves in the form and the clothes of D'Albert.

490 The Lady at the Dressing Table. The fourth in the series of *Six Drawings Illustrating Théophile Gautier's Romance Mademoiselle de Maupin by Aubrey Beardsley*, published by Leonard Smithers and Co. [*sic*], London, 1898. Signed with the artist's initials. Pl.490
From the photogravure, 9¼ × 7½ inches
Mrs Pierre Matisse, New York

The original drawing (7 × 6 inches; signed and dated) was in indian-ink and wash and belonged to Mrs E.T.Hutchinson of Schloss Weissenstein, Austria. It was sold at Christie's for £18,000 to Mr Julian Hartnoll, London, on 25 June 1985. In *Yellow Book* days Beardsley's perspectives were often contradictory: here there are contradictions in perspective which are more plausible, less abrupt. For instance, the conflicting vanishing points, that of the figures and the tipped up table and that of the architectural background, conjure a sense of space, a sense that was later insisted upon, with turbulent stylization, by the followers of Cézanne. The composition is in the spirit, but not in the manner, of the Venetian painter Longhi, with whose pictures in general there is a much stronger affinity in Beardsley's painting 'A Caprice'(NO.329).

491   The Lady with the Rose. The fifth in the series of *Six Drawings Illustrating Théophile Gautier's Romance Mademoiselle de Maupin by Aubrey Beardsley,* published by Leonard Smithers and Co. [*sic*], London, 1898. Signed with the artist's initials. Pl. 491
Pen, ink and wash, $7\frac{3}{4} \times 6\frac{7}{16}$ inches
Scofield Thayer Collection, Fogg Art Museum, Harvard University, Massachusetts

The strange conical hat was either an invention of the artist's, or more likely a memorization of certain hats on Chinoiserie male figures. In many of his drawings after *The Rape of the Lock* the quilling of cloth, rendered by stippled lines, appeared more and more, either in curtains or in garments: here it is the main feature of the lady's overskirt. By this date the nearly plebeian, nearly *putassiere,* faces of his earlier women have become transformed, as in this illustration, into faces in which over-large eyes and lips seem to stress a uterine drive that responds to any kind of romantic sensuality, without the stimuli of gain, of greed or of aggression. The striped wall-decoration reflects the artist's own taste: one of the rooms at 114 Cambridge Street was decorated similarly; and the revived vogue for 1780 stripes can be said to have been abetted by Beardsley, and to be found at the centre of that mixture of Louis Seize and Robert Adam pastiche which grew apace in the 1900s.

492   The Lady with the Monkey. Drawing for reproduction in photogravure of the last plate in the series *Six Drawings Illustrating Théophile Gautier's Romance Mademoiselle de Maupin by Aubrey Beardsley,* published by Leonard Smithers and Co. [*sic*], London, 1898. Signed with the artist's initials. Pl.492
Pen, ink and wash, $7\frac{7}{8} \times 6\frac{5}{8}$ inches
Mr R.A. Harari, London

This is the most elaborate example of Beardsley's technique in this manner with washes of ink interpreting the intermediate tones. In December 1897 Beardsley considered switching it to his *Volpone* series, but then changed his mind and it was published later as above. The miniature monkey was perhaps an unconscious *revenant* of the foetuses of 1893, in more plausible terms.

493   Design for the book-plate of the poetess Olive Custance, afterwards Lady Alfred Douglas. Lettered 'Ex Libris Olive Custance' and signed with initials. Pl.493
Pen, ink, pencil and wash, $3\frac{11}{16} \times 5\frac{5}{8}$ inches
National Gallery of South Australia, Adelaide

The drawing is executed in a technique whereby intermediate tones were introduced by pencil and ink wash. It belongs to the group which includes 'Arbuscula' and the illustrations to *Mademoiselle de Maupin.*

494   Arbuscula. Drawing for illustration facing p.38 in *A History of Dancing From the Earliest Ages to our own Times,* from the French of Gaston Vuillier, published by William Heinemann, London, 1898. 4to. Signed with the artist's initials. On the back of the paper, in Beardsley's hand, is a pencil inscription: 'Dont *rub (pencilling)'.* Some pen and indian-ink scribbles are cancelled by brush strokes. Pl.494.
Indian ink, wash and pencil, $5\frac{1}{4} \times 3\frac{15}{16}$ inches
Mr Brian Reade, London

Arbuscula was the name of a dancer during the earlier Roman Empire. The table has been drawn mainly with a pencil. Since the artist had used pencil-shading as well as ink wash in order to render the intermediate tones in this drawing, the reproduction in the 1898 book was in photogravure. The photogravure was reproduced in green on p.75 of *Under the Hill* by Aubrey Beardsley, published by John Lane, London and New York, 1904. It had been reproduced in green in the portfolio of extra plates supplied with the deluxe edition of the book. Lane bought the drawing from Heinemann (see catalogue of Lane sale in New York, 1926). It was bought at Sotheby's by Reade on 1 May 1968. The composition seems reminiscent of J.Smith's late seventeenth-century mezzotint of Madam Loftus.

495   Design for the front cover of *Ben Jonson his Volpone: or The Foxe,* with a critical essay on the author by Vincent O'Sullivan and an eulogy of the artist by Robert Ross, published by Leonard Smithers and Co. [*sic*], London, 1898. 4to. Signed with initials and dated 'Paris 1898'. Pl.495
$10\frac{15}{16} \times 8\frac{3}{16}$ inches
Scofield Thayer Collection, Fogg Art Museum, Harvard University, Massachusetts

The design was stamped in gold on the turquoise blue cloth front covers of the edition of 1000 copies on art paper, and in gold on the vellum front covers of the edition on Japanese paper of 100 copies.

496   Volpone Adoring his Treasure. Drawing for the frontispiece to *Ben Jonson his Volpone: or The Foxe,* with a critical essay on the author by Vincent O'Sullivan and an eulogy of the artist by Robert Ross, published by Leonard Smithers and Co. [*sic*], London 1898. 4to. Signed with initials. Pl.496
$11\frac{1}{2} \times 8$ inches
Princeton University Library

This drawing was intended for the prospectus of the book. The frontispiece, five initial letters and front cover design for *Volpone* together constituted Beardsley's last undertaking, not completed at the time of his death on 16 March 1898. They were published with the text later in the year by Leonard Smithers in an edition of 100 copies on Japanese vellum, and 1000 copies on art paper bound in turquoise-blue cloth with the cover design stamped in gold. The prints, and particularly the frontispiece, came out sharper on the art paper than on the Japanese vellum. In the frontispiece Beardsley strove to recapture the qualities of a seventeenth-century engraving. The result is one of the most exalted achievements of penmanship in the history of art.

497   Design for the initial V on p. 19 of *Ben Jonson his Volpone: or The Foxe,* published by Leonard Smithers and Co [*sic*], London, 1898. 4to. Pl.497
Pen, ink and pencil, $4\frac{11}{16} \times 6\frac{5}{8}$ inches
Grenville L.Winthrop Bequest, Fogg Art Museum, Harvard University, Massachusetts

Following up his past successes in overloading one side of a composition and redeeming this effect by an intuitive visual event on the 'empty' side, Beardsley here links the upper half of a composite column, the soffit of an architrave and a decorative swag and a pendant. He has used a pencil to solidify all this with soft shading. Cancelling the whole composition, yet ranged on the outer edge of the architrave, comes a Roman V outlined in ink. In the search for tangible effects the artist has failed in structural logic and produced for once an incoherent design. This and the succeeding drawings for initials in *Volpone* had to be reproduced by half-tone because of the soft shading in pencil.

498 Design for the initial V on p. 21 of *Ben Jonson his Volpone: or The Foxe,* published by Leonard Smithers and Co [*sic*], London, 1898. 4to. Pl. 498
Pen, ink and pencil, $7 \times 6\frac{5}{16}$ inches
Grenville L. Winthrop Bequest, Fogg Art Museum, Harvard University, Massachusetts

Beardsley has now abandoned his gift of dramatizing outlines and silhouettes in an attempt to dramatize the values of highlighting. The stability of the composition is emphasized by the elephant itself, and tradition by the use of this familiar image with its basket-shaped urn full of fruits—which in the Regency would have been a 'castle' or howdah. The drawing has a thick, ponderous force.

499 Design for the initial S on pp. 55 and 116 of *Ben Jonson his Volpone: or The Foxe,* published by Leonard Smithers and Co [*sic*], London, 1898. 4to. Pl. 499
Pen, ink and pencil, $6\frac{15}{16} \times 6\frac{1}{4}$ inches
Grenville L. Winthrop Bequest, Fogg Art Museum, Harvard University, Massachusetts

This is probably the most successful of the *Volpone* initials because the *sfumato* is not overdone. Perhaps the letter S inspired the artist to recapture his old sense of design in complex curves. These curves are integral to the form of the aggressive bird, which is a monster out of his old *Bon-Mots* period, turning the corner of Beardsley's mixed feelings of humour and fear. The rectangular contrast of a rusticated baroque building and the pencil-shading symbolizing the texture of old stone form an admirable contrast to the bird's movement.

500 Sketch for a variant of the initial S in *Ben Jonson his Volpone: or The Foxe,* published by Leonard Smithers and Co [*sic*], London, 1898 (p. 55). With a slight sketch of a satyr below. Pl. 500

Pencil on a sheet of ruled paper, $7\frac{1}{2} \times 4\frac{1}{8}$ inches
Princeton University Library

The final design for the initial S was of a totally different character. However, pencil drawings by Beardsley are rare.

501 Design for the initial M on p. 83 of *Ben Jonson his Volpone: or The Foxe,* published by Leonard Smithers and Co [*sic*], London, 1898. 4to. Pl. 501
Pen, ink and pencil, $7\frac{1}{16} \times 6\frac{1}{16}$ inches
Grenville L. Winthrop Bequest, Fogg Art Museum, Harvard University, Massachusetts

It is hard not to suspect a decline of vitality behind the comparatively limp draughtsmanship of this drawing. Beardsley's former obsession with breasts seems to be gratified by a desperate realism. The pencil-shaded mother and child have the air of an ill-cleaned *tenebroso* picture of the seventeenth century. None the less he was struggling to acquire a sculpturesque sense of feeling in the round: it was as if approaching death brought an unconscious wish to assert the reality, the solidity, of his concepts, bringing also a promise of new developments, in anticipation of the rough art of the early twentieth century.

502 Design for the initial V on p. 147 of *Ben Jonson his Volpone: or The Foxe,* published by Leonard Smithers and Co [*sic*], London, 1898. 4to. Pl. 502
Pen, ink and pencil, $6\frac{15}{16} \times 6\frac{1}{4}$ inches
Grenville L. Winthrop Bequest, Fogg Art Museum, Harvard University, Massachusetts

The best part of this design is the letter V which casts into the *sfumato* background of rubbed pencil the very stable and centralized term of the great god Pan. The congested expression of this god is neither very sinister nor very amusing. Romantic trees constitute a new element in Beardsley's art, unfortunately never to be developed.

Index